DOUBLE VISION

DOUBLE VISION

A TRAVELOGUE OF RECOVERY FROM RITUAL ABUSE

by

ANNA RICHARDSON

Copyright © 1997 by Anna Richardson

All rights reserved. Printed in the United States of America. No part of this publication may be reproduced or transmitted in any form or by any means, electronic or mechanical, including photocopy, recording, or any information storage or retrieval system, without permission in writing from the publisher except in the case of brief quotations embodied in critical articles and reviews. For information address Trilogy Books, 50 S. DeLacey Avenue, Suite 201, Pasadena, CA 91105.

Cover design: Joanne Stevens Art & Design

Publishers Cataloging in Publication

Richardson, Anna, 1958-
    Double Vision : a travelogue of recovery from ritual abuse/ Anna Richardson.
    p. cm.
    Includes bibliographical references
    ISBN 0-9623879-7-5

1. Richardson, Anna, 1958- 2. Ritual abuse victims--Rehabilitation. 3. Adult child abuse victims--Rehabilitation. 4. Incest. 5. Child sexual abuse. I. Title.

RC569.5.R59R53   616.85'82
                                QBI97-40311

Library of Congress Catalog Card Number 97-60210

TO RICH AND TO L.
who walked with me through the valley of the shadow

"You need only claim the events of your life to make yourself yours. When you truly possess all you have been and done, which may take some time, you are fierce with reality"

— *Florida Scott-Maxwell*

Acknowledgements

Without Margaret Robinson and Joan Larkin, who read each chapter as I wrote it, and again when I revised, this book would have been more pompous and less honest.

Without the women who came on Wednesday nights, who told their stories and listened to mine – who knows? I doubt I would have written this book at all.

My thanks too to the Five College Women's Studies Research Associateship and access to a different community.

And to my publisher, Marge Wood, for her willingness to learn about ritual abuse and her courage in taking on a book like this during such a time of backlash.

Author's Note

To the best of my memory, the events described in this book really happened. However, in order to protect the privacy and safety of the innocent, the guilty, and all those of us who are both, I have changed not only the names of the people who appear in this book but also distinguishing physical and biographical details. In addition I have shifted key geographical locations.

I have tried to bring to these alterations a novelist's eye in order to preserve the flavor of the original details but I have also been thorough: details have been changed in such a way that it is impossible to deduce the identities of actual people from the information given in this book. As a result any similarity between the individuals portrayed in this book and human beings known to the reader will be illusory.

FOREWORD

The sounds of the ocean keep me company as I write this. The sun is strong, the air alive and clean. The world seems bright, benevolent. How do I reconcile this world with the world depicted in this book? How can I begin to write about the journey to, through, and from that "other world," that secret, hidden, unbelievable world of sadistic ritual abuse, in which Anna once lived and then re-lived in her healing process? How do I convey the depth and variety of feelings that I too experienced on this extraordinary journey? I don't know. What I do know is how much respect I have for the courage, integrity, honesty and resilience of the woman you will meet in these pages.

In the spring of 1986, when I was the Pastor of a small-town church, a young woman began attending the Sunday service. The congregation was small enough that visitors were easily recognized. It was several weeks, however, before I had a chance to talk with this new person since she would cry during the service and leave early. My guess was that she was staying at the nearby artists' retreat. When we did finally talk I found her to be sensitive, insightful, extremely bright and articulate.

A few months later she asked if we could meet weekly for counseling. We began meeting for two hours each week. I am not a professionally trained clinician, though I had a social work background before I went to seminary. Occasionally I would see someone for counseling but more often I would refer them elsewhere. Anna and I were both wary in those early days. She was afraid that, despite my appearance to the contrary, I might be a narrow judgmental Christian who would condemn her for her lifestyle and blame her for, or minimize, her childhood woundedness. For my part, I remember feeling that I really didn't know this person with an English accent although I felt there was a lot stirring in her. Since that tentative beginning, we've been working together for nine years. The work has changed both of our lives.

For the first couple of years we focused mostly on the sexual and physical abuse and neglect Anna suffered from her mother and father, and felt our way into a trustworthy, collaborative relationship. The whole issue of ritual abuse did not surface for several years, though if we had had "eyes to see" we would have seen hints of it in her dreams and in certain memory fragments that only began to make sense much later.

The first time I used the word "ritual" (actually "ritualistic") was to describe the quality of stylized repetitiveness in memories she was having of both her parents abusing her at the same time. I had no knowledge of the category "ritual abuse" at that time.

At the end of 1989 new images which shocked and frightened me began to emerge. Anna's memories and dreams became more intense and they began to depict organized, intentional group abuse. I didn't even know what ritual abuse was until we were in the midst of it. It was confusing and disconcerting. If it weren't for the fact that we had worked together for three years already and I had learned how reliable Anna's psyche was, I believe I would have had great difficulty in taking it seriously and would have found my way toward explanations that dismissed or minimized or rendered it symbolic somehow. But by the time it came up, our relationship was well established, as was the safety and sacredness of our work together. It was as if a part of Anna knew that this was the time to deal with those very deep wounds.

In many ways I felt more like a midwife than an active agent in Anna's healing process. She was motivated. I don't remember her canceling once in all the years we've worked together. She set her own pace and did her inner work on her own rhythm. Sometimes I would make comments or offer possible connections with other memories or dream images that she had shared. Sometimes I would just remind her that she was safe here and she need not let the fear overwhelm her if she didn't want to. Often she would be very emotional during a session, and sometimes she would stammer as she recalled various instances of abuse. She had her own way of going into a sort of trance state, or dissociated state, as she followed an image or a word or a feeling through a maze of connections and associations toward its source. This process was so creative and ingenious and had such integrity that I knew it was impossible for her to be making up the content as she went along

Anna had many of her own resistances to overcome (and maybe "programming" as well) in getting to the ritual abuse memories. She would be physically affected as the material emerged. She would shake, feel cold, gag, cry, stammer and rock back and forth. I often felt helpless. At times I was shaken and scared and felt in danger myself. Once, after struggling to recall and relate a memory, she became very frightened and said, "Now that I've told you, you're going to die, they're going to get you." And while part of me was doing my best to rationalize and dismiss this, she said it with such terror and conviction it made the hairs on the back of my neck stand up, and I was afraid. Just then I heard footsteps in the hall outside my office, walking heavily toward the door. I oscillated between a panicky desire to run and the adrenaline which made me want to face whatever was coming and get it over with. Adrenaline won and I whipped open the door only to find the sexton, who normally wouldn't be there at that time, looking for something. He looked startled and I laughed that nervous laugh of relief. I relate this to let you know the power of this material and the effect it can have on one's emotions and sense of safety. There is a growing literature now on "vicarious traumatization" acknowledging the effects of very difficult material on the therapist's emotions, psyche, and sense of his or her world.

Often after a session where particularly gruesome and malevolent abuse was recalled and related, I would go home and take my two year old daughter in my arms and rock her. I wanted to protect her from a world in which such atrocities could happen, but also, I realize now, I wanted to soothe myself and to allow the experience of holding her to be a bridge back to that other world where children are loved and not abused.

It seemed as if each week more experiential memories came. They began in fragments of images or feelings and slowly evolved into connected episodes. We both kept hoping that "this would be it" and "there can't be anything worse than this." But there was always more, and some of it was worse. I didn't know how to carry this material. I felt isolated. Though I shared some of it with my wife, who is a clinical psychotherapist, I was also aware of not wanting to burden her. At a Grand Rounds lecture on dissociative disorders, the speaker mentioned case material that involved ritual abuse. The examples he shared were familiar to me. We talked several times and, through him, I made contact with a group of therapists who were dealing with people who had been ritually abused. There were monthly meetings of support and information. These were very helpful in countering the feelings of isolation and unreality that can otherwise be overwhelming.

It is probably not an accident that Anna found herself working toward healing with someone who represented God and religion. Those who practice sadistic ritual abuse often use the trappings of religious ritual and metaphysics to give them more power to create fear, secrecy and belief in their omnipotence. Those who have been wounded by such abuse often will not go near any church, or trust anyone in a robe, or take part in group ritual that includes lighted candles or sharing the "body and blood of Christ." Many of the normal rituals of church life are experienced as quite frightening by such survivors, whose wounds often come from parodies or distortions of Christian rituals. That Anna left crying for the first several weeks she came to the church is not surprising. But there is tremendous potential for healing when such rituals can be experienced positively. Powerful healing can be set in motion when one feels that one's dignity and worth are accepted and affirmed, not only through words but in the actions and embrace of an accepting community. I am not prescribing this for everyone — the healing of childhood psyches is so personal and idiosyncratic — but I did see it work as a positive healing force on Anna's journey.

Once, when she was going into the depths of pain and darkness, we came up with the idea of getting the advent wreath out of the church and lighting it. The wreath represented the community, God's love, the promise that "the light shines in the darkness and the darkness shall not overcome it." This helped her feel safe and gave her courage to continue her journey into the labyrinth. The feeling of not being alone, symbolized by the wreath or by my voice saying "It's OK, I'm still here" often provided the thread that gave her the confidence that she could find her way out again.

Anna also had several experiences as a child and later as a grown-up that I would call spiritual. Her experience of a golden egg of light with a cross in the center that came and kept her from "disappearing" or being extinguished during a group rape, was a very important and powerful one. Some therapists talk of an inner self helper, or archetypes of wholeness and mandalas. I have come to call the place from which these experiences emerge the "center that holds." However we understand or define such experiences it is important to talk about them and give permission for survivors to talk about them. I raise this because it is largely unexplored territory in the healing process from trauma.

This has been a personal foreword to a personal book. A bibliography of other writings about ritual abuse is provided in the back. My life has been deepened by my work with Anna. My beliefs have been challenged and have become more sharply focused yet with smoother edges. There is a basic mystery to life, love, wounding and healing. To walk with another in this mystery is transformative. Transformation is what happens when we cooperate with the force that intends our healing and wholeness. It is a force that leads us from the way things are to the way things could be — from brokenness toward wholeness, from darkness toward light, from diminishment toward fullness, from violence toward peace, from hatred toward love. Working together with Anna has been a transforming experience for both of us. It is my hope that reading this book may be fuel for your own journey. And together, maybe we can become a force for the transformation of our world.

Richard Fournier, M.Div.
Old First Church
Springfield, Massachusetts
April, 1995

Introduction

One evening in March 1990 I turned on the radio to listen to Outlook, a BBC World Service program broadcast by the Albany public radio station. The announcer was warning the audience that the subject matter of tonight's program was deeply disturbing. It was a program about Ritual Abuse and the attention it was receiving in the UK from mainstream children's charities such as the National Society for the Prevention of Cruelty to Children. It included a taped excerpt of an eleven year old girl describing the sacrifice and dismemberment of a baby and the drinking of its blood. I sat there stunned, listening to the girl's flat London voice describe in detail a ritual similar to one I had myself witnessed in England when I was ten years old. I had only begun to remember ritual abuse three months earlier, this particular ritual having been the first to surface, and I still clung to the hope that I was participating in some mass American hysteria: such weird and bloody practices, I thought, might happen in cult prone America but surely not in pragmatic old England. It was the very ordinary Englishness of the girl's voice which cracked my denial.

Later in the program a psychiatrist described how a boy he worked with could not speak about what had happened to him: so great was his terror, and so effective the brainwashing he had been subjected to, he literally could not form the words with his mouth. I too had, in remembering incidents of ritual abuse, found myself incapable of making the muscles of my mouth form sound into words, though I could think them quite clearly. The psychiatrist had found the boy could circumvent the prohibitions by making signs with his hands. I had found I could write down the words I could not speak.

As I listened I was shaking but at the same time I felt a fierce exhilaration: the radio, since childhood my voice of the world, had spoken, had confirmed. So too had the NSPCC who, in March 1990, declared it was devoting seven of its sixty-six teams to cases where children had been ritually abused.

I had tried to call my lover, Liz, when the program started but her phone was busy. Now I sat in the armchair in the corner of my house, the house I had designed and built and only moved into in January. I stared at the wood stove and the wall of books behind it. The uncurtained window at my side reflected back to me the contents of my little house, the kitchen counters made of cherry boards salvaged from the dump, sanded down and freshly oiled; the round table I found on the street in Brooklyn years ago; the ragged Persian rug I bought in a flea market in Algeria when I was eighteen. All I could think was, "It's true. It happens in England. It's true. It might be true."

I had had no conscious recollection of ritual abuse until December 1989. In fact I had had no memory of violence or abuse of any kind in my family until I stopped drinking in 1984. Then, within a few weeks, I began to remember sexual abuse. I remembered my mother's abuse of me and then, two years after that, my father's. In December 1989 I had my first memories of ritual abuse. Over the next three years new information surfaced almost every week. In that time I remembered abuse which took place between 1968 and 1976, from when I was ten until I was eighteen, in both England and Germany.

The process by which forgotten experience enters consciousness, often years after the actual event, is at the core of my healing from ritual abuse. I refer to the process as remembering though this is something of a misnomer. It would be more accurate, but more cumbersome, to refer to the process as one of completing the experiencing of events which, at the time of their occurrence, were so threatening to the psyche's integrity they had to be "frozen." When I remember an incident of ritual abuse for the first time what I am actually doing is experiencing it completely for the first time. It is only after it has been felt and assimilated that it can become a memory in the ordinary sense of the word.

Recovering memories does not happen in a vacuum: as with any other mental process there is a play between the worlds, internal and external. Would I have remembered if I had not had two friends,

Leslie and Tina, who had themselves begun to talk about the peculiar fragments floating into their consciousness? To be more precise, how would we have heard each other's fragments, if we had dared voice them, if we had not heard whisperings already from the wider world that such things existed? Most likely, we would have written poems, painted pictures, marveled at the dark intricacy of the unconscious, perhaps gone crazy, been drugged, locked up, gone back to drink, perhaps found a less visibly destructive way to wall ourselves from our truths, remained functional, numb, prey to incomprehensible fear and despair. These were the fates of people who remembered before there was a language for what happened, and people who believed them. I remembered ritual abuse in part because other people were remembering and talking about it. I wasn't aware just how many people were beginning to remember but I knew there were a few of us. The psyche is wise, interested in preserving its wholeness. In my experience at least it does not release into consciousness more than I can handle. I think it — I — sensed that at last it was possible and safe enough for me to know what had happened.

It was safe enough not only because I trusted Rich not to lock me up but also because, with friends and the women who came to the Survivors of Incest Anonymous weekly meeting, I had been making a context for my memories. Although the content of ritual abuse memories was new and terrifying, the process of remembering and telling was not so different from remembering "regular" incest. Memories which would have felt intolerable and impossible alone could be told and listened to and somehow they became more bearable.

Not that we all believed each other easily. Often I thought to myself, "I can't believe that happened. She really is crazy." The best I could do was to keep an open mind. I wanted to believe that this was just mass hysteria, a collective fantasy. But when I looked at Tina and Leslie I did not see women eager to jump on any bandwagon. They were struggling as hard as I was to discount the images and sensations which were surfacing. Far from embracing the new craze, we each resisted acknowledging the reality of our memories for as long as possible, by whatever means we could.

The NSPCC news release reported on the Outlook program stated:
"Ritualistic abuse constitutes the multiple abuse (involving physical, sexual and emotional abuse) of both

boys and girls of all ages. [It] involves a wide range of activities including the use of masks and costumes, the invocation of supernatural powers, animal sacrifices, the drinking of blood and urine, the smearing of feces on children, sexual and physical abuse of children.

NSPCC experience suggests that physical abuse networks are secretive and well-organized and have a psychological hold over the victims making the process of gathering information extremely difficult.

Nine months earlier a more detailed discussion document had been put before one of the NSPCC's committees. The allegations went much further:

- The involvement of large numbers of children, including the very young and new born babies

- Large numbers of adult perpetrators, including women

- Children being transported to special places where the abuse takes place, such as farms and cellars

- The use of threats to control and intimidate; survivors' fear of the power of the cult

- The systematic production of pornography to finance the cult

- The use of drugs

- High levels of physical and sexual abuse: "Victims report they are penetrated by objects and they are subjected to bizarre forms of cruelty and manipulation"

- The ritualistic sacrifice of animals and the drinking of their blood

- The mutilation or sacrifice of children and babies

- The breeding of infants especially for that purpose, or for use in sexual rituals

• INTRODUCTION •

- The eating of the flesh and internal organs of infants and young babies, the drinking of their blood

- The smearing of the body with blood or feces, and the enforced consumption of urine and excrement

- The involvement of influential people in interlinked satanic and pornography networks: "doctors, police officers, teachers, social workers, are active in abusing in both networks"

- Fear by the victims of the power of the network, reinforced by the punishment and murder of those who attempt to break away

- The use for blackmail of pornographic and video material showing members committing abuse and sacrifice

- Effective brainwashing of members to prevent disclosure

The document adds:
"The first reaction on hearing about ritualistic abuse is one of disbelief, then denial, and then ridicule."

The details of this document are cited in a book by British journalist Andrew Boyd, *Blasphemous Rumours: Is Satanic Ritual Abuse Fact or Fantasy? An Investigation*, published by Fount Paperbacks in 1991. He writes:

> I came across the NSPCC discussion document early in my research. Its observations seemed overstated and incredible; at the least implausible.
>
> *But every statement listed above in that document was later supported, reiterated and reinforced by professional carers and the victims who gave their accounts.*
>
> Few of those carers, to my knowledge, have any connection with the childcare agency. With several omissions, the above list is a clear and succinct summary of what has been described time and again as the common elements of ritual abuse, frequently observed both in advance and independently of the NSPCC disclosure, and therefore, to a measure, outside NSPCC influence. Those elements are continuing to be described and disclosed despite the profound media skepticism and public criticism of its proponents.

That is not a statement of faith, it is a matter of observation. (Boyd, pp 31–32, his emphasis.)

From personal experience I can corroborate every point in the NSPCC document except for the use of film in blackmail, which I imagine is used more against people involved as adults than as children. From listening to other survivors who were abused here in the USA I can say that the NSPCC list is just as applicable on this side of the Atlantic. It tallies with information put out by the Women's Center of Los Angeles Task Force on Ritual Abuse, for example.

Boyd's book addresses questions I choose not to engage: I am not out to marshal the proofs that ritual abuse exists, I know it does. I am interested in how one survives it, how one heals from it, how one accepts into consciousness knowledge of organized cruelty, and how one opposes it.

I am not naive about the denial which will greet my story. I have tried most of it on for size myself, defeated in the end by the consistency of my memories and the intensity of their impact. Denial is an ordinary human response to threatening information, and information about ritual abuse is very threatening. When someone accepts that these activities have taken place, are taking place in his or her country, quite possibly in his or her town, he or she confronts the same questions which face the survivor: If this is true, what can I trust? Who can I trust if the doctor, the policeman, the minister may be involved? Sure, torture and mutilation happen in small Central American countries but here? What does it mean to be civilized? What is evil? How are the people who commit these acts different from me? What will happen to me, to the people I love, if I speak out against them?

What is particularly frightening in confronting ritual abuse is not only its pervasiveness and the extreme cruelty it involves, but its organization. Ritual abuse clearly requires planning and an administrative structure. Information is recorded and disseminated: rituals in geographically diverse areas are performed in identical ways. Babies whose deaths will go unrecorded are acquired, whether from women within the cults or from abroad or from other sources. Snuff films are made and marketed. Somebody somewhere manufactures machinery of torture.

• INTRODUCTION •

Early on in my remembering I read a book of interviews with the children of Nazi war criminals. I recognized their numbness and shock, their recurrent feelings of disbelief that father could have come home from his day as commandant of a death camp to play Schubert so beautifully, to bend and admire a daffodil, to play with the dog.(1)

Taking in the reality of any kind of organized evil is a slow and difficult process for most people. In the case of ritual abuse there is a particular twist. Planned cruelty is usually directed at groups of people who are perceived as "other," but parents frequently subject their own children to ritual abuse. In most societies a person's blood family is experienced as closest to self, to "us" and not "other." How then do parents come to expose their own children to organized evil? How to understand this with the mind? With the heart?

Worrying at these problems has been part of recovery. The threat of meaninglessness posed by ritual abuse, the ways it dislocates reality, disintegrates expectation — here is my father working in the garden, here is my father torturing a boy; here is the bank manager smiling across the counter, here is the bank manager in the woods drinking blood — is a real part of the damage it causes. I am not a professional philosopher but a habitual thinker with a hankering for meaning. Being on the receiving end of atrocity gives one a new sensitivity to the wounds inflicted by people's longing to seek refuge from randomness in easy theologies. What it means and what it takes to accept the role chance plays is one theme of this book.

Why did this happen to me?
Why did I survive when others didn't?
Why me?
Why not me?

To heal from ritual abuse I have needed to draw on a strength greater than my own, but in writing about spirituality I bear in mind Elie Wiesel's stricture: "Make no assertions about God which you could not make while standing over a pit of burning babies." Though I do speak of God sometimes, the concept is not, for me, tied to any particular theology, Christian or otherwise. Rather it is a shifting and fluid notion whose reality may reside in nothing more (nor less) than the yearnings and furies of my own heart.

The people who abused me were interested in what happens when you apply extreme pressure to a human personality, through pain, terror, the imposition of impossible choices. I would rather not have undergone these experiences, but having done so I too am interested in what happened. Both the abuse and the remembering of it pushed me at times beyond reason, thought, the bounds of self, into the realm of mystery. In the eye of horror, joy is possible, available, enables one to endure. This is the province of stories, not of discursive prose. In the biggest sense that's what this book is, a story whose roots are in mystery.

Because I am most at home with story, I chose to arrange this book chronologically rather than thematically. I have shaped it not as an account of the ritual abuse itself but of the recovery from the abuse, using excerpts from my journals to tell the story.

This book is not so much about violence as it is about healing from violence. Still, it is necessary to describe what happened. I don't like reading about violence myself. It gives me nightmares. One of the key questions for me in writing this book has been, how to write about violence without doing violence? Cops and doctors settle for a clinical detachment. It separates the narrator from the events narrated. Journalists use a similar separation, calling it objectivity. But there is a kind of violence to the human spirit in describing a horrific event only as an event, excluding the emotions it arouses.

Over the years of going to SIA meetings and talking to other survivors, the stories I have found it most difficult to listen to are the ones told in a monotone. There is a lie, a lie the person is telling themselves, and asking you to join in, the lie that they can tell what happened without having it affect them. It is often an involuntary lie: in self-protection one shuts down and dissociates, the feelings may be inaccessible.

But still, when someone tells atrocity in a voice without inflection, I am afraid. They can tell more than I can bear to hear because they are not feeling what they are saying. I don't want to have to shut down myself. I don't even know if I can. I retreat into disbelief, or day-dreaming about delphiniums.

Tell the truth and tell it all. If you can cry and rage and smile, I can probably hear it all. You won't be able to tell it so much faster than my heart can bear. I try to apply these thoughts to myself as I write this book, to be wary when, either in the journals or as I comment on them, my words feel disconnected from feeling. Often when that happens they come more quickly, I feel excited, urgent. My mind is glad to shed my heart, to show what it can do on its own, how swiftly it can summarize, define, explain.

The question of pace is important. Heart and soul take longer to absorb information than the brain. When too much comes at once, they get left behind. I have deliberately included a lot of ordinary life — nature, love, money worries — in among the gruesome memories. Those journal entries are a relief to me each time I come to them, like stepping stones in a swamp full of alligators. I assume my readers will supply more of the same for themselves as they read. I myself kept a book of botanical watercolors and a canister of potpourri from the garden on my desk as antidotes.

Once I had the idea of using excerpts from my journals, I started going through the stack of notebooks I'd filled since I got sober, fifty-seven of them in all! I quickly realized I could spend half the book on the years before the ritual abuse surfaced explicitly, noting the dreams and memory fragments I had no context for at the time. But even when I limited myself to the three years of actual ritual abuse memories there were still ten notebooks, each with two hundred pages.

Selecting what in the journals to include, what to omit, has been difficult. Part of what has helped me to believe I am not making all this up for some obscure but compelling psychological reason, is the way memories have emerged as pieces of a mosaic, a huge and intricate mosaic in which the different pieces constituting one particular scene have surfaced separately and often years apart. It is impossible to reproduce here the experience of uncovering that mosaic in its entirety but I have tried to give instances of it.

Journal entries are sometimes embarrassing: since I was not writing them with an audience in mind I did not always dress self-pity or posturing in prettier clothes. Sometimes things I have written seem certain to invite disbelief or ridicule, to provide skeptics with perfect ammunition. I have tried to treat the journals as historical documents, not to tailor them so I come out looking better. Occasionally I have made minor changes in the interest of clarity. Any substantial additions are enclosed in square brackets. Omissions are indicated by ... when they occur in the middle of an entry. I kept the dates as I wrote them at the head of each entry in my journal though I know they were often approximate.

By quoting from my journals extensively I have attempted to preserve the experience of recovery as it happened, but inevitably selection transforms the material. I hope not to have tidied up my experiences so much that another survivor, reading this book, finds his or her fragments lacking in clarity and dismisses them. Ultimately my mosaic is only part of a much larger whole. I would hate to have my story used as a measure against which other survivors' memories are held and found wanting.

I believe passionately in the integrity of each individual's story, that healing comes from living from the inside out, not from the application of external Standards, Structures and Notions. For this reason I have not sought to generalize my experiences into universally applicable Stages of Recovery. While a sketch map of the general territory of ritual abuse recovery, similar to that provided for incest survivors by *The Courage to Heal,* would be useful, my personal sympathies lie with folk tales rather than self-help books as vehicles for wisdom.(2)

A story is made up not only of speaking but of listening. This is a story of my listening to others, and being listened to, and so learning to listen to myself. I have been fortunate in finding other survivors whose paths lead through similar terrain, who keep up a running commentary of their own. Dealing with ritual abuse has given me a new appreciation for listening, its difficulty, costliness, rarity, necessity. Once a week or so for nine years I have talked with a man who listens with his heart as well as his mind, who believes in story and in the power for transformation within each of us, who has not hidden behind a professional mask but has walked through the valley of the shadow at my side. And I have had a partner who, for as long and as much as she was able, listened to my story and was herself changed because she did not shut her heart away from the horror. I have friends who listened and asked questions and others who could not listen, who changed the subject, who judged me for holding onto the past, and who, when I challenged them, heard me out and tried to listen more.

Listening is not easy, it changes one's world, lays one open to the griefs of others. Linda McCarriston, a poet who writes about cruelty and family violence, said once in a reading that, though she knows her work is sometimes painful to hear, and it is hard for her to witness that pain, she works from the belief that "People of good will always are willing to lose their ignorance." This is what I ask of you, this willingness.

But I cannot ask of you more than I can manage myself. I am not willing all the time. There are times when I won't listen to the news, to friends, to the frogs and birds and dying trees. I refuse to know any more about Bosnia or nuclear waste. I switch off, day dream about poppies and swimming in green rivers. But in the end I come around, in the end I am willing to lose my ignorance, and that is what matters.

I know from experience that there is spiritual sustenance in reality, in accepting what is, not because it is right, proper, intended, but simply because it is what it is and denial insulates us from spirit in the exact measure that it separates us from truth. Always approximate, shifting, these truths, these realities, but nonetheless in them I find my succor, and can trust that you will too: they are the living waters.

1. Dan Bar-On, *Legacy of Silence: Encounters with Children of the Third Reich.* Cambridge, Mass.: Harvard University Press, 1989

2. Chrystine Oksana, *Safe Passage to Healing: A Guide for Survivors of Ritual Abuse.* New York: Harper Collins, 1994

Chapter One

In December 1983 I walked up and down Delancey Street in the Lower East Side of New York, closing one eye then the other, trying to read the traffic signs. I was worried that my eyesight had deteriorated but I couldn't seem to get myself to go to an eye doctor. I knew my reluctance was foolish and I couldn't really explain it. When I was eleven, I had become, quite suddenly, afraid that I would go blind. I used to tell people that I had overheard the optician warning my mother I might lose my sight and that was where the fear came from, but I wasn't sure I'd heard any such thing. My life was full of inexplicable feelings and reactions, and the stories I told to account for them never felt quite convincing.

Walking up and down the street, I was trying to work out a way to tell if my eyesight was worse than it should be. Finally it came to me that in order for people to drive safely they must be able to read road signs at a reasonable distance. But what constituted a reasonable distance?

Life had acquired this tentative quality in a number of areas. How did other people move with apparent certainty through a world propped on such flimsy girders as normality, probability, reasonableness?

At last I determined that my eyesight was almost certainly worse than it should have been if I were driving a car. I called an eye doctor and was given an appointment for January 24th.

On the night of the 23rd I gave a reading, with my friends Laura and Sally at a performance space in the East Village. I was drunk, which was not unusual. Two days earlier I had volunteered for a lay-off from the construction company where I was working as a carpenter's apprentice. I didn't expect to go back. My plan was to drink myself to death. I'd always assumed I'd be dead by the time I was twenty-five and here I was twenty-five and a half. I made a list of all the gay bars in New York. Might as well enjoy myself on the way down, I thought.

Under the bravado I was scared — I'd had diarrhea for months, I couldn't decide whether the fridge needed to be repaired though the apartment stank of rotting food, my cat was sick but I couldn't seem to get her to the vet, and I had a strong sensation that my fifth floor walk-up was floating in the sky, attached to the ground only by a single telephone line — but I couldn't bear to admit my drinking was out of control.

After the reading we went to Laura's apartment to celebrate. Her lover, Marla, and I started talking about incest, about the fact that people forget it happened to them. How could one be sure it hadn't? I don't know how or why we got into that conversation. I could remember very little of my childhood but as far as I knew I had never experienced any kind of abuse. Marla told me a story. She told me a story about a woman who had never been able to face the incest in her childhood until one day, watching a group of six- and seven-year-olds playing, she thought, "It wasn't my fault." When Marla said those words all the hairs on my body stood up. I felt as if I had been electrocuted. A few moments later I said, "I am an alcoholic and I can't stop drinking." I hadn't planned to say it. I didn't even recognize the voice that came from my mouth. Then I said, "Oh I'm just making this up to get attention." "Have you said it before?" "No." I cried and cried. "Do you want to stop drinking?" "Yes." "Can you?" "No. Maybe for five days." "Are you willing to get help?" "Yes."

The first day of my lay-off I was in an AA meeting and, though I drank daily for the ten years before that, I haven't had a drink since. There is always, for me, a touch of the miraculous in the stories of how people got sober, something irreducible, inexplicable. That is true in my case, and at the same time I can see that the phrase "It wasn't my fault" was the key. Those were the words that made my hair stand up. For a moment I must have believed it, thought that perhaps I did not have to kill myself after all. But what had I thought was my fault? What was the crime for which I had sentenced myself to death? I didn't know.

On the afternoon before the reading I wrote in my journal:

• CHAPTER ONE •

1/23/84

The lure of debauchery is old — reading Scott Fitzgerald at 15 — & connected to a defiant acceptance of one's own badness. The lesbian life a` la Reneé Vivien et al.

And not wanting to think. There's an old gesture, a drunken shove of the arm turned up before the face and pushing away.

I drink too much. It's the same thing. But also I need not to be so scared of being seen in my unbuttoned state, drunk or angry or self-glorifying....

I get so impatient with this tight sturdy well-able-to-look-after-herself person. I want to crack her, to say look you can be "unacceptable" and your friends won't run away. You live in a safer world now.

You just want to make a fool of yourself, says the tight voice.

But I'm so tired of having chicken frozen in the freezer and never running out of milk. Tired of being a sensible mother to myself. I want to be a lover not a mother. To dissolve myself in sweat and the touch of a breast and hands seen across a room and taut kisses in cold doorways....

I want to feel the tenderness of making love between bodies without biographies. To touch and laugh and talk, yes, not "This is who I am it's 3am" but words lean and soft as the line of a hip and the street lamp making moonscapes of two bodies.

How I longed to become a body without a biography. But it wasn't only that I wanted to escape myself, my history. I wanted the freedom and the spontaneity I associated with the erotic. I was exhausted and bored by my endless need to control not just my drinking but my feelings, my life. It was as if I had a monster inside I had to keep caged, something so bad only constant vigilance could protect me and the world.

I had used booze to stay numb, to stay far from whatever was inside me. For a long time it worked to muffle my longings and fears. But somehow it wasn't working any longer. It wasn't just the booze, the whole protective shell I'd made for myself had grown too small. It was strangling me.

The story I read at the reading that Sunday night was called "The Sea, The Sea." I'd been working on it for a couple of months. It didn't make sense to me. In it, the narrator, a woman of detached intellect who models herself on the great detectives, Poirot, Maigret,

Holmes, is walking down Mott Street in New York City when she is seized by the thought, "There's a storm among the shadows." Shortly afterwards she hears a voice chanting

> *the dark waters pull*
> *the dark waters pull*
> *my timbered hull*
> *I am a ship*
> *a prison ship   seaworthy   silent*
> *silent   silent*

The voice's name is Hannah. She talks and talks.

> Something in her words suffocated me, as if a hand on my head were pushing me under, but she followed me, our footsteps rhyming in the brittle air. Since I couldn't get rid of her I resolved to discover the thread which would draw sense out of this melee of memory, mysticism and half-baked poetry. Only by making out of her monologue a story I could tell myself, one with a beginning and an end and some logic to what went on in between, could I return to the street the solidity it so strangely lacked.

The narrator listens, and her listening helps the chanting words resolve themselves into a story about a journey Hannah took from Africa to England when she was ten. She and her mother and father and brother were on a ship. There was to be a fancy dress contest. Hannah and her brother were to go as the mermaid and the fisherman, he holding a rod with a hook caught in her hair, she wearing the fish's tail her mother was making out of silver foil. Hannah wanted to be the fisherman. Angry at this costume which bound her legs so she could barely move, she got drunk for the first time on her mother's gin.

She and her brother won first prize. In front of the crowd and the judges she proceeded to do a striptease, removing piece by piece the costume her mother had made for her, frightened by the alien rhythms of her body's dance, entranced by its power to draw the eyes of the crowd. In the course of the telling of this last story, the voices of Hannah and the narrator merge until they are one voice speaking.

Writing the ending I thought it absurdly optimistic. I felt no such possibility of integrating within myself the inchoate voice of my feelings and my ever-watchful and critical rational voice. But the ending insisted on itself.

In retrospect, "The Sea, The Sea" appears to me to be an oddly accurate depiction of the process of remembering and healing on which I had not yet embarked. Over time I would learn to pay attention to the feeling that there is "a storm among the shadows," because it often meant a new memory was on its way. I learned to listen to the voice of that child self, telling her truth from the shadows, and gradually I learned not to separate myself from her and all she knew.

In writing the fancy dress contest scene in "The Sea, The Sea" I drew on a memory of the first time I got drunk. It was at a cocktail party my parents were giving. We were living in Germany at the time. I must have been thirteen or fourteen. I drank six or seven Screwdrivers and went up to my room which overlooked the street. Down below chauffeurs sat waiting in the cars. Standing in my lighted window I did a striptease, drink dimming the voice which insisted this wasn't a good idea. I wanted the drivers to see and at the same time I was afraid they would look up. I don't remember it being a sexual feeling particularly, more a compulsion to be seen. Look. Everything may look glittering and polite down below but look upstairs, look at the bedroom window. The truth is always trying to tell itself. Denied direct expression it speaks symbolically.

As a teenager the longing to tell, to have someone see, for someone to know what was happening, both compelled and frightened me. When I was sixteen I made my hands shake for six whole weeks while I was at school in the hopes that somebody would see, would ask what was wrong. I knew I was making my hands shake, I wasn't really crazy, but on the other hand perhaps it was crazy to make your hands shake?

I used to fantasize about going crazy: if you were crazy you could say whatever you wanted and nobody could hold you responsible. It would be like being drunk only more so. Here was the crux of the matter: I needed desperately to be heard but I couldn't afford to be believed. I wonder how many people in mental hospitals are there because going crazy was a way to resolve this dilemma.

When the housemaster at Elmsbury, the last boarding school I attended, suggested that a drunken wrist slashing was a cry for help, I denied it. I didn't know, consciously, what it was I was trying to tell people. The abuse was going on all through this time, but all I had were isolated memories of odd experiences, like buoys bobbing on the surface, marking the site of the wreck. Knowing that I had suddenly become afraid of going blind was one of those buoys.

Looking at the weeks before I got sober I see that the way of silence and self-control was no longer working but spontaneity, self-expression, the desire for connection — the erotic — still meant death, danger, degradation. Living in this tension I just wanted to get it over with, to surrender, to give up control and so die.

But by the strange alchemy of the Self another possibility had been preparing itself, a possibility I could barely glimpse: that I could surrender and find new life.

Where before sex had been my only real experience of letting go, of spontaneity, in the year before I got sober I had begun to experience through writing the sense of partnership with an invisible, mysterious and trustworthy process. Imagination, God, Self, whatever you want to call it, I had begun to feel it again. Stories appeared from inside me, whole stories showing a logic of emotion and symbol I perceived but knew I had not devised. Some were stories from a childhood I thought I'd forgotten. A new channel of communication had been opened up between conscious and unconscious. It soon became apparent that my old means of experiencing moments of release from rigid self-censorship, booze, was blocking the new channel. I'd come home from work, planning to write, have a beer and another and be too drunk to think by the time I got to the typewriter.

Ultimately I can't account for why I got sober when I did. The thirst for dying had grown so strong I couldn't fight it any more. On the other hand for the first time in years I felt there was something worth living for. What I was offered when, for a moment, the door of my self-hatred swung open, in the minutes after Marla told the story of the woman whose fault it wasn't and all the hairs on my body stood up, was the paradoxical way of freedom through defeat.

Admitting that I could not control my drinking and that I needed help terrified me but it was also a relief. Getting involved in Alcoholics Anonymous I said to my friends, I'm afraid this is a cult. If I change too much, please come and get me out.

On January 24th, my first day without a drink in about ten years, I was sitting at the eye doctor's. My eyes had indeed weakened, though not badly. He fitted me with a pair of contact lenses and left

• Chapter One •

the room. I sat in the chair, panic stricken, thinking over and over, "I don't want to see this clearly."

I shook my way through the first weeks, went to meetings and got a sponsor, a woman I talked to every day. I was haunted by the sense that I had a black hole inside me into which I could fall and be crushed into nothingness, and by the image of my family as a house of mirrors in the dark. After listening to this for a while my sponsor gave me the name of a therapist and suggested I go see her.

3/29/84

Dream
I go to an AA meeting early, talk to this middle aged woman. She wants me to open the door. I have keys to the bathrooms. She gets me to unlock them. I say, "I haven't done the fourth step yet but I can show you upstairs."

Inside this building are two bums decapitating a pure black, healthy cat, slicing off its head, ready for food, the bright red of blood and flesh, the neck like salami. There's blood all over the floor. I scream at them and someone else, "There's blood in my house." It's everywhere, in fat drops and rivulets. "There's blood in my house."

Later I think I'm glad not to do my fourth step until I've done one, two and three.

The fourth step in AA is to take "a searching and fearless moral inventory of ourselves." I had this dream three days after starting therapy with Esther. I certainly wasn't ready then to unlock all the doors of my house, to see just how much blood had been shed, but I was ready to open the first door.

I told Esther about my respectable upper-middle-class family and the revulsion I felt for them, particularly for my mother. I told her about my drinking and screwing around and a suicide attempt when I was eighteen and the drunken wrist-slashing and my endless self-hatred and anxiety, and how I couldn't remember anything much before the age of twelve. I told her about the story Marla had told me and the effect it had on me. She asked me if I had ever been abused and I said no, the only thing I could think of was a story my mother used to tell about how, when I was three, I started to wet the bed again and she took me to the family doctor. According to my mother I told the doctor the *au pair* was being mean to me and my parents fired her. End of story.

I told Esther about an image I'd had when I was twenty-three, shortly after I came to America: I had attended a training to work as a volunteer in a shelter for battered women and their children. To help us identify with the feelings of children coming out of violent homes we were asked to think of a childhood experience of violence of our own. I was embarrassed. I thought, "Oh no, I'm going to be the only person in the room who never experienced any violence." There was a guided meditation and, to show willingness, I closed my eyes and emptied my mind. Suddenly I felt as if I were standing at the bottom of some stone steps looking up at a closed door, longing for somebody to come and take me out of wherever I was. I had no idea what this was about so I just filed it away in my mind along with all the other inexplicable fragments, the lies I told — about not being able to remember who I lost my virginity to, for example — and the weird reactions I had.

The third time I saw Esther she asked if there might be a connection between the stone steps, the mean *au pair* and the image of the black hole. As she finished her sentence I felt myself to be in a room half underground, terrified. My body felt very small. There was a sharp pain in my left shoulder. It felt, in the present, as if my shoulder was jerking up and down. A part of me was in that underground room feeling the terror, another part watched. I saw my blue pleated skirt being pulled up, my bare thigh, the handle of a hairbrush being pushed into me. I could hear someone talking German. I stared at the stone steps leading up to the closed door. I longed with all my being for somebody to open it and take me out of there.

After a while Esther called my name, told me I could come back. I felt terrified, begged her not to call me that name. I cowered, feeling she was going to stride across the room and hit me.

I was shaken afterwards. I had never experienced anything like it before, but it felt real. I knew somehow it was not all one memory but a composite. I assumed the woman with the hairbrush was the *au pair,* that the room was in the house in Austria where we lived from when I was three till I was six. Once I came out of the memory my shoulder stopped hurting and I realized with surprise that it had been hurting for as long as I could remember, for so long I no longer noticed it but I had developed a habit of massaging it.

In the next session, Esther asked me if I thought it really was

• CHAPTER ONE •

the *au pair* who abused me, or if it might have been someone in my family. She explained that people mostly found the thought of incest so unbearable that it was easier to ascribe the abuse to someone else. I said no, I didn't think either of my parents had abused me and she agreed, saying my family did not sound like an incestuous family to her.

I don't know quite what she meant by that, but I think it had to do with the emotional temperature of life in my family as I had described it to her, which was cool to the point of frigidity. Early on, when I had talked about the image of a house of mirrors in the dark and told her about some of my guilty teenage secrets — compulsive stealing, lesbianism, the suicide attempt — she had startled me by pointing out that my parents in fact knew about all these things, they just hadn't talked about them. She was shocked, I think, that parents could know that their eighteen year old daughter had tried to kill herself and never mention it to her. Mostly I remembered begging the school not to tell them and my relief when they seemed not to have. For my parents to know anything of what I felt or cared about was unbearable to me.

In the present I could see she was right. From the point of view of an outsider, especially an American outsider, it was rather shocking that they had never talked to me about it. I didn't know how to explain to her how completely in keeping it was. It was how my family did things and it was how my culture handled emotional intensity.

Some years after the suicide attempt I found out from a family friend that the school *had* told my parents and that they had consulted a psychiatrist who told them not to worry as long as I kept getting good marks at school. I did. Two months after the suicide attempt I took the Oxbridge entrance exams and won a scholarship to Lady Margaret Hall, Oxford to read English. Well done, said my father. Yes, well done darling, said my mother and we all heaved a sigh of relief.

My father was an engineer, consulting with foreign governments on the design of power grids. He worked with a company which specialized in generator components and, by the time I was a teenager, his work involved making and maintaining connections with politicians, civil servants and industrialists in whatever country he was assigned to. My mother hosted and attended countless cocktail and dinner parties and looked after my brother and me. Bill, four years younger than me, was at a minor public school, having failed to get into a big name one, rowing and playing cricket.

In England, the class system is the skeleton. I can't begin to talk about my family without placing them in that intricately differentiated hierarchy, a hierarchy which dictates not only where people live and the jobs they do but the way they talk to each other, the way they express love and hate, the form their violence takes.

My father did not come from an upper-class background: his mother had grown up extremely poor, going to work in a woolens mill at fourteen, later going on to own her own haberdashery shop which she ran until she retired. My father's father had run away from home when he was fifteen. Eventually he became a successful businessman, one of the "nouveau riche." My father, the oldest son, (he had one brother and two sisters), was I think the first on either side of his family to go to university: he won a scholarship to read engineering at Cambridge. Then he went on to do a Ph.D. in electrical engineering.

Shortly after he got his doctorate my father was hired by a prestigious engineering firm, a company founded in the 1930s by the younger son of an Earl who had been sent to Rhodesia (as it was then) to make his fortune. The company was studded with men who had been to Eton, Harrow and Winchester. Even in the mid-1950s such companies excluded the middle and working class products of the new "red brick" universities. No doubt my father's passport in was his Cambridge degree.

As it happened one of the partners in this firm was my mother's godfather. My mother at this time was working as an assistant to a Knightsbridge antiques dealer. She was young, attractive, well-bred and she had the right sorts of friends. Her pay was meager but she was given an additional allowance to buy clothes. In return she gave parties for prospective clients, primarily from abroad. On one occasion she was giving a party for a particularly tall Norwegian princess. When, at the last minute, one of her tame bachelors caught the flu and backed out, she could think of no other man of sufficient height to take his place. Then she remembered the young man she'd bumped into when she was visiting her godfather in his office.

The party went so well she ran out of Pimms and decided to brew up some cold tea as a substitute, reckoning everyone was drunk enough that they wouldn't know the difference. My father caught her at it and decided, so the story goes, "This is the wife for me."

• CHAPTER ONE •

My mother told this story often. My father hid behind his newspaper. He almost never told stories. I've noticed before how revealing these oft-told stories can be about a family. It's as if they are so smooth from being passed from hand to hand that nobody notices just how much they are giving away.

In marrying my mother my father married someone with the necessary social savoir faire. She dressed him and coached him in the finer linguistic distinctions of class, as she did later with Bill and me — "Don't say pardon, say what; it's sofa not couch, loo not toilet" — especially after any visit to Ma and Grandpop, my father's parents. My mother herself came from a complicated mix of Spanish, Scots and Anglo-Irish minor aristocracy. She had the blood but no money. An only child, her father was killed at Dunkirk when she was five, and her mother, whom I called Granny, never remarried. Granny had lived in East Africa until my mother was born (only just making it back to British soil in time), and was later a professional harpist. She lived most of the rest of her life in the Lake District in straitened circumstances, making occasional trips to London where she stayed in small, dignified upper-class hotels. My mother's coming out ball as a debutante probably ate a large hole in Granny's capital.

When I think about my parents' marriage there are so many social forces converging that it is hard to see the individuals. My mother was devoted to being a Woman, finding her worth in the mirror of men's eyes, and my father too seemed content to play his traditional part, being the breadwinner, the rational one, leaving emotions to my mother. As a teenager I thought they had divided the attributes of one human being between two, they needed each other to be whole. That was the ideal in their time, and they lived it. They have been married for almost forty years.

It is always hard for children to write about their parents. In the context of a book about violent sexual abuse, it is tempting to try to point to the monsters lurking in the shadows, but the thing about my family was that the surface was so well-polished one could not see what was underneath. Perhaps it is the very absence of cracks and contradictions that is the warning sign.

Here was my father, a successful engineer, tall, thin, blond-haired and blue-eyed, handsome in a boney way, fond of golf, chess, fishing, a good swimmer. He liked to do a little work with his hands, did a lot of the renovation of the Mill House, the house my parents bought in 1964, himself. He dreamed on retirement of planting a vineyard and making his own wine.

And my mother 5 feet 2 inches, plump and always on a diet, with green eyes and auburn hair. Wherever we went in the Mediterranean, she looked like a native. Artistic, emotional, acquisitive, filling the house with beautiful antiques bought for a song, she was an ardent gardener. Beauty of any sort really moved her. She yearned after a bohemian life but needed the stability of convention. Family was very important to her, perhaps because she had so little of it. So was her image of herself as a passionate, sexual woman. She proclaimed herself stupid, regarding intellectuals as bloodless bores, but was always chosen to head committees (which she despised) because of her grasp of the necessary information. She loved to ride and read the biographies of queens and courtesans. As a young woman she won trophies show jumping. My brother too played golf and fished and swam, and planned, from early childhood, to be a rich man ("So you can look after your poor old mother in her old age," my mother always said.) He was sent to boarding school at seven, as was the custom for boys of his class, though he was miserable and homesick and my mother didn't want him to go — "but what could you do? He wouldn't fit in later if he didn't start now." Perhaps in reaction to his older sister he was determinedly unintellectual and conservative. For his twenty-first birthday, at his own request, he was given a dinner jacket. His Christmas cards, when he was at university, were all from couples, Jock and Sue, Sandy and John. But he ended up leading a far less conventional life, climbing mountains all over the world and, eventually, settling in Nepal where he organizes climbing expeditions in the Himalayas.

There was always this adventurous streak in my parents too. It's one of the things I'm grateful for: we didn't stick to the expatriate British ghettoes in the various countries we lived in. We swam on dangerous, beautiful beaches in East Africa and drove through deserts to game reserves where we watched hippopotami wallow and ate antelope steaks for dinner when I was seven and eight and nine. We traveled in Iran, making friends with the secret service agent sent to follow us, and explored the Atlas Mountains of North Africa. Each of my father's consulting jobs offered new possibilities. We were never quite sure where he would be sent. As each assignment neared its end we would spin a globe and take turns closing our eyes and putting a finger down on the turning world: Addis Abbaba; Moscow — oh God no, too bad for my cystitis — Baghdad, that's better; Melbourne.

Chapter One

I suppose I was the crack, the fissure, the one who had the police car drawn up outside the house in Germany after I got caught shoplifting wine from the local supermarket, the curtains in all the neighboring houses twitching. I was the one who got thrown out of school at fourteen after the Italian teacher saw me making out with the English teacher. I was the one who got drunk and did a striptease for the waiting chauffeurs.

In the end I was the one who couldn't keep to the pattern of drinking approved by my class: gin and tonic or a whisky soda at lunch, sometimes followed by wine, the same before dinner, wine with the meal, now and then brandy or a liqueur afterwards. That was how my parents drank. I don't remember a day when they didn't drink. But they rarely got drunk. The way they drank was not unusual for the world in which they lived. I doubt they could have kept up the perfect surface without it.

I wanted to keep up that surface too, it was the only world I knew. But for whatever reason I could not manage my drinking the way they did theirs. A few weeks after I got sober I had a dream in which my mother and father and brother were all in a speedboat. They were wearing bright colored clothing and smiling as if for a photograph. The sun shone, bouncing off the surface of the water. From the dock where I was standing I could see a shadow moving under the water. I was terrified. I wanted to call out to them, to warn them, but I couldn't make the words come, and they kept on smiling.

Chapter Two

In the years following the surfacing of that first composite memory in April 1984, as I remembered more and more of the incest I experienced as a child, the strange business of remembering completely repressed experiences became ordinary to me. Each new memory had its own charge, of course. At first I was simply stunned to discover that my past was not what I thought. Then there was the specific pain of facing what each of my parents had done. Gradually the ways I'd felt and acted over the years began to make more sense to me, and there was a sort of relief in that, though always mingled with grief at what I now knew.

It was relentless, the wave upon wave of new information beating down on me. At different points, first with Esther and then, after I moved to Western Massachusetts in 1986, with Rich, I was sure I'd reached the end, that this was the last, worst memory my psyche had been holding back until I was ready to face it. But then, a few weeks later, another memory would come. Memories almost never came, whole and finished, out of nowhere. There was usually some kind of leakage first: fragments of feelings, images, anxiety. I learned to take all the bits and pieces to therapy, to talk about first one then another, paying attention to my feelings, to what felt hardest. With Esther, at the beginning, I would often stutter at a key word and then I would feel my consciousness slip sideways. Sometimes I stared at her glass-topped coffee table, or rather at the light reflected from it, until I felt myself begin to trance out. With Rich, I would talk, paying attention to "casual thoughts," following apparent digressions, and then there would be a slight internal movement, as if a trapdoor had opened in my diaphragm and I had dropped down deeper into myself.

It is a distinct state, the remembering state, though the difference from ordinary consciousness is subtle. It is as though one has stepped sideways, out of the traffic of everyday life. It feels similar to the state I'm in when I'm writing a poem, consciousness collected, focused inward, detached from the chatter of the intellect. The length of time I stayed "under", in the remembering state, varied but it was rarely longer than half an hour, usually less.

Mostly the shift into the remembering state happened only a moment or two before the forgotten experience broke through into consciousness and then I would be inside the experience and watching it at the same time, the watcher commenting, 'No way, what the hell is this, who does shit like that? You're making it up' while I went in and out of feeling what had happened.

Often I was afraid I wouldn't be able to come back, I would be sucked into the past, maddened by it to some point of no return. Sometimes I shut down suddenly, in the middle of a memory, overwhelmed by a wave of sleepiness, or I would find myself thinking about algebra or grocery shopping. Sometimes I came back to the present abruptly, sometimes slowly. There was always a moment when I crossed the line. Sometimes I could talk, tell what I was seeing, while I was in the memory, sometimes telling had to wait until afterwards.

And after the surfacing of the memory there was the shock of it. Often I cried for a long time. Mostly in the end I would switch into intellectual mode, making connections, seeing how the new information had been presaged, how it affected what I already knew. This was the beginning of integrating it into my story. It was also how I separated myself from the feelings and readied myself to go out into the street.

It was exhausting and disorienting, traveling between worlds in this way, but I didn't have a lot of alternatives. I almost always tried to delay whatever memory was coming up, but experience taught me that it would come in the end, and that the period when a memory was on its way to the surface was often more painful and disruptive than actually facing the memory.

Though it's hard to work up much gratitude for this, I think I am lucky that I was able to remember. There are people for whom it is not an option: at the moment when repressed information is about to surface, the psyche goes on red alert, fearing that the information is still too threatening to its integrity. The information is pushed back down again and there is none of the relief that follows when a memory has truly become conscious.

I say memory, but in fact what surfaces is more like raw experience. It only becomes a memory, in the ordinary sense of the word, at the end of the process when it has been felt and thought about and integrated into the self. The "memories" I was recovering had not gone through the usual process which transforms experience into memory. Instead they had collected, unassimilated, inchoate, in a state of suspended animation. There they waited, some of them for more than twenty years, until something, some internal wisdom, judged that I was ready to let them start moving down the path from experience to memory.

So when I talk about remembering forgotten experiences what I am really talking about is completing the process of experiencing that event for the first time. That is why the images and emotions and physical sensations are often so much more vivid than in ordinary memory: I am feeling the experience fully for the first time. Once I have done that, the experience begins to turn into a memory. It loses some of its clarity and detail, and becomes more like any other childhood memory.(1)

The transformation of experience into memory is a natural process: it takes energy to interrupt it. And although one can keep experiences frozen for years they are always in an unstable state: they exist inside the psyche but they have not been assimilated into it. Like shrapnel or a splinter, however embedded, they remain alien, an irritant.

The point at which I got sober was somehow the point at which my psyche decided it was costing me too much to keep the deep freeze running. Or perhaps I was ready to start remembering earlier but subconsciously I was using booze to put off the moment when I would have to start knowing the truth of my life. Once I did start remembering what happened to me, though the process was painful and tedious and frightening, something in me understood that this was what I had to do if I wanted to live an authentic life. I'd always wanted to feel alive — that was what I tried to get from booze and drugs and sex and danger — and somehow, when I got sober, I understood that all the artificial ways would only leave me feeling dead inside (if they didn't actually kill me.) It wasn't that I wanted to remember all that pain. If I had known exactly how much of it I was going to have to face, I probably would have gone out and gotten drunk. But somehow I did know that it wasn't pointless suffering, to remember. Still I was always hoping I'd done enough of it.

In the summer of 1989 I thought that finally I really had dredged up all the forgotten experiences lurking about in my psyche. Rich thought so too. I felt freer than I ever had before, and less of a stranger to myself. I still had a few inexplicable reactions to things, a few memory fragments which didn't seem to fit in anywhere, but they were so few compared to how it used to be they seemed insignificant.

I'd been sober for five years. I'd finished my first novel and was starting on a second. Working as a freelance carpenter, I made enough to support myself and my writing habit. And I was finally in a calm and viable relationship.

I'd been lovers with Liz for a year and a half, a record for me. Eight years my elder, Liz grew up in a Hampshire village forty miles from the Mill House, the house my parents had bought when I was six. The same height as me — 5'10" — but with straight reddish hair and blue eyes (mine is curly and brown, my eyes green), what had drawn me to her, beyond a powerful sexual attraction, was her kindness, her probity, her passion for accuracy. For the first time I felt I was in a relationship that might last.

Liz had emigrated to America in her early twenties. After a few years in Seattle she bought land and built a house for herself in southern Vermont, in a town whose population of six hundred was a zany and on the whole amiable mix of hippies, lesbians and Yankees. A few months after we got together she offered to give me a piece of her land. In December 1988 I went to live with her while I built my own house next door to hers.

In retrospect it was probably exactly this new level of material and emotional security which made it possible for me to recall abuse I could not have coped with before.

That summer, putting in a couple of hours' work each morning on the novel then working on the house until it got dark, I began to remember what I thought of as formalized abuse: my mother watching while my father had sex with me. He would only stop when I came. Sometimes they tied me up. This was supposed to make me straight. I also remembered my mother giving me to a group of men at the riding stables where we kept a horse. Sometimes she watched them rape me. All of this took place in Germany where we lived from when I was thirteen until I was seventeen.

What made these memories different from all the earlier incest memories was the element of premeditation. There must have been some discussion between that group of men and my mother. My father must have bought the rope he used to tie me up, or at least gone down to the basement for it. Or did he add it to my mother's shopping list?

Whatever half-conscious excuses I had made for them — my mother disoriented, a split personality, driven to re-enact her own abuse on me, my father in spasms of uncontrollable sexual need — disintegrated in the face of their collaboration and planning. The horror that grew in me then was a shadow of what was to come a few months later.

I had a lot of questions about these new memories. Why hadn't I run away? When I got in the car with my mother to go to the stables did I think we were just going riding? Did I know I was going to be gang-raped and get in anyway? I was a teenager by then, how could I have been so cowed at home when I was such a rebel at school?

How could I have blanked all this out while still maintaining a fairly continuous recollection of day to day life at home? I'd had near total amnesia concerning my childhood up to the age of twelve: clearly I had protected myself from the incest that happened during that time by forgetting everything. But I thought I remembered my life as a teenager. How could I have remembered the colors of the carpets in the house in Germany, the windowsills, the views from the windows, and forgotten being raped on my bed? I thought I remembered how I spent my days, sleeping as late as possible, working my way through Western literature at the rate of a book a day, drinking whatever I could lay my hands on. How could I have forgotten and remembered at the same time?

By this point in my recovery I'd had plenty of practice in the discipline of listening to the promptings of my psyche, however crazy or frightening or shameful or plain improbable they might be. I'd learned not to try to make a finished story before I even had the first draft down. So I let the questions be questions and went on listening.

Dream hints and images began to coalesce into the sense that I had gotten pregnant by my father when I was sixteen or seventeen.

10/10/89

"I can't talk. I feel really trapped. I can't make the words come. It started when I was about to say miscarriage.

I can see myself very drunk on gin hitting my stomach? To make it come out?

Can you talk to me? This feels stupid but I can't talk."

That was a note I handed to Rich. I was trying to say I thought I'd had a miscarriage but I couldn't say it. Couldn't make the word come — any words — afraid I'd start screaming no No NO

Scary to be silenced. Terrifying. Breathe, try to accept. This is a part of me who is afraid to speak, who's stopping me. I couldn't cross the line between my mind and the muscles of my mouth, my tongue.

The memory felt real though of course I wanted to believe I was making it up. That struggle I was used to but I was puzzled by this new element: willing myself to say a word and not being able to.

To protect myself from the emotional impact of the memory, I focused on practicalities. Was it in the bathroom at boarding school that I had the miscarriage? How far along was I? I remembered having suddenly gained a lot of weight the fall after I turned sixteen. Was it then?

Usually after a few weeks of sitting with a new memory the details sorted themselves out and I'd have an idea of roughly where and when something happened. Mostly too, the experience would lose some of its charge once I'd remembered it. But in the case of this memory the details remained hazy and for months afterwards the sight of blood in the toilet bowl when I got my period left me frantic, crowded in the head, panting with anxiety.

When a memory is not complete it exerts a sort of magnetic pull on every day life, drawing circumstances which will trigger the release of whatever remains hidden. I don't understand *how* this works but I know that it does.

In early November of 1989 Suzanne, a Jungian analyst with whom I had worked, helping to take groups on a white people's version of a vision quest, asked if I wanted to come to a gathering at her house. It was to be a circle of women, mostly in their forties and older, who had not had children or had lost them and wanted to talk about their feelings. This seemed timely to me, still reeling from the memory of the miscarriage, but I was leery, having decided not to

• CHAPTER TWO •

work with Suzanne any more. She assured me she wasn't expecting me to help her lead the ceremony. There was to be a fire ritual: participants could bring things to give to the fire. Frantic with doubt — should I go? shouldn't I? — I made a clay figurine of the fetus I had miscarried.

When I arrived I saw a circle of women mostly my age, mid-thirties, with a life-size baby doll in the middle of the circle and another woman nursing a new born. Suzanne acted as if I was helping her lead the ceremony and I didn't refuse, I shut down and stayed. When it came my turn to offer something to the fire I put the clay figurine in it, explaining what it represented. I felt numb and desperate at the same time, as if I was violating something just to fill a role I hadn't wanted anyway. As soon as the ceremony was over I felt a fireball of rage rush through me and left without a word. I had no idea where the feelings were coming from, only that I had done something terrible.

11/27/89

Why are so many of the people I feel close to or drawn to turning out to be ritual abuse survivors (and multiples)? [People with Multiple Personality Disorder.] I feel thoroughly chilled by talk of RA.

My intense unease with ritual lately?

Stuff about a deformed baby?

Hoods — people in hoods.

Memory of a "past life" as an Aztec priest cutting out the heart of a human sacrifice.

11/28/89

Such sadness and — fear — has moved down into my belly from my heart — I wake up with the ache, don't know what I've been dreaming but I think all night I've been trying to think everything all right with my stomach muscles but I can't.

Instead I feel bleak, I want to cry, but it's the kind of sad which is leaking out from way inside my body.

It's gray outside, windy and raining.

11/29/89

Saw Rich. Talked about the grief, rage reactions to the sounds of people eating, the anger at feeling watched — sense that there's a memory which will tie it all together. Perhaps Mum was eating while watching Dad fuck me.

I wanted to say there's something to tie up food and sex and feel-

ing like a prostitute but I couldn't say the words — couldn't say "tie up," no way to make the words — like with the miscarriage memory. I wrote it down, aware of a different voice there — tie up ha ha she wrote — sense of her intense rage — one great scream.

She talked, this other one — I don't remember all of it clearly — about her murderous rage, how I wanted to kill them, how I tried once. "Anna was scared when she came to in their bedroom holding the knife I'd taken from the kitchen."

Grief and sadness as well as rage — Mum sitting eating. Both of them eating, just watching — me tied up, exposed. They talking about me — how much I cost to feed. This was for me to hear, though not spoken to me.

Also Mum asking Dad how it is, how do I feel inside.

This is for their benefit, their little power play.

I can't see much — Dad's black shoes. I think I'm on my stomach.

At one point in the remembering my back cramps. I think I had my arms tied behind my back. How I went in and out of trying to shut down completely alternating with trying to get into feelings of arousal, to submerge myself completely so the feelings were like the ocean and Mum and Dad became small by comparison.

Sure does tie up (ha ha) food and sex and feeling like a prostitute. Shit.

At some point the voice said Anna wants to come back and then I was there again.

Rich used the word ritualistic of it all.

Yes, I thought with relief, my abuse was ritualistic, that's what it was, that must be why I'm feeling this odd connection to ritual abuse survivors.

Over the course of the next week, the first week of December, 1989, I had my first explicit memories of ritual abuse. The initial stage in the surfacing of a memory is rather like a cook assembling all the ingredients on the counter, only the cook doesn't know, consciously, what's on the menu. In the weeks leading up to the first explicit memories, I assembled hoods, human sacrifice, MPD, bleakness, a memory of rage and holding a knife, splitting, the sound of eating, something about babies and fire and feeling implicated.

To switch metaphors, it's as if a whirlpool develops in the psyche, drawing to it the bits and pieces of feeling, thought, observation which float around, organizing conscious but unnoticed material in relation to the center, the source of that centripetal draw: the will of the story to be told, the will of the psyche to complete the process by which an experience is absorbed and transformed into a memory.

12/1/89
Bar Harbor, Maine

In the car driving north, Liz and I inventing a detective story to stay awake: Muriel Norridge, English village postmistress, uncovering a satanic cult. She's noticed an eleven year old girl acting strangely, finds her a safe place to stay in the woods. At last the girl trusts Muriel enough to tell her about the ritual abuse. Who can Muriel trust? Is the village policeman involved? the doctor? the vicar? I kept embellishing the story.

Then L. asked if I thought I was going to remember any ritual abuse.

I felt dread, wanted to say no but couldn't, that cold silence — went inside — not to teenage stuff with Mum and Dad but click to the man in the brown suit, me at 10 or 11 putting a cross of my blood on Mum & Dad's bedroom door, my sudden fear of ghosts and supernatural stuff. [These were memory fragments I'd not been able to place.] Flash of this man's genitals up close — click — they or he must have told me I'd go blind if I told — the origin of that fear.

At a gas station — look in the mirror in the bathroom — eyes not recognizing me but more, looking for something behind me — him? — something I expect to be there which isn't. Weird feeling.

L. says: Is this the man who you and your brother watched fucking your mother?

I'd forgotten about that memory.

The up close feeling of seeing his genitals, his hairy thighs.

Inside there's an eleven year old keeping these memories, afraid if she tells I'll go blind.

Asked her to show me.

I see the hands of the man holding a long knife to Bill's little boy penis — horror and terror in me — my mother afraid too then (and out of it on ? codeine) — he made a cut at the base of Bill's penis and smeared the blood in an X on my belly and genitals — said, or I thought? — 'This is where you do it' then fucked Mum.

L. asked if he was naked. Sense that no, he was wearing something weird? Something with a hood? (I found myself thinking about hoods in the last week or two, and about my terror watching "The Omega Man" when I was fourteen: men in hoods in an underground garage, pouring lighted gasoline on people.)

The smugglers' tunnel in the Mill House — underground — the stone steps?

Jesus, I'm sad and tired of this, ask God for strength and willingness to go on. This a.m. I was aware each bit of recovery is not for me alone but for my people, for all the survivors who need desperately to see and believe healing is possible.

That felt good — that it's for us as well as for me.

When Liz asked me if I was going to remember ritual abuse, I felt cold to the bone. I hadn't really registered what I was doing as I pushed the plot of our detective story towards the uncovering of ritual abuse. But when I couldn't answer her question and I felt that cold, I knew. I didn't want to know, and soon enough the doubts would come flooding in, but in that moment I knew.

Fragments of memory and information which had never fitted in anywhere began to come together. Instead of finding myself thinking of the "ritualistic" abuse when I was a teenager, to my surprise I was brought back to the period when I was ten and eleven. We had just returned from Kenya to England where we lived in the Mill House. A sixteenth century cottage with an Edwardian addition, the Mill House had what was reputed to be a smugglers' tunnel, reached by stone steps which led down from behind a door in the laundry room. I had some, though not a lot, of ordinary memory of that time. I knew I had gone from being an excellent student to playing truant and stealing, that I had gone quite abruptly from loving ghost stories to being terrified of anything to do with the supernatural, that I'd suddenly become afraid of going blind and that I'd started having nightmares. I remembered going to see Granny often in the middle of the night. She was always awake, and kind to me. (She had come to spend the last few months of her life with us. She was dying of cancer: it was pain that kept her awake, I realized later.)

There were odd fragments of memory which had surfaced over the years: my first year in therapy I'd remembered making that bloody cross on my parents' bedroom door when I was ten or eleven. I'd assumed it was an expression of anger at my mother for having an affair while my father was away. It seemed a little on the weird side but hey, I was a weird kid. A couple of years after that I'd remembered

• CHAPTER TWO •

"a man in a brown suit." That was how I always thought of him. I figured he must be the man my mother was having an affair with though it surprised me, he didn't seem her type somehow. In the summer of 1989 I remembered my brother and I being made to watch him having sex with my mother. The memory never felt quite complete and I "forgot" it again.

12/2/89
Bar Harbor

Dream.

There is a bank with an old apple tree and a drainage ditch. A toddler comes with me, Sophia [a friend] saying be careful. I see the little child's face turned up to me, blond hair, and then faster than I can stop she toddles to the edge where there's a lake, where looking down I saw a sunken boat — she falls in and sinks like a stone. I dive right in over her, go straight to the bottom. It's too dark to see but my hands fasten around what I think is her body, sense a little warmth — swim right out and toss her onto the bank. Somebody can do first aid and they bring her back. I'm told she'll be OK.

I wake up.

Later

The ice covered granite at the thunder hole, ultramarine water reaching up into the crevices of rock

water & weed

rock & ice

Felt this is it, is exactly what I need, this is what I came to Maine for, this harshness, this throb from the rock. I need this now to make it, to live what I have to live, the opposites present, the green rocking sea, the still rocks, the hard rock, the matted spongy seaweed & further down barnacles and purple glints of mussels cleaving to the rock

pink & gray

No more words really than to keep describing the water, the rocks, the coexistence of opposites.

Initiation. Descent. The choices one makes — to accept the strange and ragged intuitions, to stand before the empty page.

Those first days of sobriety, haunted by the sense of a black hole inside, by the stone steps. Now I think again about the steps from the secret tunnel....

L. dreamt of a wounded baby bear — the peril of helping it, that it's mother was around — a wound such that it could not survive in the wild.

1. I have found the writing of Dr. Ivor Browne particularly useful in understanding my experiences of remembering. Dr. Browne is Professor of Psychiatry at University College, Dublin, and chief psychiatrist for the Eastern Health Board, Dublin. C.f. his paper, "Psychological Trauma, or Unexperienced Experience." *ReVISION* 12, no.4 (Spring 1990): 21-34.

Chapter Three

12/5/89

Liz's and my second anniversary.

Saw Rich.

Talked about the maybe memory of ritual sexual abuse — tapping into the split off parts of me.

Trying to tap into it a bit more.

The room underground in the Mill House — the smuggler's tunnel. The hood. R. pointed out I'd noticed this man's clothing in earlier memories of him — the Man in the Brown Suit. Flash — candlelight (no wonder I don't find it restful), the man, my mother and I naked — something whirling over our heads? him having us touch each other? That's not really it.

My mind veered away. Then I was thinking of the eleven-year-old self who said no, who split off.

Rich was visibly shaken while I was trying to picture what happened — he got up and moved around, heart racing — he had an image — I asked him to tell me — of candlelight, the man, a long knife, the killing of a baby.

I was running hot and cold chills but not exactly connecting.

Yes re Suzanne and my "past life memory" from a year ago, both of us witches in a coven, me responsible for the death of her baby. I associated that life then with the Mill House, the underground passage. Suzanne in present life, the babies at the ritual at her house where I felt so nuts.

My dream of recovering the baby (toddler really).

L's dream of an injured young animal.

Phone rings.

> *R. smiles. Phone call was to ask if the church wants a box of small animals for children.*
>
> *I ask him again, what was that symbolism of the bloody cross I put on Mum & Dad's door?*
>
> *Chill — the sign the Jews put on their doors so the Angel of Death would not take their first born children when the last curse fell on the Pharoah.*
>
> *Tears came a little but I think the feelings are shut off with the split away person.*
>
> *R. said I can see him Thursday if I need to.*
>
> *I've felt off red meat for the first time in years this last couple of weeks. Keep thinking about Tina going vegetarian when she began to remember the baby killing stuff. Baby eating.*
>
> *Where do the babies come from?*

As the first memories began to surface, I heard the constant hammering of doubt in my mind. I must be making it up. I must. A part of me knew there was no point in trying to decide now. Only time could tell me whether these were experiences surfacing or mere chimera, without root in real life, part of a mass hysteria. My longing for the images not to be true fought with the knowledge I'd won of myself and of the process of remembering.

There was something familiar about the way disparate elements were coming together, a whole cloth starting to weave itself out of so many separate threads. In dealing with the incest memories, I had come to trust this process. But the image of a baby actually being killed with a knife had come from Rich's mind, not directly from mine. I knew we had a strong psychic connection, I trusted him not to jerk me around, but still it was possible to that this was his image, not mine. He agreed. He had been very hesitant to tell me the image, and had stressed at the time that it could well be a figment of his imagination.

Occasionally, in the past, Rich had had an image come and, if I wanted to hear it, he had told me it. Either I would respond instantly, usually by bursting into tears, or I would feel only a polite interest. It would be clear immediately whether he was indeed mirroring an image from my mind, or projecting one from his. This time it was a little different.

I had seen Rich's agitation while I sat there stuck, my mind veering away from the emerging knowledge. Trying to think about

Chapter Three

what was coming up felt like trying to hold two magnets together, north pole to north pole. I felt frustrated, disconnected, guessing rather than being able to look at whatever was pushing at the membrane separating conscious from unconscious. So when I asked Rich what was up and he said he had a powerful image, I urged him to tell me it. I thought from previous times that I would be able to tell by my reaction whether the image was real for me or not. This time, though, I felt neither the instant click and release of feelings I'd have expected if it were true, nor the indifference I would normally feel if it were off base. My body was responding with intense changes in temperature but I couldn't feel the image emotionally. I could see, however, how it was in a sense already woven into the cloth: Suzanne, babies, the meaning of the bloody cross, meat, the man with the knife, so many images prefigured this one.

Rich had not simply imposed an image of his own, but had brought together several of mine. A few weeks earlier I had told him a dream about a dead baby I was trying to bury. In the dream there was nowhere deep enough to put it. Parts of the baby kept poking out of the ground. Still I felt I couldn't be sure about Rich's image.

Part of what was disrupting my usual process, and would do so for a while, was the split I was finding in myself: "Inside there's an eleven-year-old keeping these memories, afraid if she tells me I'll go blind." It wasn't so much the sense of having an identifiable eleven-year-old self inside which felt new to me, as the fact that she was in control of information I did not know about. In order for that information to enter consciousness I had to step aside and let her talk. It felt a little weird, but I soon got the knack of it.

Over the previous three years I had developed an amiable relationship with what I called the tribe, a cluster of internal characters, from a joyful two-year-old to Miles, an extremely practical and scientific eleven-year-old boy, to Marin, the vain teenage girl I never was. I didn't feel out of control or threatened as an adult by these aspects of myself. They didn't take over, and anyway, having written a novel, I viewed the presence of different characters living and talking inside me without much alarm. I enjoyed a playful relationship with them, and had learned that relating to myself as an inclusive circle, a kind tribe rather than an authoritarian family in which the conscious adult has to dominate, gave me a new serenity and balance.

There are a lot of labels which could be applied to what I was doing, from reparenting myself to managing Multiple Personality

Disorder. I'm glad I didn't bother with them. The emergence of this new eleven-year-old, however, unnerved me. I didn't want to start having the kinds of experiences my two friends with MPD talked about, of losing time, finding they'd done and said things in the present that they did not remember. I was afraid that I, in my adult, witness self, might not be able to remain present while the eleven-year-old told her story.

There was another more familiar split I was finding in myself: my feelings were separate from my knowledge. It felt as though I was getting a lot of information without being able to work it through emotionally. It wasn't that I was completely numb. Instead of being attached to particular memories the feeling permeated everything. This in the end helped me believe there must be some reality to the new images.

12/6/89

Cry cry cry — a broken heart? a heavy heart. Most of the day I worked and was o.k. — splitting firewood (a good semi-dangerous task requiring muscles and concentration) and a little bit laying my floor.

Cried on my way to the SIA meeting — spacey — missed the exit.

I think there's a psychic event happening, like the Berlin wall coming down, re ritual abuse. So many people remembering dead babies.

I'm moving much faster than usual, hardly any time to feel.

12/7/89

I did not know [when I had the "past-life memory"] that Suzanne had a daughter who died as a baby.

[I'd asked Suzanne to find the clay baby I'd put in her woodstove during the fire ritual at her house and give it back to me.]

I open the packet containing the charred clay baby from that ceremony I was so angry about.... I say, sitting with the clay baby, what if it wasn't a real baby they killed, it was just a doll — then I see a knife being plunged in and the flesh? quartered? carved?

Split the rest of my firewood today and moved another 1/3 cord down near the cabin — tired, headache after talking to Rich on the phone, but maybe it was the fumes and the noise of the splitter. (Oh, ha ha, the splitter.)

Miserable in the evening, cold and headachey and nauseous but remembered it would pass and dozed and it did.

Thank God for this relationship with Liz — I don't know how

CHAPTER THREE

I'd do this without her — think of Tina, of Carol, alone with this — God I'm grateful for the security I do have.

12/9/89

Dreamt about knives — different kinds — and about everything being built of ice.

Dear God dear God spare me and protect me, my heart aches and I cry when I relax. God what if it's true, what if I watched, what if my hand was on the knife, what if I lived at the baby's expense

What if it's true

Great gasps of sobbing after a wild no no no as I reached for the bread-knife and was thinking about what I'd written here and I remembered then screaming no no no and the man shoved the handle of the knife into my cunt, the knife he used, the long blade sticking down between my legs, bloody.

Fine walk in the woods by the beaver pond — so many tracks, raccoon & fox & deer & skunk & maybe possum — a stream skimmed over with ice, water falling down a waterfall under ice, hollow, reverberating.

There's no evil in nature but plenty of suffering and death.

My lovely pink and blonde oak floor.

12/11/89

Read at the church yesterday as part of the 150th Anniversary Celebration poetry reading. It was great — the response strong and warm.

Jack Donahue's going to barter honey from his bees for poems.

Sodden with grief I sob whenever I slow down, driving especially — saturated — keening helps a little — I ache & ache & ache — I suppose perhaps it's true.

12/13/89

Voices driving to the SIA meeting. "Drive off the road." "Drive at that light." Crowded somehow inside. Programming?

12/15/89

I feel much better having told L. last night all of what I remember — slices of the baby's flesh, the knife handle in my cunt. My eye stopped twitching after I told her.

Cried in the Common Ground Restaurant — deep anxiety ris-

ing up in me — *after passing the life-size creche scene in which a man in brown knelt over the crib?*

Flashes in the drive home through the snow of the knife going into the baby, of the silence which followed

Can't believe sometimes I'm living this nightmare

If it was a doll
If it was an animal
If it wasn't

Assimilating shocking information takes time: denial is a necessary stage, a natural means of self-protection. "What if? What if it's true?" rang in my head over and over. I found some shelter in the conditional while beginning to take in the possibility that I had witnessed a baby being murdered in front of me. My psyche, trying to complete the experience, seized on like experiences in the present: my hand on the handle of a long bread knife; the figure of a man in a brown gown bending over a cradle. Through these breaches in the dam which was holding back all that I knew poured images, feelings. These came directly from me, without any suggestion from Rich or anyone else. This undercut my hope that the sacrifice was merely the product of Rich's imagination.

I tried out the idea that it had all happened but not to a real baby. I'd heard a woman in a meeting say she'd gone to see a therapist who specialised in ritual abuse, who was a survivor herself, and this therapist told her the cults never killed real babies, it was always an illusion, theater intended to terrify. I couldn't buy that that was always so but perhaps, perhaps in my case.

Mostly I felt a sort of aching shock and a grief so pervasive I thought perhaps I was at last feeling the sorrow of my grandmother's death. I'd felt loved by her, and safe with her, and I'd never been able to remember her death or the funeral or anything much except a vague sense that she had been cremated. Perhaps, I told myself, all this sorrow was about Granny and not about dead babies at all.

I knew from experience that telling someone else what I was remembering would help, but I felt more than usually reluctant. When I did finally tell Liz, I felt better, and the odd tic in my right eyelid stopped.

I'd never had such a tic before: it started when I began to remember the ritual abuse, and I've had it, on and off, ever since. It's

• CHAPTER THREE •

irritating but also validating — it's not something I could make happen — and useful, like the oil pressure warning light in a car. It comes when there's something I don't want to see, goes away when I've looked at whatever it is and told somebody about it. Sometimes it serves as a more general indicator of my level of stress: it came back, for example, when I finally got myself to type out these first explicit memories for this book.

In some ways I was fortunate that, when the ritual abuse started to come up, I already had five years' practice in dealing with incest memories. I had come to trust the internal wisdom which governs this journey when it is allowed to do so. I knew that the more I trusted it, the less frightening and disruptive the process would be. This trust had not come easily.

At the end of my first year sober, when I began to acknowledge the incest with my mother, I remember standing in front of the little altar I'd made on my chest of drawers, thinking, "I know something is helping me. I don't have the courage to face this, I never have had, but I'm doing it, so something must be helping." On my altar were four statuettes a friend had given me. I'd told her about getting sober and, haltingly, about my need somehow to connect with a Higher Power, and she'd said "Oh, you're the person I brought these for then, I didn't know. It was just before I left India. I knew I had to buy them." They were four aspects of the Divine Mother, and though I knew so little of Hindu iconography I couldn't be sure which was which, I prayed to them every night.

That first year I would listen to people in AA meetings say "You only get what you can handle," and I'd think "Oh yeah, what about Auschwitz?" I felt overwhelmed by all the new information. My family wasn't what I thought it was. I wasn't who I thought I was. Without alcohol to dim them, feelings I couldn't even name roared through me. I wrote and wrote and when I couldn't write fast enough I painted with my fingers until all the colors merged into a mud brown. When even that didn't work I tried acting as if I believed that, just for today, I wasn't going to get more than I could handle, and I found it helped. I had a series of provisos which enabled me to pretend I believed it: I got what I could handle with all the help now available to me; it was my own psyche which only released to me what I could handle. (I couldn't — still can't — believe that some great controlling god metes out traffic accidents and fatal illnesses only to those who can "handle" them.)

Pretending to believe I wouldn't get more than I could handle in any one day allowed me to unhook my feelings about the feelings I was having from the feelings themselves. I couldn't get rid of the fear and pain but I found I had some control over my fear of the fear, over that screech of anxiety: I can't bear this, it's too much, I'll go crazy, I won't be able to work, etc.

I knew all this. I had learned to do what works, not what makes sense. I had learned how much more tolerable it is to accept the presence of pain and terror, to live with them in the moment, than it is to try to drive them away. I had learned the power of trust, but as the ritual abuse came up, I could not hold onto it for more than a moment or two at a time.

12/18/89

Dream.

Tina and I get a job cutting up first apples then fish for a woman. She doesn't leave clear instructions about what she wants so we're guessing a bit. Tina's been doing it a while longer — points to more bruises which need to be cut out of the apples. Then I'm cutting up a huge side of smoked salmon. It almost wraps itself around me like a blanket when I move it. It is beautiful. It's all right cutting the flesh into squares though I'm not sure how big they should be. Then I cut up a flat fish? (a bottom feeder). At first I see it as a stuffed animal made from Black Watch tartan. Start to cut then realize I have to take out the backbone first — some comes out easily, the main spine, but not some of the smaller bones — I pull them out with pliers.

The next morning we go to work and the woman has us sit, smudges us with sage. I draw in smoke, grateful for it. Nothing much happens. We sit a while. Then there's a group of us, all women. We throw a ball around. I catch and throw fairly hard, my competitive edge comes out, and with it a tinge of aggression. The woman approves of that which makes me happy.

Then she asks us each to answer some questions with a couple of sentences, which we do. She tells us how each of us has revealed something of ourselves: K. has anger as her core emotion, J. throws up psychic screens, then she looks me in the eye, says "Sorrow." I feel it all show through my eyes as I look back at her then drop them.

I feel seen and accepted, loved really, and in the presence of strength. Seen above all. It was OK not to know what was happening

if she was running the show.
I woke happy from this dream.
Apples: the knowledge of good and evil (bruised no less, from the Fall?) Fish: food from the unconscious. The bottom feeder made of Black Watch tartan: the depths of evil I have seen.
How small to cut up the fish? How much can a person swallow at one time — without biting off more than they can chew!

I can still feel the happiness I felt, waking from this dream. In those first weeks of remembering ritual abuse, my dreams did much to sustain and reassure me. The dream of the child falling in the lake told me I could rescue what had sunk below the surface and, with help, bring it back to life. In the dream of the apples and the fish I encountered, more clearly than ever before or since, what felt like an embodiment of female divinity. I felt blessed by the woman who smudged me with sage. She acknowledged my feelings and approved of my strength. She gave me something my own mother could not give me: a mirror of my true self, and the feeling that I was acceptable in her eyes. These are experiences which make trust possible, and it was trust I needed to go on. In the dream I felt it: "It was OK not to know what was happening if she was running the show."

I try to make room for my dreams, to listen and let their meanings grow in me. The wisdom which guides the process of remembering speaks their language. Some dreams have a lot of "juice," many layers which only reveal themselves over time. The dream of the apples and the fish was a "big" dream in this way. It was giving me what I needed for my journey — sacred food, the fish, a common symbol of Christ, the apple from Eden — and it was showing me the importance of sorting the good food from the bad, that archetypal folk story task. (1)

I felt exhausted at the thought of more memories, more flashbacks, more years of grieving, and horrified at what had already come up, which I sensed more and more clearly involved cannibalism, the eating of the baby's flesh. In the dream, the salmon, a fish which makes a dangerous trip every year from ocean to mountain stream, "almost wraps itself around me like a blanket when I move it. It is beautiful." This mantle of protection is, I suspect, not only the salmon itself but also my ability to see its beauty.

Over and over through three years of facing terrible cruelty I've been sustained by a delight in beauty, as I was in those first days by the purple glints of mussels cleaving to rock, the sight of water moving under ice. There is more to watch than blackness. Even when I feel no trust in anything I can pay attention, and beauty is food.

Remembering ritual abuse taught me that when pain is acute enough, I no longer have the luxury of amplifying my suffering by dwelling on it. Instead I have to live from moment to moment, drawing sustenance where possible, from the colors in an oak floor, animal tracks in the snow. This is neither denial nor evasion. The psyche refuses to endure horror without some rhythm of respite. I have come to count on this rhythm where once I feared it, thinking that if I could feel happiness in the midst of pain, the pain was invalidated, proven unreal. Facing ritual abuse has taught me to notice joy, to welcome it when it comes, whatever it's source. I've learned to cultivate it by paying attention to the particularity of the world: this rock, this tree, this face.

12/19/89

Saw Rich.
The detail that keeps getting me is the eating — eating the literal flesh. Can that be true?
R. told me it was one of the earliest rumors about Christians — they killed babies and ate them — in a bunch of Roman records. And of course that one has been around about the Jews too.
Re the Christians, a misunderstanding of the sacrament.

This is my body, this is my blood,
this is my heart, this is my hand,

hand in hand we'll dance for the man
bland man stand with a knife there

there there quiet my little
quiet you bundle of hope

hope hope the man will stop
his knife above the heart

heart heart break in my chest
he carves we eat this

• Chapter Three •

*this this is my body, this is my blood
this is my heart, this is my hand.*

A burst of optimism after going down to the cabin to stoke the stove at 11 tonight so the third coat of urethane can dry — the oak boards shining up through the layers of gloss like something seen underwater, under that slow shining water just before it skins with ice.

Tonight the sharp bright stars and half a moon coming up, the sleeping heaps of wood, oak and birch from this land, black cherry, quiet guardians of my house.

---

1. See, for example, the Russian story of Baba Yaga and Wassilissa, discussed in Marie-Louise von Franz. *Shadow and Evil in Fairy Tales.* Dallas, Texas: Spring Publications, 1974

Chapter Four

12/19/89

Saw Rich — heart aching on the way over — the voices saying drive at that sign, that, that — yellow signs with black marks, arrows, forks

Sharp sobbing when I thought "they," "they" did something to me, not just "he."

Babble of voices in me.

[After talking a while about the week] I can feel the edge of trance, talk of feeling I could black out — get out of the way and another voice would speak.

Fear of what I'll see and that I'll fragment.

But maybe I feel this bad because I haven't remembered enough — OK. I'll try to let it through.

Rich fetches the advent wreath and lights candles to make a safe place for me to come back to. (Not that candlelight is so safe for me — give me a nice 100W bare bulb any day.)

Closed my eyes, prayed, and bang, erupted into desperate sobbing — in the woods at night they're burning a puppy alive — golden puppy — the noises — horrible horrible horrible — desperate — sense someone making me watch? — then I'm above it all looking down circling. They say my spirit's in a bat. A kind of exhilaration, not caring — body feeling weird — like a square, a canvas they'll paint on but they won't because Anna's listening in. My body feels off to my right a little, tingling in my arms and legs, odd feelings — I begin to realise I've been given some kind of a drug. I go numb — some kind of anaesthetic type drug? They're going to paint something on the canvas — a warning maybe? A sheath knife, blade up with hilts — an upside down cross, and out of that a live snake — then realise this is my body, this canvas. A man in a hood has a knife and carves in my belly the upside down cross. I'm cold — feet away from the fire, head near it — I'm on something cold — stone. One of them has got his thing out (this voice has trouble with "dirty" words — doesn't know how to say he's going to rape her) — she's on an altar, rectangular, grooves around it which collect the blood.

They want the blood of a "virgin." (Went to sleep here.)

12/20/89

Memory cont...

The drug began to wear off — the manic elation long gone, so was the sense of detachment, of watching, began to feel pain in my body from the man doing his thing (I couldn't say the words.)

I began to come down — literally, a sensation of dropping levels, sense of my body shifting, limbs tingling a little, very cold except for top of head.

Then a blast of panic and grief, that heavy sobbing, "I shouldn't have told you" — wail — "you'll die now. They said anyone who sees will die and now I made you see" — deep hard sobbing.

Rich made some reassuring noises — in my adult witness mind I knew it wasn't true.

What haunts me now — the puppy — I feel desperate horror, and what I felt then, "I don't want to see." No wonder I've felt afraid somebody would do something weird to the Scrap — the little kitten L. and I are looking after.

I feel sick just thinking about it.

When I asked if any of it seemed credible, Rich said that as soon as I said I was on something cold he'd had an image of a rectangular stone altar with grooves around it and a place for collecting blood. He'd found one once, an ancient one, in the woods here in the Valley.

The sense of participation, of having been a part of everything happening, that it was all me, like the poem of sorts I wrote the other day —

  This is my body, this is my blood,
   this is my heart, this is my hand

boundlessness, like positive mystical experiences — result of the drug? or the ritual? or pain? Weird feeling anyhow.

Outside, blue sky and flurries, sun on my small beautiful house

• Chapter Four •

> *there where nothing was seven months ago — the house I've built while traveling this particular circle of hell — Jung with his stone tower — building is an anchor on this rough sea.*
>
> *Diane cried when I talked about the dog — it haunts me now, that image — can't look at Emma and Ben [L.'s and my dogs] without thinking of it.*
>
> *US invaded Panama — yesterday? — so much for the great good cheer of world news lately*

As I began to remember more, and to see that a whole group of people was involved, not just "the Man in the Brown Suit," I felt in desperate need of an anchor. Everything about these memories was weird.

Remembering incest, I had sometimes experienced physical sensations without knowing what to make of them, but the sensations themselves had felt as if they belonged within the ordinary realms of what a body might feel. As the ritual abuse memories began to surface I found myself not only witnessing grotesque events, I was experiencing their traces in my body. I felt myself circling above it all, like a bat. And then I felt like a square of canvas. This wasn't just a thought. I felt flat and stretched, my texture coarse.

There was some relief in finding explanations, however incomplete — they were using hypnotic suggestion so I experienced myself as a bat, or whatever else they said I was; I was cold because I was lying on a slab of stone; I'd been given some kind of drug — but the explanations only begged more questions.

It wasn't just when I was inside the memories that I felt weird. I didn't know what to make of voices saying, "Drive at that sign." Where were they coming from, these voices which told me to drive off the road? Was I going crazy? Was I really feeling suicidal? I didn't think so, but I knew I shared the human capacity for projecting feelings I found unacceptable onto other people. So why not onto other voices?

I'd heard ritual abuse survivors talking about programming, brainwashing, but I'd been skeptical. It seemed such a convenient way to disown awkward feelings, puzzling behaviors. On the other hand these voices did not feel like a part of me, even a disowned part. They only showed up when I was driving to or from therapy or an SIA meeting.

I didn't want to believe they were the product of brainwashing.

The idea horrified me, that people could have tinkered with my brain, implanting messages which would be triggered years later if I tried to tell. If it was true, how much could they still control me? If it was true I felt as if they were still, now, raping my brain.

I tried simply to observe the voices, to notice what triggered them, for example yellow signs indicating a fork in the road. I refused to believe the voices had the power to affect my actions.

12/21/89

Intense love and sense of pride in us, respect for this heroine's journey — this at the Newcomer's [SIA] meeting which I chaired with a heavy heart — a new woman talking of being stripped of all crutches — of all means of winning approval (as I was in a way at Yale in the end) — the self rebelling against false food — journey down into the dark.

But yes all of us coming to trust ourselves and our truths against the outside world, against all representatives of authority, and against our own fear of pain. My god but this takes courage — and is worth it — the alchemical fire. I felt all this in waves of love and joy. I felt strong and full after that meeting where before I'd felt weak and despairing.

Dream.
In a house, on my way downstairs I see a Black woman who I think of as Cora or like Cora [a friend]. I only see from her neck to mid belly — naked — dunes of golden flesh — ample and smooth and lovely & then I look again & see somebody has cut with a knife from nipple to ribs on each breast — not sure if I see blood and milk mixing or just think it will be there.

Mother of milk and blood. Symbolic. Something in Macbeth? Mythology.

But it won't quite stay as mythology — did something happen?
Mother is same color skin as the baby I think was murdered?

12/22/89

1:30am
Terrified — don't want to go to sleep — talked about ritual abuse to Abigail [a couples' therapist Liz and I went to see briefly] and now here I am feeling I'm going to be killed.

Stayed up till 1 a.m. wrapping presents when the thought began — What if it's true? What if it's true?

It's like reaching a particular stratum in this psyche's archeology:

> *the stratum of terror.*
> *Of what, says L.*
> *Of the man coming behind me and putting his hands around my throat and strangling me — the man who's also the devil.*
> *I think I live with this terror all the time — viz. my need always to be able to face the door, to see who's coming in.*
>
> *Christmas Eve*
> *Vertigo — holding the knife with the man as it goes into the baby's chest — the crowd in church — L. and I in our quilt "robes," being wise guys with Jack the 35-year-old donkey in the living crèche — the baby dead again — the knife against the flesh then pushing through — a baby crying in church then the moment of silence — it's what I remembered this morning and have suspected for days — that my hand was on the knife. You didn't do anything wrong said L. — oh but I did, said a voice inside and I cried and cried, shook with the horror*
> *I talked to Leslie on the phone. I ate lunch. Made chocolate mousse pie. Tested my new knowledge like a new tooth.*
> *Rich preached about faith that the dark won't win, about making a difference — it helped to hear.*

I kept hoping that the image of a baby being killed was just a figment of Rich's imagination, or failing that, that the baby was really only a doll. But, in church on Christmas Eve, I felt the feeling in my hand of the knife being pushed into the baby's chest. The past hovered over the present and the silence in the church when a baby stopped crying was the silence when the baby died twenty years earlier. I could not pretend to myself anymore that the baby had been just a doll.

The part of the memory I fought hardest was the knowledge that my hand was on the knife too. In addition to terror, ritual abuse cults use guilt to stop people breaking the silence. To remember is to face one's own guilt, to tell is to incriminate oneself.

Even without being forced into direct participation in the abuse, simply witnessing it creates a sense of complicity. The very fact of having survived, when others didn't, comes to feel like a proof of one's guilt.

One of the core purposes of ritual is to create communion, to take the participants beyond the boundaries of the individual self into one-ness, the "participation mystique." In the language of the Christian sacrament, we are one in the body and blood of Christ. In some form I had experienced that union in the terrible perversion of the sacrament which took place: it was my hand on the knife and my heart which was pierced. How was that sense of participation created? With drugs, and with some of the traditional means by which religious ritual seeks to shift one's state of consciousness, the hypnotic effect of candle or firelight in the dark for example. But also the stress created by being made to witness cruelty was used as a kind of pry bar applied to the psyche, a way to force the mind out of its customary groove.

Under intolerable pressure the psyche struggles to protect itself by whatever means available. Suspending the process by which experience is taken in, digested, transformed into memory helps to limit the long term impact of the experience but it does not provide complete protection at the moment when it is happening. Two other tactics the psyche uses are merging and splitting. By merging I mean that the psyche can temporarily flood its own boundaries and, losing the sense of separate identity, become one with everything that is happening, exactly the 'participation mystique' that ritual seeks to create. What this meant for me was that I felt identified not with the life-giving forces of the universe (as I had in some spontaneous mystical experiences as a teenager) but with hatred and brutality. This kind of experience is not illusory, it is real and ineradicable. The psyche sustains some forms of damage in order to avoid worse.

I suspect that my psyche made greater use than most of the tactic of merging rather than splitting, perhaps because I have a natural aptitude for it. But I did split too. Forced to witness torture, the self who saw split from the self who felt.

Like merging, the psyche's tactic of dividing empathy from observation, response from perception — "I'm above it all looking down ... a kind of exhilaration, not caring" — is a common form of self-protection. In certain circumstances it is called professional detachment. It is common among doctors, or any one in a job where one is required to witness suffering. It has its uses, but it is also what makes it possible for otherwise decent people to inflict terrible suffering on laboratory animals in the name of science. It is helpful to soldiers in their business of killing. In the cult this split is the first step towards shutting off the capacity for empathy altogether, thereby creating the next generation of abusers.

When I saw Rich again three days after Christmas another

• Chapter Four •

memory surfaced, this time of a Black woman who was tied to a tree.

They push my face at her breasts and I suck and milk is in my mouth. Then I look and see her breasts have been slashed with a knife like in my dream.

They rub my face in the blood which is blood and white — physical feeling of head being rubbed

The church bell chimes two. I heard chimes back then, a lot in a row. Midnight?

There's a cauldron on the fire bubbling. I think, they put the baby in there.

All this comes while I'm trying to talk but I can't make words come at all, only images and movements of my body.

I look at the woman again and there's a knife in her chest. The handle is sticking out. It has detailed, intricate patterns on it — a red and white zigzag — I can't see it all.

I can't bear this. Is she dead? Was she ever alive?

The eleven-year-old asks Rich if he really wants to hear. She says he might get killed or go blind....

I feel numb, immobilized, incapable of transmitting orders from my head to my body, but slowly, subdued voice, slightly blurred voice, I tell it. Now I can talk but I don't have any of the body feelings except for the sense of the drug....

I am angry. I want to see the people who are there but I can't see. I'm confused. I don't know if they're so well hooded and masked that I can't see or that I can't bear to look and know. I'm pretty sure my mother's there. I think, "We're the same size, she and I," and everyone else looks huge.

After the woman's dead a man's voice says, "She will come again," something like that. She's not really dead. They call her names. One sounds like Bitch Goddess but maybe isn't. The others I don't understand.

Eventually the drug starts to wear off a little. Until then it's the way I've heard people describe Thorazine: my body is immobile but my mind is working. I begin to thaw from the outside in — in the center is a cube covered in gray fuzzy material like my old Teddy and I say it's mine, nobody can get to this. This last square at the core.

How to think it — that's what I don't know.

Could she have been a doll?

Warm milk, blood, says Rich.

57

12/29/89

Woke feeling rested after eight hours sleep.

After a dream in which an old woman and I become allies. She knew about some crime, wasn't going to tell me but decided to.

Somewhere in me I think I should have died rather than let them kill her — have tried to stop them at whatever cost — and that's part of why stories of self-sacrificing courage make me cry so easily.

I was a child. I was drugged.... It is my own unfelt guilt which is — the way to forgiveness.

1/2/90

Saw Rich

Talked a while about Abigail, letting her push me in couples' therapy into talking about the latest memory when I didn't want to, then pounding headache, terror and fury.

I need to covenant with the eleven-year-old.

What do I need? Her to keep telling me what happened.

What does she need? Me to keep her anonymity except in very clearly safe places.

After a while I could hear the eleven-year-old saying okay, enough talk time for you. We fished out the old advent wreath and I closed my eyes and prayed. No abrupt jerk into the eleven-year-old — all grayer and number — man on the other side of the fire wearing a wooden goat type mask with curled horns like ram's horns — my mother there, hair pulled back, no weird hood — me on the altar stone — the people doing a sort of low growling chant — anger in me and over and over saying it's stupid, it's stupid — the woman's on the tree. She's dead already. The man in the mask has a phallus sticking out — shiny — wood maybe — too big for life — I lying there, everything looking distorted, then through the trees out of the dark a skull with flaming eyes — it's stupid, it's stupid, it's a fake — a moment of feeling pure terror, I cry, but quickly go back into the defiant anger.

The masked man and my mother fuck over me, almost over my face — the wooden phallus — the smell surrounding me — the people are around me, chanting again — they're stupid, they're wearing stupid masks, stupid masks like fancy dress, all black, store bought, some shaped like birds — then the man's holding my shoulders and forces the huge phallus into me — tearing me — I feel wet on my leg — blood — it all feels very far away, the hurting — somebody injects something into my arm.

A man says, "You're the Devil's child, the Devil's maid, the

Chapter Four

Devil's bairn you'll bear."
It's stupid, it's stupid, I know him, he's the man in the brown suit, he works at the bank in the village.
Then I'm very sleepy, fade into a sort of sleep peopled by weird images. When I wake up it's nearing dawn, the fire has died down, the man in brown is there, and my mother. He kneels by me, he has gray eyes and black eyebrows — he stares in my eyes and he touches my left eyelid. He says if you tell what you have seen we will burn your eyes out. My mother starts to cry. He stands up and hits her hard across the face. He says if we tell anyone we will be killed. I've got blood on my face and on my legs, dried. Then it's starting to rain, we follow the man out, winding through woods, nettles, wild garlic, big trees — I don't know what happens when I get to the road.

Did I really see a woman being murdered? Who were these people? How could they get away with murdering a grown woman? Who was the woman? Didn't anybody report her missing? What was my mother's role? Where was my father? My brother? Why didn't anyone see fires in the woods at night, hear chanting? Why did they do it? Did they believe in what they were doing, or were they just a group of sadists who played with the trappings of ritual in order to terrify their victims?

Most of these questions I can still only speculate about. The woman and her baby for example, perhaps they were recent immigrants, isolated and far from home, perhaps undocumented. Poor women looking for work abroad are vulnerable to all sorts of exploitation.

As to why nobody noticed, I'm not sure what precautions were taken. The will not to know is a powerful force in itself, viz. the ignorance claimed by the villagers living around Nazi concentration camps. It is frightening to have answers to some of the questions: I am uneasy writing that I recognized the man in brown from the bank in the village. If I'm right then I have in my possession explicit information about organized crime. But maybe I'm wrong. This kind of specific information could, perhaps, be proved or disproved. What if I were proved wrong? Would that mean I'd made everything up? That I am crazy after all? Details in memories don't always fit together easily. If the Black woman's baby was in the cauldron it seems unlikely that that was the same baby I saw sacrificed in the smuggler's tunnel. I can't quite imagine the man in brown storing the little corpse somewhere and then bringing it into the woods. On the other hand, perhaps the baby wasn't in the cauldron. After all that was only a thought I had during the memory, I didn't actually see it in there.

The whole thing is so unimaginable it's hard to know what standards of probability to apply. Mostly I trust memories I experience physically more than thoughts I have or words I hear. My memories of ritual abuse generally seem more densely physical than those I've had of incest, perhaps because, over the years of recovery, I've become less dissociated from my body. Perhaps also the drugs used in ritual abuse have something to do with this. Whatever the reason, I have often felt a physical sensation — heat on my head, cold stone under me — early in the surfacing of an experience, before I remembered the source of the sensation — the fire, the altar. This has helped me trust the truth of my memories. Where I didn't have the sensation, for example I did not actually feel the man carve the upside down cross into my belly, I have doubted the literalness of the memory. Certainly I don't now have any such scar on my belly. But this does not necessarily mean I made the incident up, it may be that the man who told me he was going to do this did not physically perform the act. Ritual abuse works with illusion and suggestion in a sophisticated mind game: what matters is that the victims believe in the power of the abusers. If the layers of illusion and actuality are so intermingled, the experiences so weird, that the victims cannot believe in themselves, so much the better.

"How to think it — that's what I don't know." I felt a schism in my mind between the world where women were murdered and children had their faces smeared with blood and the flower-lined High Street of the Surrey village where we lived. For a long time I could not remember the actual journeys which must have taken place across that schism, from my primrose yellow bedroom in the Mill House to the stone altar in the woods and back again. Mostly I could not identify the people who participated in the ritual abuse, in part because they were masked but also because I didn't want to make that bridge to the everyday world. It was only when faced with the choice between that fear and the fear that the man in brown was really a satanic power that I identified him: "It's stupid, it's stupid, I know him ... he works at the bank in the village."

How to think it? How to think about the murder of a nursing woman and her baby, the rubbing of a young girl's face in the woman's milk and blood, the rape of that girl with a wooden phallus used moments before in intercourse with the girl's mother?

There is a sort of internal coherence to the actions, however grotesque they are. From the perspective of modern Western culture, with its scientific cast of mind, such actions are senseless, but in the realm of myth and archetypal symbol, they make a shadowy sense.

They seem to constitute a kind of puberty rite in which the girl loses her mother and is given to the devil. She is weaned from milk to blood. She is carried across the threshold of puberty on the Devil's penis, that wooden phallus wielded by the man in the goat's head mask. "You're the Devil's child, the Devil's maid, the Devil's bairn you'll bear." Now the girl is a woman like her mother, both are possessed by the same phallus. The girl thinks of her mother, "We're the same size, she and I."

The killing of the woman has a symbolic quality too. The fragments, "She will come again" and "Bitch(?) Goddess," suggest some sort of Persephone/Kore myth in which the female embodiment of nature's fecundity must descend into the underworld each year.

It is easy to write about these rites as if they were scenes depicted on fragments of ancient pottery, recently unearthed, or perhaps the rituals of a tribe deep in the rain forests of South America — Western culture has made a science of projecting its shadow onto other cultures, finding them oh so interesting — but these were rites I witnessed in the woods of Surrey, thirty miles from Buckingham Palace and the Houses of Parliament. They didn't happen to a girl, a woman, they happened to me, to my mother, to a Black woman whose name I don't know, whose breasts I touched. How to think it?

The people performing these rites, they did not come from some other country, they lived in Abinger and Guildford and Godalming. Did they believe in these rituals? Did they believe the sacrifice of the woman was necessary to ensure the fruitfulness of the earth for the coming year? If not, what ends were these rituals intended to serve?

I doubt that most of the participants believed in the rituals in the fullest religious and spiritual sense. I can't know that for sure. What I do see is that the rituals clearly performed specific functions for the cult.

The two most constant elements in the rituals were rape and being made to eat blood and flesh and feces. Both reinforced the sense of participation in the cult, and of being possessed by evil.

As I write this book news is coming out about the rape camps in the former Yugoslavia where Serb soldiers organized the mass rape of Muslim women, and boasted of their intent to make these women bear Serb children. This is the ultimate expression of rape as occupation. In ritual abuse cults, girls and women are deliberately impregnated to produce undocumented babies for sacrifice, but the goal of the constant rape is not simply utilitarian in this way. Nor is it solely an enticement to the male participants, a promise of constant sexual opportunity. Rape is one of the tools by which the cults seek to take possession of their victims.

Killing and eating the victim is another kind of possession. Turning the victim into a perpetrator is yet another. The cults require silence in order to survive, but they must also reproduce themselves by creating new generations of rapists, torturers, murderers.

My hunch is that while some of the rank and file cult members may believe the rituals are truly in the service of Satan, and that Satan is an independent, supernatural force, the leadership is more cynical in its use of ritual and the concept of the supernatural. They use the idea of the Devil as a way to terrify and control.

It is very effective. As a child the only way I could protect myself against it was to refuse to believe in it, to tell myself over and over that it was stupid.

I still cannot face the possibility that some of the things I saw during the ritual abuse were supernatural occurrences rather than theatrical tricks intended to terrify. This is not a reasoned position, I simply am unable to tolerate the fear engendered by thinking these people had access to a power greater than themselves.

The calculated use of fear to manipulate and control people is one of the hallmarks of evil, whether one believes evil to be an independent force or a distorted aspect of human character. As I began to face the ritual abuse, I found I had to face the concept of evil. I had always avoided the word, uneasy with any theology which implied a principle separate from good/God, but now I needed it. I could think of no other way to describe what I was remembering. It made me uneasy though: even to believe in the concept of evil felt like playing into the cult's hands, because they had tried to make me believe in a supernatural power for evil.

Glad I started a few months ago overhauling my conceptual

framework of God, good and evil — started then to erect the scaffolding for this stuff.

So I wrote in my journal right after remembering the murder of the nursing mother. A scaffolding, so that I could build from the blocks of memory as they arrived an edifice of thought, a place I could walk in and out of. This was my fantasy. In reality I had to learn to live among the rubble. No conceptual framework was adequate to protect me from the senseless sense of ritual abuse.

As a teenager I was drawn to the soldier poets of the First World War. I understood in a visceral, and at the time inexplicable, way their feeling of having been separated from their country, their homeland, by an experience of atrocity most civilians could not or would not imagine. There was such a disparity between the language of glorious patriotism and the anonymous slaughter of mass warfare that the soldier's experiences were never woven into a transcendent collective story. Always, afterwards, there was that chasm separating the two worlds they had lived in.

At sixteen I was greatly relieved to come across F. Scott Fitzgerald's comment that,

> The test of a first rate intelligence is the ability to hold two opposing ideas in the mind at the same time, and still retain the ability to function. (1)

Though I could not say exactly what those opposing ideas were, I felt that the world was discontinuous, and so was I, and that I was struggling to hold together. I was in good company, I told myself, reading T.S. Eliot, sifting the "heap of broken images." My suffering was probably proof of my "first-rate intelligence," (I yearned to be a genius) — only stupid people could be content in such a world. But after all, Eliot converted to Catholicism, and I longed for a story which could make my world whole, which could somehow hold within itself all the fragments, placing them so they made sense at last.

Above all I needed a story which talked about evil. I needed it when the abuse was happening and I needed it now, as I was beginning to remember. In a way, the whole of ritual abuse recovery has been about searching for a story to tell about what happened.

The first memories of ritual abuse afforded me a glimpse of the country of cruelty which spread out on the far side of the abyss I had always sensed at my feet. The abyss itself was in a way only the crease, the fold in the page dividing the world from its shadow. But to see both worlds at once required me to rethink not only my personal story and my family's story but also the story of my country and my culture: I knew people committed acts of atrocious cruelty — in Uganda, in South America, but in the woods of Surrey?

1. F. Scott Fitzgerald, *The Crack-Up,* New Directions, 1956. p.69

Chapter Five

1/7/90

Dreams of being chased by two men, sometimes with knives, sometimes with flaming torches — I don't think they catch me

Days of rare calm and peace with L. — astonishes me that it can be this good — that I can feel this good in a relationship — this much in love and in a different sort of love than that fevered omnipotent high at the beginning.

1/8/90

A burst — a blast — of fear in the Shady Glen diner tonight after eating — heart pounding anxiety — at first I thought it was some chemical — MSG? — but when I closed my eyes and asked, I learned a man had walked by who looked like a man in the satanic cult.

1/9/90

Grief again — grief grief grief burning in my belly — seeing Rich I thought about the way the old sexual fantasy of being passed around a circle of men has been pressing in and how I know it really happened. The eleven year old wanted to tell it herself — wants to be acknowledged. She's survived these damn experiences, she gets to tell them — so I slid out of the way — saw very fast being passed from prick to prick — couldn't feel the lower half of my body — my upper part so cold, sometimes cold and hard, sometimes gummy, the hands holding me sinking into my skin.

I see blood on a penis.

Then endorphins kick in — I'm on a sea, bobbing up and down, then a shark comes and eats my legs and then my body. All that's left

is a point of consciousness and, dimly, a shadowy body still being passed around, then the point of consciousness begins to shrink. I think I'm going to vanish then there's a circle of light coming toward me with a cross and at its center an eye and I am warm, so warm, and the wave of dark is thick and huge swelling over me and there's an almost chant telling me "I am of the dark, I will sin with the dark" but I am in that small circle of light, at first clutching the foot of the cross then for a second I am on the cross — then fading into sleep then no, let the terror in — I do a bit — then something — what? — I don't quite remember — then memory of eating the baby's flesh — being of the dark.
   Jesus.

   Afterwards, intellectual, fumbling over why one is — why I am — drawn to recreate situations, e.g. sexual fantasies of abuse that really happened....
   How bodily these memories have been compared to how they used to be — the body's experience of gang rape — mostly not about the penises at all but about cold & warmth, substance & shadow, presence & absence.

   It has always been easier for me to talk to Rich about sex than about God. I told him about the circle with the cross in it but we didn't talk about it much. The Christianness of it bothered me. It's just because it's my tradition, I told myself: these are the symbols that stock my psyche. If I were a Jew or a Sikh or a Hopi, the image would have come wearing different clothes. Under my fidgeting I recognized the sacredness of the experience, and I did not want to demean it, or talk away its power. Three years after remembering it, when I was typing out these journal entries, I painted the image on a piece of oak and put it on my desk. It is a kind of mandala. It is at the heart of my healing from violation, that inviolable circle of light.
   To have faith in it, in this center which cannot be possessed by any power, however great or clever or cruel, is to be healed. Such a faith is not a thought, a good idea, it happens in the heart. In my case it happens slowly, fitfully. I sense for a moment how it might be to live from the knowledge that in my core I cannot be violated, dismantled, devoured — then I go back to living from the fears.

1/11/90

   Waves of aching-hearted grief, after the fury had evaporated (osten-

sibly at L. for not respecting my writing time), furious grief at the dead animals on the roads after this warm spell, sobbed on L.'s shoulder when she came home but patches of good cheer and peace too — a peace I don't think I knew in the first 2 - 3 years of recovery and here I have it even while recovering RA memories.

And then L.'s fine cotton face on the pillow, the look of happiness she gets in bed, of basking contentment — how I do love her — more deeply now than before — every day I learn something about love — that it exists continues to astonish me.

1/14/90

Thoughts from reading about MPD
— the territory feels familiar, especially from adolescence: they're talking about experiences I've had.
— it explains how I could have lived in the same house as them, while they abused me, with no conscious memory, only feelings of disgust and despair.

1/15/90

Saw Rich
Talked about the Multiple stuff being a good language and of the mythical connections, e.g. one article described a woman whose "executive personality" was called Athena. How is what they call executive personality, the one who knows, sees, orders, different to God-within?

Rich said: psychosynthesis' idea of "sub-personalities," Gurdjieff's the many "I"s; Seth books. The possible and probable selves.

I wanted to talk about my sense of an enemy to my core self — one who wants me to fragment completely — but my mind scrambled — I couldn't think the thoughts straight at all.

OK OK all this is a way to warn you I think something's going on between the different people. I ask him to light the candles — trance out a bit — a smallish child? / fear self says, "They're trying to kill me, they're trying to make me into somebody else." Then I'm holding the little box they've implanted in me, the one I've painted and written and dreamed about for years, and Anna wants to open it but it's too dangerous, if it gets out it will poison everything. Sense of almost animal presence — her terror — and then she [the child/fear self] begins to go to sleep, waft away — I felt my body changing, sliding into sleep and dreams.

Rich a little nervous. I said it's OK, I'm here watching. She sleeps *and I'm going to open the box — I, the organizer self (God self?). Help me put it in a circle of light. We do and I brace myself to open it. As my hands touch it I find it's not really there and in it there is nothing, only gray air and voices — the cult man's: "You're Satan's child" — and Mum: "Bad bad bad" while she raped me with the hairbrush.*

I want to let go of the voices.

Let go, says Rich.

To the south wind I give the voices which tell me I'm bad.

To the west wind the voices which tell me I will do evil.

To the north wind (here the tears come) "Look at what you've done." My bloody hands.

To the east ?

Came back very shortly after this. Felt very shy. Felt airy in my chest.

What wisdom, said Rich. He'd girded himself to do battles with monsters — but there was nothing there. It's fear that gives the monster power.

Though I will walk through the valley of the shadow of death I shall fear no evil.

I'd had images of that buried toxic box from the moment I got sober. I dreamed about it once as a concrete bunker containing radioactive waste; I painted it as a box with a child inside it. It was both womb and grave, my hidey hole and the black hole into which I would be sucked and crushed to death. It was my protection from the world and the place where I protected the world from me. The box was the safe center of myself, and it was "implanted in me."

As I began to remember the ritual abuse I thought often about this box. I had tried to keep locked away in it my badness, the proof that they had "gotten me." I felt if I could succeed in holding within myself the poison, not letting it touch anyone else, then, although they had contaminated me, I would not have become one of them because I would have refused to victimize other people.

The idea of opening the box created major conflict in me: until now my psyche had been organized around the task of keeping it locked. I felt more disintegrated than I ever had. I tried using the language of MPD to describe what was happening — "something's going on between the different people" — but that language soon shaded into spiritual language: "She sleeps and I'm going to open the box — I, the organizer self (God self?) Help me put it in a circle of light."

• CHAPTER FIVE •

As I came to open the box I had a peculiar sensation, I felt quite literally my fear-filled self, and with it my physical body, going to sleep, but instead of my consciousness going to sleep too, as would normally happen, "I" remained awake. "I" was, briefly, identified with my God self, not my fear self. My fear self believed in the power of the evil contained in that box and could never have opened it. My God self did not believe in the power of it. "As my hands touch it I find it's not really there and in it is nothing."

It is impossible to describe or understand this experience using the concept of a single and unified I. Nor does a psychiatric model of the disintegrated self help here. There are spiritual traditions from all over the world which do offer insight but I am not familiar enough with them to make good use of their terminology. Instead I use an image to help me think about the way the "I" of my consciousness moved from identification with my fearful self to a fearless one. The image is of a free standing glass map I once saw at a large train station. There is a light which shows you where you are, and if you type in where you want to go, the light will move, tracing the path to your destination. I think of this map as a floor plan of the house of the self. The light is the point of consciousness, the place where one is aware of oneself as "I." This point moves around the house. Sometimes it is in the room of fear, sometimes in a child's bedroom, sometimes it comes to rest at a window looking out on a tree, sunshine, a bird singing. To some extent one types in one's own destinations: we have a degree of choice over which rooms in the house we stay in. Most people keep their favorite armchair in the room of one particular emotion. As the woman in my dream of the apples and the fish told me, that room for me is the room of sorrow. For others it may be rage or fear or cheerfulness.

The small light of consciousness moves from room to room but at the heart of the house, the hearth, there is a holy space where another light shines, steadily. Many spiritual traditions teach practices through which one learns to bring the moving light to the still light at the center.

1/16/90

Meditating this morning — which came easily — I looked at the tribe — new eleven-year-old included — but something was missing: the god person, the one who sees all — ah, the one in that circle of light as I was losing consciousness during the gang rape — the circle of light with the cross with the eye on it (the I). That's where the all-seer stays — only so is she able to see and feel all. I see her and then the circle of the tribe is that circle of light, we are it, a clump of light, no longer separate in a way, but no big bang of unification either. Subsumed in the fire of that presence.

The circle of light at the heart of the house is a paradoxical place: it is the center that holds, the place where the I can bear everything without fragmenting, where the eye can see all the opposing worlds at once. It is a place of unity, but that unity is only possible because the self unites with something larger than itself. The small moving light becomes one with the steady light at the center. In a sense it is no longer itself but is "subsumed in the fire of that presence." Perhaps that is why, though it is bliss, and ease, to be in that place, I avoid going there.

1/17/90

First real night in the cabin — more or less moved in upstairs — exhausted and happy and scared and thrilled and lonely and relieved and and and

1/18/90

Joy to wake up here — a sunny morning — to be closer to the trees again, to the outside, to daylight — it is so BEAUTIFUL — and yes I do love the feeling of waking up alone to this deep silence.

Now, after the doubts and fears of yesterday, I feel sure this is good — a Good Thing — the chimney creaking and the fire downstairs is all the sound there is and under and behind it the wind through the trees like distant surf.

Here, in this house, I thought just now, I might be able to make love again.

1/20/90

Moved Sido [one of my cats] in with me after watching Mystery *and* Masterpiece Theater *and "Murder She Wrote" with L. who cried when I left for the night — I look forward so deeply to waking in the morning and going to my desk — as if I have thirsted for a year — Sido's pleasure in this place, her great purrings and rubbings, reflect my own, as if she were expressing my own relief at solitude and less domesticity — all the while I feel loyal to L. and full of love for her.*

• CHAPTER FIVE •

I remembered the circle of light and I opened the toxic box days before I moved into my house. I think the central act of moving into the house I had been building for myself drew other symbols of healing into orbit around it, like moons around a planet. Houses are potent. They are the place where so many needs converge: physical, emotional, aesthetic, spiritual. They volunteer themselves as symbols of the self.

When I was designing my house, my main concern was to balance the feeling of being sheltered with the feeling of being open to the outdoors. In Liz's house I had felt too separated from the outside: it was super-insulated, the walls thick, the windows small. Before that I had lived for two and a half years in a twelve by twelve foot cabin which I loved. There the membrane between inner and outer felt so thin it was almost non-existent. In fact there was so little insulation the wind ruffled the papers on my desk and in winter the cats' water froze overnight. I wanted a middle ground, a balance between wall and window, vulnerability and protection. The shaping of this idea in the world, as a physical structure, was also reshaping my internal structure.

Emotionally, over the years, I had gone back and forth between being too impermeable and too porous. Growing up I tried to protect myself from my family and from the cult by throwing up a great wall of invulnerability, a constant No: no, I didn't care whether my mother told me I smelled or not; no, I didn't believe the cult had supernatural powers; no, they couldn't make me into somebody else.

It didn't work. With rape and torture and brainwashing the cult broke through defense after defense. Desperately I tried to make some small final part of me unreachable, inviolable, locking it up in a tiny box. At twenty, traveling alone in Thailand, I became acutely aware of a deep cold cave in me which nothing and nobody could enter. I was sad that the experiences I sought out could not touch me in my depths but I was also relieved. I couldn't be overwhelmed or changed.

Still it is unbearably lonely to live behind such thick defenses. My need for connection and company runs deep. I experienced that need as an enemy inside myself and I identified it with the enemy outside myself — the cult — who wanted me broken. This was a false identification. In fact if the cult had succeeded in getting me to wall off my need for human connection entirely they would have succeeded either in driving me crazy or in making me one of them, heartless and violent. But for years, believing that my only safety came from the wall, I feared anything in myself which threatened it.

I rocketed back and forth between trusting nobody and trusting anybody, blindly and without discrimination. Then I would get hurt — raped once — and this would prove to me, again, that I should trust no one. I would turn on myself savagely for having been so stupid as to make myself vulnerable to harm.

I craved connection and I felt my craving as a betrayal. Building my house was an attempt to create a structure which could hold and balance these opposing impulses.

The whole idea of building my own house was rooted in childhood fantasies of solitary self-reliance. By the time I was seven I had started collecting useful facts for when I was grown-up and living alone off the land, whether on a desert island or in Alaska. Safety would come when I did not need anything from anybody.

But, as it turned out, my house, far from being an emblem of triumphant self-sufficiency, was proof of what could be accomplished by accepting help. Quite literally I could not have done it alone: I had two thousand dollars, some tools, the necessary skills and a ten-year-old car to my name. Liz gave me the land, my grandparents gave me nine thousand dollars, a woman at church offered me windows she'd salvaged and stored in her barn, neighbors came to raise the walls, Liz and other friends helped me build when they could.

I worked alone most of the time but, at a point of total discouragement, a woman I'd never even met called up, wondering if she could pound nails for a couple of days. She helped me pour the concrete posts on which the whole structure rests. I don't own my house because I wrested it from the world with my two strong hands but because I was able to receive the gifts which were offered to me.

I was learning in the building of my house what I was learning with Rich, that security does not come from self-reliance but from being open to help.

1/22/90

I said the other night [at an SIA meeting] I don't want to trade my past for another. When L. asks what I need I always say " A new past and an AK47," but it's not true because I know I am how I am partly because of the past and I feel a fierce loyalty to myself as I am.

This seems amazing to me when I consider the past I'm talking about.

CHAPTER FIVE

1/23/90

Intuitively: I need to release the tension in my core personality — the bracing against these threatening parts — my own rage, a self or voice which wants me broken. To do that I have to let fall apart what's taken years to cement together.

Scary as shit.

1/24/90

This thick grief again — for my isolation and aloofness (how to keep the skill of solitude but out of different motives now?)

Isolation's roots in rage and humiliation, having been seen in the most horrifying and degrading circumstances, how shy I am of eyes (and yet how I court attention) — under the shyness is fury.

In the woods at eleven, that dark clarity — my parents are strangers, I don't know them, I don't care. The birth of I don't care?

I've always remembered that moment in the woods. It happened, I know now, a year or so into the ritual abuse. I was playing truant from school, sitting in an oak tree. I felt tangled. Nothing held together in my mind. I felt like a caterpillar trapped in the dark, bound in my cocoon. And then I thought quite simply, "If they weren't my parents I wouldn't like them. They are strangers and I don't like them." I felt hatched then, wings stretched in the sun. Everything seemed so clear.

I suppose that was the first time I had been able to use a thought to resolve a conflict which I could not resolve in reality: my parents were my parents but they did not act as parents were supposed to. Not only did they not protect me, they hurt me. Also my mother at least seemed unable even to protect herself. I could not hold in my mind at the same time the two opposing ideas that they were my parents and they behaved like strangers. To resolve the conflict I changed their name: these are not my parents, they are strangers. Because they are strangers I am free not to like them and not to care about them. Renaming them was a way to resolve the conflict between what I thought I should feel and what I felt. It was also a way to cope with conflicting emotions: I cared about them and I was angry with them. I could deal with the conflict now by choosing not to care about them. Rejection and invulnerability became my way of dealing with anger and ambiguous emotions.

These were not defenses which would evaporate at a touch the way the box had. Moving into my house was a move out of the box locked inside me, but the house itself was a kind of box. Moving into it was proof of my ability to take care of myself but also of my continued unease around other people.

Liz and I lived together for a year while I built. I'd lived alone for five years before that. I found, during that year, that, however much I wanted to, I could not completely relax with another person in the house. Instead I felt a continuous low key buzz of adrenaline. I could not turn off the radar scanners in my head which monitor every movement around me. I had been clear with Liz from the start of our relationship that I needed a lot of time alone and she accepted that, needing it herself, though to a lesser degree. Solitude is a pleasure to me, not merely a means of avoiding tension. But I can also see how my habits of isolation were and are sad adaptations to the abuse I endured.

Chapter Six

2/5/90

'O Lord, I believe. Help thou my unbelief" is all I want to write just now, and writing it makes me want to cry and outside the snow is thick and pure and glittering. I lay in bed this morning, aware of the life of my body, so close here to the wild and beautiful life of trees.

I ache because I am going to remember savage humiliation tomorrow seeing Rich? I just remember shit and feel a twinge of the I-want-to-die feeling.

We eat things to incorporate them.

Oh God I believe. Help thou my unbelief.

Oh God — oh Granny — did I pray in my fear a prayer you'd taught me? Did they make me eat shit then? Is that it? I don't know but I feel cold — it is cold in here, the fire didn't catch last night — but it's more than that. I look at this beautiful clean forest and am grabbed by grief — besides this I feel so — filthy. Oh God help me I'm afraid — and now I'm thinking about building cabinets. Hah!

2/7/90

Saw Rich.

On the way there I wanted to eat chocolate, or anything, then said no, saw an image of licking shit off a dick. Almost threw up in the truck, couldn't shake the picture. Told Rich, not wanting to, still don't even want to write it. Circle of men, me on my hands and knees being fucked like an animal. Muck or shit on my body. Other kids there.

'Girls?'

Nnno. If I let myself trance I'll see more, and did, not a full scale split, sense of being held up in the air, very airy, far from earth (drugs?

drink?) held up by men, licking shit from one man's dick — told to — knife blade in my asshole, they pushed it further in until I did what they said. It hurt. They were laughing.

Bill was there. They'd made him put the shit on the dick I think. Made me put shit from a pile on the ground onto a dick for him to eat, pat it around the dick. They made him eat it too, knife in ass. Image of one of them fucking him in the ass, him bleeding.

No wonder the poor fucker hardly talked and was afraid of the world.

Old memory (one I've always had) of shitting in the bath in the Mill House. Ambiguous feeling, shame and haste to clean it up v. wanting to let Mum find it. 11 or 12? Same time period as new memory.

How did they get access to us? Mum, totally afraid of this man, old Brown Suit?

This new memory was more immediate and physical than any I had had before. The divide between my forgotten experiences and my everyday life was becoming more permeable. The day before it surfaced I could make out the outline of the memory, feel its shape. Nor did I have to split so much to let it enter my consciousness. In fact, over the next few weeks, I and the child who experienced this abuse became less and less separate. It was easier to see links between the new memories and my life as I had always known it. I had always remembered sitting in the bath when I was about eleven, shitting. Now I had a possible context for that incident. Similarly, the way I remembered my brother — his mute withdrawal, his inability to defend himself at school, — seemed as though it might make sense as a response to the ritual abuse. Though I went on feeling disbelief that such barbarity could have happened in England, the worlds, internal and external, forgotten and remembered, no longer felt quite so far apart.

More than any connections I made in my mind, my body was beginning to serve as a bridge between the worlds. This body which lay on my bed watching the sun come up through the trees was the same body which was raped and forced to eat shit. No wonder I had been wary of living in it, kept my "I" outside of it as much as possible. I feared its vulnerability and I feared its knowledge.

As a young child I protected myself from the incest by dissociating myself from the body that was enduring these humiliating,

Chapter Six

painful experiences. By the time I was sixteen I could trance out almost at will by unfocusing my eyes. In that state my friend Katarina, intrigued, could pinch me, even stick a pin in my thigh, and I wouldn't react. I knew she was doing it, I was not oblivious, I simply did not have to respond because I was not in that body. Then at some point I would choose to slip sideways and be back inside my body, able to move and blink my eyes and speak.

In rejecting my body I was trying to reject my powerlessness. In ordinary life, being disconnected from one's body makes one more vulnerable, not less, but at home and in the cult, the times when I chose not to leave my body, in the hopes that I could make a difference to what was happening, deepened my feeling of powerlessness. When I was fifteen and my mother was watching my father rape me, I knew they wouldn't stop until I responded sexually. I had some control in the situation — I could influence how long the rape went on — but only by being in my body. Being in my body, responding, made me feel they were succeeding in raping not just my body but me.

2/14/90

Saw Rich yesterday — talked of grief at not seeing Grandma and Grandad before they die, of memories of them, normal childhood memories, the joy of sneaking out into the garden before they got up, of Bill and me covering the bathroom walls with foam soap, my mother's hatred for them.

Said I'll check in with the eleven-year-old, see if Grandpop did seem implicated, closed my eyes and pictured him, over his shoulder I saw a sort of wooden rectangular shape with a pattern but no eye holes. I thought it was a mask but I couldn't "read" it, make sense of it. 'No,' said the eleven-year-old, brushing Grandpop aside, "he's not relevant."

I told Rich this but added there's something to do with the mask, closed my eyes. It was closer to my face. Either then or later I heard their voices saying, "Your eyes are ours, they belong to us. What you see belongs to us." Something sharpish pressed across my forehead. There was a yellowish energy/light in my eyes — I mean I could sort of see my eyes from inside my body. The "mask" came closer, nobody behind it, then I thought it's like a lid, this mask, and they're putting it on me, and then realized it was the lid of a box, a wooden box, a coffin in which I was lying. No room to move around. Oh God. Then the box was moved and then, as if I'd been buried, I couldn't hear anything.

I lay there in horror and panic. I thought they might have buried me alive and were going to leave me there. Mostly I thought I mustn't panic, I mustn't start flailing. I'll go crazy if I do. Something in that feeling, the fear of panic, of going out of control in a situation over which I had no control, in which I had no room to move, feels completely familiar. My head said, 'Oh you must be making this up, you'd be going completely nuts otherwise.' My body started to jerk and flail — me trying to prove to myself that I have room to move now, in the present, I thought, but then realized the movements themselves were confined, as if by the walls of a box. My voice, stuttering and high, talked again and again of terror at what would happen if I panicked, plunging, unstrung, mad.

At some point I saw a high arc of yellow/white light and I felt calmer. A room of quiet opened up inside me, but then I felt confused: did this light belong to them? How could I trust it? Time passed in the calmer state. At last the box moved (I don't have any idea how long it was) and a man, brown hooded and either masked or made up, red rings around the eyes, opened it. They wanted to know what I'd seen. I didn't want to tell them, to make the light theirs, but I did because I was afraid. One held a knife and made a tiny cut in the center of my forehead (on my third eye) and at the base of my throat. It was an initiation. Then they fucked me with the wooden phallus.

The dark vision quest — oh God I just wept and wept.

No wonder I fear being trapped and confined.

No wonder I know a lot about vision quest ritual.

However ambivalent I was about being in my body, however skilled at stepping outside it, my body experienced everything. The mind can deny but the body does not lie. All through the years my body has lived in the world as a body which was once locked in a coffin. In remembering the ritual abuse I was not only becoming conscious of previously unconscious thoughts, I was releasing experiences which had been trapped in my flesh and bones and nerves.

As I remembered it seemed as though the division between my consciousness and my body began to dissolve. Thinking about the dog being burned made my stomach spasm. When the memory of licking shit began to surface I was literally retching in the truck as I drove down the highway. In Rich's office I jerked and flailed and gagged as memories surfaced. It frightened me sometimes, as I sensed that it frightened him. Would I go out of control, would I really throw up, would I start to scream and scream, frightening the other people working in the building?

Instinctively I know that in order truly to inhabit my body I need to re-experience what happened physically and so release it. And I have felt in my body some of what happened to me, I have screamed myself hoarse in the woods, in my car, but there is a limit I reach, a place where, all of a sudden, I am no longer feeling terror or agony, instead I am sleepy or I find myself thinking of the cabinets I'm about to build. I never have screamed in Rich's office. I have not felt myself go into uncontrolled physical panic in the present in the way that I surely did during some of the ritual abuse. I feel the beginnings of it then I shut down.

I noticed this limit early on in the remembering. I thought then it was the child self, the one who held the memories, who was protecting herself and me from the raw, crazy-making terror. Perhaps it was. Or perhaps the mind is simply incapable of experiencing its own unstringing. Perhaps this is the limit to the power of the torturer.

I am inclined, these days, to accept with gratitude any natural limit to the body's vulnerability to suffering, to doubt the benefits of trying to push past those limits. Though I have a blanket willingness to do whatever I need to do to heal, I have very little specific willingness to re-experience consciously everything my body has endured. I hope I don't have to.

If I let myself picture for a moment being shut in a narrow wooden box with no way to get out, my heart begins to pound. That kind of utter helplessness is almost intolerable. If I could have focused on some plan of action, however improbable, it would have helped me keep the panic at bay, the maddening, futile panic which had me, even in the remembering, clawing at the walls of the coffin. But there was nothing I could do to get out.

In *Regeneration*, a novel about the First World War, historian Pat Barker writes that Rivers, a doctor, was

> fascinated by the differences in severity of breakdown between the different branches of the RFC [Royal Flying Corp]. Pilots, though they did indeed break down, did so less frequently and usually less severely than the men who manned observation balloons. They, floating helplessly above the battlefields, unable either to avoid attack or to defend

themselves effectively against it, showed the highest incidence of breakdown of any service. Even including infantry officers. This reinforced River's view that it was prolonged strain, immobility and helplessness that did the damage, and not the sudden shocks or bizarre horrors that the patients themselves were inclined to point to as the explanation for their condition.

For me too I think the grotesque games the cult played with blood and shit were far less damaging than the experiences of prolonged, utter helplessness.

The damage arising from such experiences does not come so much from the experience itself as from the ways the psyche tries to deal with the experience. If one can somehow accept one's powerlessness it is not so bad. But absolute powerlessness is so hard to bear that the psyche, unable to effect real change in the situation, searches for other ways to regain a feeling of control. It tries to claim power one doesn't and didn't have. This is the seed from which a great kudzu of distorted thought and feeling may grow, throttling spontaneity and smothering the flow of life. For example, when I was three and my mother was raping me, it was easier for me to believe that I was bad, that somehow I had caused her to do this to me, than it was for me to accept that I had no influence on what was happening to me. To this day, when somebody hurts me, my first reaction is to feel that I am bad. I must somehow have caused this person to hurt me.

It was some weeks after the coffin memory surfaced that I recalled how, when I was a year and a half sober, I had acquired a coffin myself. I'd been renovating a Victorian house on Staten Island for a theater director. His theater was throwing out some old props, including a genuine metal coffin. He asked jokingly whether anyone wanted it and, somewhat to his surprise, I did. I was all set to bring it back to my apartment, ostensibly as a present for Nanette, my girlfriend at the time, who had a fantasy of making love in a coffin. (She had a difficult childhood herself...) I got as far as getting the coffin to the job site where, temporarily, I stored my tools in it. In the end I couldn't face lugging the thing up five flights of stairs and freaking out my neighbors. Still I'd contemplated it in a way that, even at the time, felt a little odd to me. I had no idea that I was trying in the present to rob the coffin of the terror it once held for me.

CHAPTER SIX

Sexual fantasies which, like the fantasy of being passed around a circle of men in the woods, contain elements of abuse experience have functioned in the same way for me, I think. A fantasy of a rape is not the same as a rape because this time around I can say stop any time I want. This time I am in control even though the fantasy itself is of being out of control. There is always somewhere the hope that in repeating the past I can remake it.

At four years sober I began to apprentice with Suzanna to lead groups on ten day "Quests for Vision" in the wilderness. The core of these quests was three days of solitary fasting and praying for a vision for one's life. Surrounding those three days were assorted archetypal rituals of death and rebirth, some of them taking place at night around a fire, sometimes including the use of masks. At first glance I should have thought this would be the last thing in the world somebody with a history of ritual abuse would get involved in, and yet there I was. I was even quite good at it: I had a curious intuitive grasp of such ritual. Suzanna commented on this, and I felt it in my bones: I know about these rituals. Once again I think I was motivated by the desire to remake the past. This time round, instead of being in a group intent on appropriating other people's visions, I would help people to find their own vision and keep it safe. It felt important to me to suggest to people that they not share the core of their vision with anyone but to keep it in their hearts, a sacred gift.

2/17/90

Got the grief again — and the anxiety which comes from pushing it away — at what they did to me — buried alive — and also a grudging sense of that experience as a source of — strength, a kind of toughness in me — is that romanticizing? Probably. It certainly wasn't the kind of experience which created faith and trust in me — but — but — something.

I felt better just writing this — acknowledging it — the wind shifting shadows in this cabin — I eating bagels and bacon at my dusty table.

2/20/90

Saw Rich — more memories — coming out of the coffin they wanted me to tell what I'd seen — I felt confused, didn't want to. They put shit in my mouth. They jeered at me. Then I saw Bill. I saw the flat withdrawn look on his face. They had a knife across my throat. They did that first, before the shit. They started passing him around — rap-

ing him anally — I started to talk. I couldn't stop. I was trying to stop them by talking. They were laughing at me. When I talked I got the shit in my mouth. I don't know how long it went on.

I sobbed and sobbed.

I'd been thinking a lot about how loving somebody makes you vulnerable to being hurt — it gives "them" power over you. A hostage to fate, I read somewhere. I'd been fearing Liz dying — had forgotten to connect that fear to "them" getting her in England [where she had gone to visit her family.]

A core issue for me — ambivalence about caring.

Was my mother there? If so, leaning against a tree bleeding from her crotch.

Jesus.

2/21/90

[At the SIA meeting] Elsa shared the memory she found when she went digging to find the roots of feeling humiliated — a memory of being put in a coffin and lowered into the ground.

Oh God.

She said how they wanted what she could see — wanted the light in her mind to use. I think we're talking about the same thing.

I had not told Elsa about the cult wanting to know what I had seen while I was in the coffin so I was particularly struck by this similarity in our memories. Her abuse happened in the southeastern US, mine across the Atlantic. Since then I have heard other people describe similar cult experiences.

I know from reading about vision quest rituals in different societies that physical privation, fear and some level of confinement are fairly common denominators. Discomfort and the feeling of powerlessness are not ends in themselves but ways to open the door to another dimension or consciousness or world. Whatever the questor meets at the threshold is powerful and sacred, a gift to bring back to the everyday world, and often an expression of his/her individual nature and destiny.

What were the cults after in using a coercive form of these rites? I don't know very much about the philosophical underpinnings of ritual abuse — whether they really believed they could make use of another person's mental energy, for example — but I sense that the primary motivation of many of the rituals was to increase the power of the people performing the rituals by taking possession of some-

• Chapter Six •

thing which ordinarily belonged to someone else, whether that something was a vision or blood or the life spirit itself.

Ritual abuse as I experienced it was all about power, and power was treated as something which could be taken and accumulated. It was also about having power over others. To apply the sort of malevolent ingenuity they did to refining and intensifying their victims' experience of powerlessness, the abusers must surely have experienced their own power in proportion to the powerlessness of their victims.

The cult was not only good at preventing the victims of physical torture from fainting and so escaping, they were also skilled at preventing one from escaping emotionally. When they raped my brother in front of me I couldn't not care, I couldn't shut down completely. They set up a situation in which I was not entirely powerless: I could make a difference to what happened to him by telling them what I had seen when I was shut in the coffin. I had a choice and therefore I felt responsible for what happened to him. Of course I had no power to determine the terms of my choice, but in the territory of powerlessness, any sensation of choice, however circumscribed, is crucial. But the choice itself was unbearable: I could protect myself and betray not only my brother but my own capacity for compassion, or I could protect my brother and give away the one room in me where I had been able to escape the power of the torturer. Choice was a bitter illusion which underscored my powerlessness.

Contemplating suicide gave me back a sense of power. I could refuse to do and be what anyone wanted. I could go somewhere where nobody could get me. Katarina says I told her when we first met that I had been obsessed with suicide since I was eleven. That may have been an exaggeration but I know that by the time I was fifteen I thought about it all the time.

When I was eighteen I tried it, and came quite close to succeeding. In my suicide note I nobly exonerated family, friends and school. As the reason for my action I quoted Camus' contention that committing suicide was the only way a human being could prove the existence of free will.

For years afterwards I thought of that note only as proof of how far from my emotions I had been, to think I was killing myself for a philosophical tenet. But when I began to remember ritual abuse and to understand the reality behind my feelings of powerlessness I saw that that note had been a precise statement of the facts of my life.

Suicide did feel like the only free exercise of will left to me.

But suicide is a typical power of the powerless: rather than opening the way to a future where one has greater choice it is the end of all choice. And though the sense of choice gained by thinking about killing myself may have been essential to my psychological survival, keeping my hand on that door knob also prevented me from committing myself wholeheartedly to anything.

I think now — it is easy to think now — that the light which came to me in the coffin, like the light that came to me during the gang rape, was not a light which could be taken from me by the cult. That light had the power to protect me from being possessed by the cult, from becoming their possession. If I could have trusted in that perhaps it would all have been a little easier. But I don't know if I would be able to trust it now, if, God forbid, it were all happening again.

I know, but I am not always sure how deeply I know it, that the versions of power the cult was interested in are not the only sorts of power around. There is another kind which is not power over but power to — power to create, to survive, to feel compassion and connection. It cannot be accumulated and its value does not depend upon its scarcity, nor does this power require somebody else to be powerless. The laws which govern it are fundamentally different from those of the bank and the army.

The mind is not the right tool with which to grasp the nature of this power. Most of what I have learned about it I have learned through experiences of powerlessness.

I could not get sober until I said "I can't stop drinking." As long as I struggled to control my drinking I kept on getting drunk. Whatever else I question, whether I understand it or not, whether I like it or not philosophically, admitting my powerlessness in this one area gave me freedom. No fancy metaphorical freedom either but the freedom not to throw up and pass out and wake up hungover, the freedom to sleep without a bottle of warm gin by my bed, the freedom to dance and make love without being high.

I wonder how it would be simply, directly, to accept my powerlessness over the ritual abuse, to cut off at the root the great complicated tangle of guilt and denial with which I have tried to hide from myself the reality of being a child at the mercy of a group of adults intent on extinguishing my spirit by whatever extravagantly malevolent means they could dream up.

Chapter Seven

2/26/90

The squirrel in the snowstorm ran between the wheels of the car in front — I thought it was OK when I saw it emerge on the other side. It ran onto the snow bank and began to turn and turn in a circle of agony, swirling up the snow. I drove past. I didn't know what to do. I cried. The image has gathered to itself all abused children, all incidental, pointless, terrible pain, all hope and despair, all powerlessness.

I've always found it painful to see animals dead in the road, like so many discarded coca-cola cans. I carry gloves in my truck for moving the corpses off the road so other animals can eat them without getting run over too, or at least so the flesh can be taken back into the earth, not smeared across the asphalt. I shudder at the powerlessness of the soft animal body against metal and rubber. Shortly before the ritual abuse surfaced I started actually sobbing whenever I saw a road kill. For the next three years my throat swelled with a furious grief and I wept for each dead animal I passed. Sometimes the highways felt crowded with corpses, with creatures wounded in passing, turning in their circles of agony.

It was the pointlessness of their deaths that got to me. If a fox ate a rabbit, or even one of our chickens, that was a life taken to make more life. But the animals killed on the roads were extinguished like cigarettes, and the people who killed them rarely noticed what they had done.

As memory followed memory I struggled to keep my head above the tide. It wasn't only my own pain, it was my brother's, and the pain of all the other children and the babies and the animals and the grown-ups too. This pain was inflicted intentionally by the cult but it felt just as incidental, as unbearably pointless as the suffering of the animals on the roads.

I thought it would help if I could understand why people were deliberately inflicting such pain. But the sheer excess of the cruelty defeated me. Who thinks this stuff up? I would ask Rich as each memory surfaced. I could see no logic to most of what was done beyond the impulse to be as nasty and brutal as possible.

The cruelty served a purpose. I saw that. It kept us silent and terrified and compliant. It was part of the process by which each new generation of perpetrators was created. It was a useful tool for people interested in breaking apart the human psyche. But the cruelty wasn't purely functional. It was too elaborate for that. I felt sure the perpetrators enjoyed it, some of them at least. What pleasure did they find in inflicting pain? Proof that they had power over somebody else? I knew that in anger and frustration and fear I could lash out at someone. I could be glad at someone else's discomfort when I was feeling inferior. But to enjoy someone else's suffering enough to seek out, actively, situations in which you could inflict it? That felt different.

I tried to look at the bigger picture: perhaps, I thought, institutional Christianity, in going too far to the extreme of light, in requiring people to reject their own shadows, had given rise to an equally extreme opposite. Certainly some of the rituals I remembered involved a deliberate inversion of Christian rites, in a spirit of gleeful sacrilege. But what about the casual viciousness of making my brother pat shit onto a penis so I could be made to lick it off? What about the myriad meticulously planned acts of gratuitous cruelty? Was the point just to be as bad as possible? Was that the way they worshipped Satan?

But why were they worshipping Satan, if they were, and what would that mean? None of this helped me understand why a particular group of people got together to organize the inflicting of pain. The idea that they did it for the love of evil felt true to me, but I didn't know what it meant. I still don't.(1)

Human beings are pattern makers and whatever doesn't fit the pattern worries at us. And not only that: whatever remains outside that weave of meaning, the text/textile of our world, has the power to awe and intimidate. It keeps company with the gods and ghosts, the whole supernatural rag bag of things beyond human comprehension.

The senselessness of the cruelty I endured is as much a part of the pain and terror of the experience as the actual physical suffering.

As a teenager I knew pretty much the whole of King Lear by heart. I loved Shakespeare's later plays, and the works of Webster, Middleton, Turner. I felt a strong connection with these men who, living in a time when the old guarantee of meaning, the medieval cosmography, was crumbling, sent their characters again and again to the edge, to look down into the abyss where chaos and randomness rule.

> We are the stars' tennis balls, struck and bandied
> which way please them,

says one of Webster's characters. In the actions of Jacobean tragedy, experience outstrips the stories people have to tell about their world, bringing both audience and characters to a shivering acknowledgment of that uncharted gap between experience and meaning.

At seventeen, I sat for hours in my bedroom in my parent's house, immersed in Webster's world of intentional cruelty and gratuitous violence, with no conscious knowledge of its similarity to my own experiences, reading and re-reading to find what shape he could make to hold it all.

I was afraid there was no shape, and my despair frightened me. Its gray breath crumbled flowers, leached delight from the world, leaving me a handful of ashes. An outspoken atheist, at seventeen I was sneaking into the school chapel at night, praying to be converted.

At thirty-one, memories surfacing, I found myself sweating with fury in AA meetings anytime anyone mentioned "God's plan" or commented that "There are no accidents." I took it personally and felt alienated. I resented that they could feast on comforting pap when my mouth was full of bones. It wasn't that I had ever bought the idea of an omnipotent and controlling God, but for a while I had not found it necessary to fight against it. Now, knowing what had happened to me, I desperately wanted there to be a reason for my suffering, some meaning to it, but the notion that God had planned it was horrifying: God the sadist in the sky, the Great Perpetrator. How could one do anything but shrink in terror from such a God?

It was with a certain angry pleasure that I took to repeating in meetings that stricture of Elie Wiesel's: "Make no assertions about God which you could not make while standing over a pit of burning babies."

References to "New Age" philosophy provoked a similar fury in me. There, the basic line was that I chose everything which happened to me in this life. My soul selected the educational curriculum I need for my spiritual growth. Out from under the thumb of the patriarchal God, I was no longer subject to events beyond my control because I was in control. I chose the family I was born into, my class, my race, my gender.

Oh yes? I wanted to say, Can you look me in the eye and tell me I chose to be raped for seventeen years? And what about the babies I saw being killed and eaten? Was that their idea? And the souls of the murderers and rapists, had they decided this was what they needed to do to "grow" in this lifetime?

I felt then — I still feel — that, in the context of atrocity, anything less than recognition of the rule of chance insults the living and the dead.(2)

In 1988, when Liz and I were driving back from a concert we found two raccoons lying dead in the road. I got out and carried them to the edge of a field and then I got back in the car and we sat in the dark quietly and at last I thought perhaps I should bring them home and skin them. I had told somebody once that that was what I did, to honor their spirits, to try to make up for the waste. It was a lie then.

All the time I was skinning the raccoons I thought I was crazy, it was so difficult, so repulsive. I was in a frenzy to get away from the flies, the stench, but I knew I mustn't quit. Something important was at stake. I kept trying to figure out what it was. I was interested in my thoughts, about giving one's word, about commitment, about waste and lies and abstraction. I watched myself turning what I was doing into a story, trying, unsuccessfully, to distance myself from the blood and the stink of it.

Skinning the raccoons became a metaphor for finding meaning, but part of its power as a metaphor was that it also kept on being just skinning the raccoons, first one, then the other. I wanted the meaning of the experience to come easily, to slip free but instead the thigh fat gripped the hide and I was held in that messy wrestle until

> the sun
> nailed me to the boards and I began
> to see everything from the inside
> out including my body which I
> have tried for so long to climb back
> into ...

When I had finished, when I had nailed the hides to the boards and smeared them with mashed brains ("Every animal has brains enough to tan its own hide," I read somewhere) and scraped them down, I thought I should write about it in my journal but then something said no, let it sit in you overnight. The next morning a poem came. I couldn't quite grasp the shape but I knew it was whole in some way and that I should not fiddle with it too much.

Looking at that poem now — I called it "Pulling It Through" — I can see how exactly it mapped for me the journey I have since taken, the journey from the separated mind to the body in the world,

> my skin soft and greasy
> retching with the stench
> I've taken on, the mess,
> hands in the body
> doing what was promised

Accepting life, not because I chose it, not because every single thing that happens is guaranteed a meaning by God's will, but simply because it is, I can take on the work of making something out of "incidental, pointless, terrible pain," out of waste, futility, randomness.

This sounds like a nice idea but in reality it is a stinking business one gets into sideways, as I got into skinning the raccoons, pulled in deeper than I ever planned by an unthinking boast.

I thought I was making something sacred to honor the raccoons and all the other creatures killed on the roads but in the end it was myself I was transforming. I still have those skins — they are not especially soft and supple, I didn't do a terribly good job. They sit in the attic in a plastic bag. But I kept my word and I kept going and I let myself be touched by the experience, and out of that came a poem, a map which took me into territory I had not yet traveled.

With luck the stories I tell when I try to weave myself and my experience together can add to the collective map, a map which does not explain why but which shows that this is here and that is there and here is a possible route from one place to the other.

1. See Dr. Phil Mollon, "The Impact of Evil" in *Treating Survivors of Satanist Abuse* ed. Valerie Sinason. London & New York: Routledge, 1994.

Mollon, a British clinical psychologist, writes:

There is something about the existence of evil that is difficult to grasp and comprehend. It is the idea that someone may be not just a *bit* bad, dishonest or cruel, not just psychopathic, but *dedicated to being bad....*

What I find personally most helpful is to have a concept of *'the satanic.'* By this I mean an aspect of the psyche — in Jungian terms an archetypal energy — characterised by its extreme destructiveness, an envious hatred of life and love, a gross narcissism that opposes concern for others, a hatred of vulnerability and weakness, extreme pride and arrogance, and above all a devotion to lies and confusion as opposed to truth." (pp.136, 140)

2. See the poem "Bashert" in Irena Klepfisz, *Keeper of Accounts*. Watertown, MA: Persephone Press, 1982.

Chapter Eight

3/5/90

I *feel tainted by what was done to me.*
I'm tapping the roots of my invisibility, my fugitive life. If I want to see the terror — here it is woven into the fabric of my life — into the core choices I've made.
Dear God help me.
Could I have made all this up?
I doubt it — my body memories.

Four months into remembering the ritual abuse, the struggle to believe myself continued. It was a long and gradual process. There was no single moment when I said, "Yes, this is true." Those moments came, but they were followed by further uncertainty. Instead what happened was that it came to seem less and less likely that I was making it all up. This was painful since my doubts helped me to hold back the terror and pain which flooded in when I thought it might really have happened. If I couldn't deny it I had to accept, not only that it had happened, but that it had changed me. I still feel an instinctive rebellion against the fact that, although what happened to me was neither my choice nor my fault, it affected and continues to affect my life profoundly.

3/6/90

Thoughts of Rich talking in his sermon about the victim becoming inhuman like the abuser brought on a huge wave of rage and I was screaming, as long and as hard as I ever have — No No No
They don't have the power to make me be like them.
That rage stayed around.

Feeling that they won. Fear.

Memory. Bill on altar — looking up at me — I'm in the circle looking down at him — his look of fear and wanting protection and puzzlement. What was I doing there? They had a knife with a sort of oval blade. They had me pushing it in. One of them was leaning over watching his face. Someone got a kind of brand — long and thin and hot — held it near his genitals. I lost all separation from his body and began to scream. Someone clapped a hand over my mouth and I was held almost upside down and caned on the soles of my feet until I passed out (which was a relief.)

3/9/90

How did they try to destroy my center? I can't talk about it. Attack of horrible fear this evening — that they got L. [when she was in England] — I don't know who to trust or how to, and then the terror swooping in. I said, strangled voice, I can't let this fear take over, I'll die. You don't understand. L. saying, 'you're right, I don't.' Then later she was trying to say something, her voice insistent, persuasive, pushing at my mind — like their voices programming me when I was terrified.

The fear that they brainwashed me to kill someone. They said with such certainty that I would do it that it was almost as if I already had done it.

I was terrified that the cult had succeeded in making me into one of them. As soon as I let go of my denial I had to face not only my experiences of powerlessness but also my guilt. I remembered with horrible clarity that puzzled look on my eight-year-old brother's face. What was I doing there, in the circle of abusers standing over him? I was pushing a knife, or something like it, into his anus.

I did what the cult wanted me to. I inflicted suffering on Bill and on other people. I did not refuse to do so whatever the consequences. I was not a hero. From the start this was the hardest part of recovery from ritual abuse for me: coming to terms with the blood on my hands.

In the world of ritual abuse, the line between being done to and doing, between "what was done to me" and "what I have done," blurs. Among those who are not killed there are few pure victims. Intellectually I understand that the cult habitually implicated everyone present in whatever crime was being committed. Guilt is a great silencer. I know too that I was a child, I had been raped and tortured into submission, but emotionally I still feel responsible for my actions.

• CHAPTER EIGHT •

To let go of some of the feeling of guilt and responsibility is to accept yet another level of powerlessness: the cult had the power to make me do things to other people which I did not want to do. This feels frighteningly close to saying they had the power to make me be somebody I did not want to be: one of Them.

This was exactly what the cult intended. I was clearly not an ideal sacrificial victim. Aside from anything else I was a legal and social entity. I had a birth certificate. I went to school. If a child like me died it would be hard to cover up. I was there to become one of them. Most of them had probably started out as I did, as the recipients of sadistic abuse. Ritual abuse has simply formalized a more general tendency: abusers tend to have been abused themselves as children. Abuse begets abuse.

My fear that the abusers had succeeded in making me into one of them was rooted both in my guilt and in real experiences of utter powerlessness. I had seen members of the cult wield the power of life and death over and over. How could I trust that there was a limit to their power? How could I be sure they hadn't accomplished what they set out to accomplish? Rationally I could point out to myself that, as an adult I had never been violent, nor taken pleasure in inflicting pain, nor been abusive to anyone but myself. But I had harbored for years the secret fear that I was inhuman, monstrous. Though the black box in which I had tried to keep my evil self locked away had proved to contain nothing but voices, those voices were powerful.

Rich's response to my anxiety that they had gotten me, made me one of them, was to point out that in my present life I do care and feel compassion. He was right, I think, to focus on the capacity for compassion as the key. The cult certainly focused on destroying it. They continuously set up situations in which identifying with the person suffering pain was itself unbearably painful. When "I lost all separation from [Bill's] body and began to scream" I was tortured until I passed out.

Even more than being powerless to alleviate somebody's pain, being forced to be the person inflicting the pain makes empathy for the sufferer intolerable.

What does keep alive the capacity for empathy when empathy becomes a source of pain — as it must in many situations? There is a vivifying power in feeling connected to other beings certainly, but why one person stays open to that while another doesn't is mysterious to me. Suffering, despite some of the myths of Christian culture, does not necessarily make for greater compassion. Just as often it hardens and isolates one.

In my second year of college friends persuaded me that I needed help with the black clouds of depression which descended on me periodically so I went to see a counselor. I wept and talked and wept for weeks. Then I made some reference to myself as an emotionally frigid person. I was startled when the counselor disagreed. It was one of the things I knew about myself, a source of shame and regret but simply true: I didn't care, really care, about anything or anyone. "What do you think you've been talking about all these weeks?" she said. "Feelings. You feel a lot." I could see she was right about the sessions we'd had. But I still felt the other version was true too. I knew there was a kind of shut off point in me, and when I reached that point I stopped feeling anything. I thought that the fact that I could do this invalidated all the rest of my emotions. How could my caring be real if I could just stop feeling it? I never quite knew what would flip that switch either, so I couldn't even be sure of when I would be feeling and when I wouldn't.

Now I know that the ability to shut off is called dissociation. Along with denial, it is one of the most common forms of self-protection. But I didn't know that then. I had no idea other people did the same thing. I felt inhuman and as though I must keep myself separate from other people. Isolation begets isolation.

I see now that the fact that I shut down occasionally was far less important than the fact that I never shut down altogether. However much I did feel alone and different, some part of me kept reaching out. I used booze to stay numb, yes, but I also used it to over-ride the feeling that I must remain silent and separate.

Once I got sober AA gave me both encouragement and opportunities to talk about what was inside me, and to listen to other people talking honestly. I learned to listen for the similarities not the differences, to use talking to connect not to compete. "Identify, don't compare."

3/11/90

Nasty descent yesterday into depression and anger. I felt separate and alone — watching through a glass — separated by the weirdness, the nightmare of what happened to me — unable to see the everyday world as real — and unable to care about people at all. My heart felt heavy with anger and hate — and then I felt as if they'd won, they

• CHAPTER EIGHT •

did get me and make me like them.

And there I was feeling there's no damn point in talking about this — but fortunately I began to cry and through the crying talk — tell that bitterness — L. said she felt like that for years. My God. And I saw how I liked watching the dogs run in the snow — began to talk about going home to Humpty the imaginary pet pig who was lying on Liz's sheep patterned flannel pillows, hooves delicately crossed, a black pig with one rose pink half of a hoof and a brown patch on his cheek. He likes warm goat's milk and wheatabix for breakfast, asparagus and lemon mayonnaise for lunch, and crabmeat and salmon enroullade for dinner.

I quite cheered myself up — and L. — with this.

Liz had not endured ritual abuse but as we talked I understood that she had lived with a depth of despair and isolation which made me shiver. I was not alone in my feelings of hate and anger and separation.

Over and over I have found that whatever the details of my experiences, other people recognize the feelings. It was hard to believe this with the ritual abuse. The details seemed so dramatic and extraordinary, the experiences of being buried in a coffin or eating a baby so far from the everyday world, I couldn't believe a bridge existed. And the specifics were off-putting to other people too. It was easy to feel like an exotic specimen when I talked about what I was remembering at AA meetings. I needed the Survivor of Incest Anonymous meetings where other people had endured similar horrors, but even in the AA meetings, when I talked about what I was feeling, my fear and rage and grief and loneliness, people nodded their heads.

Telling and listening. The simple, strange magic of connection. The antidote to all that poison. If I had held that bitterness inside me I would have continued to feel alone and separate and I would have found it harder and harder to care about other people. Locked in my tower, knowing nobody could understand how I felt, self-pity would have corroded my heart. But fortunately I began to cry and talk and Liz listened and responded and then I saw how I liked watching the dogs run in the snow. Delight could find me again. The everyday world felt real once more and I could laugh and make Liz laugh with silly stories about Humpty the gourmet pig. In that laughter as much as in the tears and furies I was doing the work of knitting the world and myself back together. "It really happened to me, and it's still happening" *and* I can laugh and be silly.

The abusers did not, in the end, have the power to make me inhuman. I have the power to isolate or to connect, to focus on my differences, or on the similarities which bind us all together. If I talk honestly, other people with open hearts understand what I am saying because we do share a common language of the emotions. It takes faith and trust to do this, and often those are in short supply. But just as abuse tends to beget more abuse, healing too acquires its own momentum. After a while one accumulates experiences of being listened to and feeling better, and talking about the next hard thing doesn't take quite so much faith.

It does however go on requiring someone to listen. Rich and Liz listened and listened. I was afraid they would burn out, I was afraid for them and I was afraid for myself. When, in the middle of March, Rich said he needed a week off, I could hardly bring myself to ask if it was okay to go on talking about my memories, I was so frightened he would say, "Well, it *is* too much for me." I suspect it was overwhelming to him at the time, but what he said was, "Where else better to bring it?" I tried to spread the burden, to talk about it at meetings and with friends, but in truth I needed to talk about it to my therapist *and* my lover *and* my friends *and* at meetings.

Talking was what helped knit the worlds together, the kindly everyday world where I lived most of the time and that other world where incredible cruelty was ordinary. Believing my memories meant accepting that both worlds were true. In order not to feel torn apart I had to tell each world about the other. I had to tell the terrified child self that another, safer world existed, and I had to tell the safer world about that place of terror.

I felt deeply grateful to Rich and to Liz for their long listening, and at the same time I felt an abiding rage. I didn't want to have to be grateful to people for listening to me talk about shit I never wanted to happen in the first place. It wasn't my fucking fault it happened. I hated feeling I was too much and I knew I'd always feared that I was, that in the end I would be left alone with my terror and my despair.

I hated that I needed something which it was difficult for people to give.

In the past, in dealing with the incest, I had been able to talk out a lot of memories and pain with other survivors. To a limited extent I could do this with the Ritual Abuse but it was so new and raw for all of us, the information so volatile in our psyches still, that it often felt too risky to listen to the specifics of each other's memories. They might trigger a flashback, bring on a new memory. And, because there are similarities between rituals enacted by cult groups in different states and even in different countries, when I listened to another survivor tell about rituals I did not remember experiencing myself, I wondered uneasily, Did that happen to me too? Am I going to have to remember that? Some of the time I warded off the unease by thinking how much worse the other person's abuse was than mine and/or wondering once again whether the whole thing wasn't just completely implausible and ridiculous and I'd gotten caught up in a mass hysteria. Other survivors probably used similar tactics to protect themselves when I was talking.

Early on in the time when a lot of people started to remember ritual abuse there were even moves within the SIA group to restrict what people could talk about in the meeting. Some people felt unsafe because other people's sharing of details triggered frightening feelings and images in them. Others were frightened of censorship. If *we* didn't believe that the truth would set you free, who would? If people couldn't talk about what happened to them here, where could they? Ultimately the anarchistic traditions of twelve step programs helped the group to accept that we had no business telling people what they could and could not talk about. We couldn't make meetings safe for everybody. Still it was a difficult and bruising debate.

Because listening was often so difficult for other survivors, I tended to rely, for one-to-one conversations, on friends who had not themselves experienced ritual abuse. But many of them were on overload too: one can't listen to the news with half an open heart and not feel overwhelmed by the weight of suffering, the pervasiveness of greed and cruelty, the blind stupidity of plundering our only home for burgers and the plastic to wrap them in. The sheer volume of information available to us is exhausting. Then, too, many of my friends had gone through traumatic experiences of one kind or another in their personal lives. How could I ask that they listen to more horror, take in that the world was an even more brutal place than they thought? The kind of listening I was asking for was not the uh-huh variety. I needed people to walk with me through the valley of the shadow, and to do that they had to face the reality of evil *for themselves.*

Often my friends felt the need to protect themselves from what I was saying. This was easier when they said they couldn't, in themselves, cope with the intensity and horror of it, much worse when their responses implied either that there was something wrong with me for needing to talk about it or that it hadn't really happened at all.

Judgment and denial were hardly unfamiliar forms of self-protection to me but still I was angry and hurt when I encountered those reactions.

Sometimes I wondered, what if I *was* making it up? What if the gory details I was asking my friends to listen to were merely figments of my imagination? The fact that I found it hard to believe myself made me terribly vulnerable to other people's incredulity.

I wished that, by closing my eyes, I could make it all go away. How could I blame other people for feeling the same way? And yet it hurt desperately when people who cared about me wouldn't push themselves to deal with this aspect of my life, this aspect of the world. I took personally their need to protect themselves.

I needed more validation from outside myself for what I was remembering. Bill was an obvious source, but he had not yet come to terms with any of the "ordinary" incest which happened in the family and he was, from what he himself told me about his drinking, an active alcoholic. He also told me he was not interested in the past or the present, only the future. He was not likely to corroborate my memories any time soon

3/13/90

Rich showed me an article in a Christian newspaper about Satanic practices on the rise among teenagers. Half of teenage suicides in Rhode Island are connected to it. Connecticut police have set up a special department for it. Rhode Island police held an information seminar.

One telling sign — when your kid draws pentagrams everywhere.

Driving away from therapy I remembered how I doodled pentagrams all the time as a teenager, always noticing if they were upside down or not. Weird.

Though I felt dubious about the interest Christian newspapers took in Satanism, the information contained in that little report Rich showed me was useful. Police departments were beginning to pay attention to Ritual Abuse. Somebody somewhere believed it hap-

• CHAPTER EIGHT •

pened. Teenage suicides were linked with it. It seemed likely that my own attempt had been. Best of all was that odd detail about kids doodling pentagrams because it linked up with a piece of information which belonged to the realm of my everyday memory, not to the world of unconscious information surfacing years later. I knew for sure that I had indeed doodled pentagrams myself for years as a teenager, and I remembered a curious attention within myself to whether they came out upside down (indicating "black magic") or right way up ("white magic"). Perhaps it was insignificant, but even such a small connection is helpful when there is so little external validation.

A few days later, on the 19th of March, I caught the Outlook program on ritual abuse on the radio. After writing down the too familiar details of the girl made to watch the killing and eating of a baby, the boy terrified into silence by being forced to watch the killing of animals, I noted in my journal,

> *All the grown ups saying they believed the kids, that the kids' stories stayed consistent. They said this is where incest was seven or eight years ago — people could hardly believe the scope of it. They were human and angry and determined and hurt and sad and shocked. The victims were not on trial.*
>
> *I stood there, stunned, tried to call L. a couple of times to get her to listen too but her phone was busy. I felt excited and frightened. This was England, English people, it does happen in England. The details were familiar. They believe us. It's real. And at least some grown ups are going to do something about it.*
>
> *Then the radio was talking about Chinese herbs and skin diseases and I was still walking around with all that excitement and fear — left T. a message, called L., cried a little — it happens in England, it's real.*

As I listened, and afterwards, my heart pounded with a mix of fear and relief. People *knew*. The pain and loneliness from when I was a child and it was happening and I knew nobody would believe me, let alone help me, mingled with the loneliness I felt in the present. I realized how much I had felt put on trial, by myself and by other people.

Mostly though, the answers to my questions about the reality — or otherwise — of Ritual Abuse had to come from inside myself. The first woman I ever heard talking about Ritual Abuse used to say,

"If all this horrible abuse had happened to me, I'd be crazy and I'm not." She was married with children, a responsible job. "I'm just not fucked up enough," she kept saying. The fact that she was an alcoholic and had been so agoraphobic she couldn't leave the house for seven years didn't seem to count. I teased her about this, but when I began to remember myself, I felt the same way. When citing my shining mental health as proof that I had to be making it all up, I seemed strangely able to ignore two teenage suicide attempts, alcoholism, a lifetime of feeling like a stranger to myself, the fact that I jump a foot in the air when someone comes up behind me unexpectedly, inexplicable attacks of terror and revulsion, an adult life shaped by the need to live under cover.

Over time, though, holding the light of this new information to my life as I knew it, I began to see the landscape differently. Events and familiar feelings cast different shadows. Things which hadn't made sense before began to make sense. Not a lot, but a few things.

For example, the ways in which I had lived in hiding began to make sense to me when I thought of myself as having been caught up in a powerful and secretive cult which I believed wanted to recruit me as an adult member. I lived in America for a number of years illegally. The life of an illegal alien requires a level of caution, secrecy, and invisibility which is tedious, a strain. I sensed, well before remembering the Ritual Abuse, that living in hiding was serving some emotional purpose for me. I could see that it gave me an excuse not to go back to England and not to see my family at a time when I was not yet strong enough to say no directly. Once I began to remember the ritual abuse it seemed likely to me that, in being here illegally, I had been living out my unconscious need to keep myself out of reach of the cult.

When I looked at my life with an open mind, signs of the kinds of trauma Ritual Abuse might inflict were not so hard to find.

When I cited my mental health as proof that it couldn't have happened I was also forgetting what I was like before nine years of therapy and other recovery work. I was ready to die, I was seeing faces in the dark outside my fifth floor apartment windows. I couldn't even tell if the fridge was working.

There is in any case an irony in using my sanity to prove that I'm crazy. Why on earth would I invent all these memories of torture? Why would I put myself through three years of shaking and gagging and a grief so deep it felt as if my bones themselves were sobbing, let

Chapter Eight

alone a guilt of such intensity I wanted to leap out of my skin? To punish my parents? I haven't been in touch with them since I confronted them with the incest in 1987, and they denied it. That was two years before the first ritual abuse memories surfaced. To feel important, one of the real victims? I don't like feeling like a victim, my impulse is to deny my vulnerability, not to amplify it, and as for feeling important, in whose eyes? Even my friends looked away. To make sense of my life? My fears and foibles felt well enough accounted for by the incest I'd remembered. Shortly before the Ritual Abuse started to surface I thought I was finally coming to the end of remembering old abuse. Whatever shadows and mysteries remained I was quite willing to let them be.

No, if I'm not fucked up enough for all this to have happened, I'm certainly not fucked up enough to be inventing it.

Chapter Nine

4/7/90

Marvellous day yesterday — mostly outside in cool spring sunshine building a new vegetable bed.
    [Later I went to a dance.] Felt closer to L. and more sexual, but when I was taking down the sheelchair ramp at the end of the dance and L. said to screw the wing nuts back onto the bolts, I crashed — irritated by the unnecessary task, overwhelmen somehow and totally out of sorts and not at all clear what had happened to me.

4/8/90

    Memory — associating wing nuts to thumb screws — tightening screws — torture — me doing it to a boy with dark hair. He or I will die. Terror. Me tightening the screws until he fainted and they carved a pentacle in his back and then I was sure they would kill him because otherwise somebody might have seen it. Feeling in myself I should die. I should have died, shouldn't have let him die instead of me. Was I more scared of dying or of the pain? It was an old thumbscrew — an ancient machinery of torture.
    God, whatever's good, I prayed and prayed — afraid of the memory coming.
    'I am here in your remembering.'

Later

    Full moon. The lovely shadows and the trees — started to cry thinking of the boy slumped forward, pentagram carved on his back — the horror of his pain.
    L. said, "All of us would choose for somebody else to die in our place."

When I saw Rich two days later I couldn't tell him about tightening the thumbscrews right away. When at last I had forced the words out, I huddled on the couch, eyes shut, feeling his horrified gaze on my skin, willing him to speak, to say something to redeem me, to tell me I was still human, that I might somehow be forgiven. The longer the silence stretched, the more deeply I felt convinced of his repulsion. The saner, witness voice told me this probably wasn't so, that I must speak, ask him to help before I slipped into the dark water I felt rising around me. But I couldn't bring myself to ask for what I most wanted. If he couldn't tell me voluntarily that I was not a monster, I did not want to try to squeeze the words out of him.

Why wouldn't Rich help me out of this pit of guilt? I felt angry as well as hurt. When we talked about it later, he said that my ability to feel bad about what I had done was the best proof that they did not get me. I still feel a twinge of anger when I think about those long silences while I begged him in my mind to contradict my self-recriminations, to tell me that I was OK, that I deserved to live. But it is true that my guilt is one of the ways I know the cult failed in their efforts to turn me into one of them.

The capacity to feel guilt is essential, but guilt itself is dangerous. It is a form of self-exile. In a way it is the application to oneself of the most common form of social sanction: exclusion. When I feel guilty, I feel disconnected. The guilt is a veil between me and other people. It makes no difference whether the guilt is merited or not. Guilt travels with a band of other feelings: self-hatred, resentment, despair, defiance. The more entrenched the guilt, the worse its effects: if one feels irredeemably bad then, out of sheer self-protection, there is an impulse to reject the world one already feels excluded from. If I'm this bad, I might as well be worse. When hope of forgiveness, acceptance, inclusion is gone then guilt, or any other form of punitive exile, tends to make one behave worse, not better. Exile is only an effective deterrent when there is some hope of belonging. The need to belong is fundamental to human beings. We are pack animals. We can't help making societies. Excluded from one, we seek another. Satanic cults, like other cults, know and use this.

Making me participate in torture and rape not only ensured my silence, it was part of the process of recruitment. As I was implicated in ever more violent acts I began to despair of myself. Perhaps I did indeed belong to Satan, as they said. If anybody in the ordinary

Chapter Nine

world knew what my hands had done, what my eyes had seen, they would run from me in horror. And even if nobody else saw, I knew. I had forfeited my right to belong in the ordinary world. Meanwhile, here was the cult telling me I belonged to them. If they could convince me that I was hopelessly bad, then in my despair and rage and loneliness and need, I would identify myself with them. I would *want* to be one of them.

My first impulse, in dealing with feelings of guilt, is to try to work out whether it is "real" guilt or not. Do I deserve to feel it? Have my actions merited it? If not, I try to argue myself out of it.

Arguing myself out of guilt doesn't work any better than arguing myself out of any other feeling. I think now that the first priority in dealing with guilt is to reaffirm the possibility of belonging: however badly one has behaved, the banishment is not absolute. For me, the pain at the bottom of guilt is always loneliness. The hurt of that can be so frightening that I go numb, and then I'm unable to feel that empathetic pain at having wounded someone else which is the useful part of guilt in the first place.

When I think about myself hunched in mute desperation after I'd told about torturing the boy, longing for Rich to say something, what I wanted was not so much for him to make the pain of having collaborated go away as it was for him to tell me that, however bad my actions had been, *I* was not hopelessly bad. I wanted him to tell me I still had a right to exist.

I once had a lover who grew up in a large and happy family. I felt there was something unfamiliar about her, as if the sun shone in her belly. She took for granted her right to exist. She assumed she had a place in the world. I warmed my hands before that certainty in her, but it made me sad. I wondered if one could acquire such a feeling later in life, or if it had to be fed to you, spoonful by spoonful, at the beginning. I could see in myself how many tensions and faults arose from straining to prove my right to exist. Anxiety, envy, competitiveness, defensiveness, the need to control, to manipulate, all these feelings cluster around that central uncertainty, like flies on a wound.

If I make a mistake or behave badly it still feels like a matter of life or death, as if somewhere inside there is a court always in session, always about to reach a ruling: do I have a right to live or not?

Perhaps it was because guilt was so much on my mind at this

time that a new piece of information about my grandmother's — my mother's mother's — death surfaced. I had long been aware that I had a blank spot where her death and funeral should have been. For a while I thought perhaps I didn't remember because I was away at boarding school when she died but then I learned that she died in 1968, when I was ten. I didn't go to boarding school until I was twelve.

I'd always remembered Granny coming to live with us at the Mill House shortly after we got back from Kenya. It was around that time that I started having terrifying nightmares and I used to go into Granny's room in the middle of the night. She was always awake — from pain, I think now, as she was dying of cancer — and kind. I sat on the edge of her bed and told her my dreams. Thinking about it, I could picture her false teeth in the glass on her bedside table, and the round pink top to her bottle of Appleblossom perfume, and on the chair her bra with one padded cup for where she'd had a mastectomy years before. I could remember the prayer she taught me to say at night, "Matthew, Mark, Luke and John, at the four corners of my bed," and the local hospital where she went sometimes, but I couldn't remember anything about her death other than a vague sense that she had been cremated.

When I first began to remember ritual abuse I told myself it started after Granny's death, that my mother, desperate with grief and weakened by the codeine she took every day back then, had been drawn into the cult, via the man in the brown suit with whom she was having an affair. I thought perhaps the man had promised that the cult would help her contact her mother's spirit. It felt pretty flimsy, this version, but it had the virtues of establishing a definite beginning, a relatively benign motive for my mother, and it kept my father out of the picture.

But then, at the end of April 1990, making a phone call to a bank in England to clear up some minor miscommunication released a flood of terror. Rich pointed out that I'd remembered that the man in brown worked in a bank.

Hysterical fear, the way I think I woke from those nightmares when I was ten and eleven, when I would go to Granny for comfort. I think that and then I'm realizing this abuse started before Granny died and I believed they made her die. They wanted me to say some words after them and I wouldn't. They told me they would make her die but I thought they were stupid except then it came true and I thought it was my fault.

It is common for children to blame themselves for deaths and other catastrophes in the family but in this case it was the cult who had told me her death was my fault. Uncovering this much, I could feel a tremendous charge of guilt but I could remember nothing more. When I tried, it felt as if a curtain were drawn across my mind, a great thick velvet curtain of sleepiness.

5/15/90

Saw Rich. Mostly chit chat.
He suggested finding an image of integration, wholeness to be able to draw on when getting into the heavy stuff.
I saw the earth — land and sea — all linked.
Somewhere a self hot and angry, more out-going. I pushed that away as irrelevant.

I pushed but it wouldn't stay away, that hot, angry self. I had a series of dreams during this time in which it was pointed out to me that repressing my anger didn't make it go away, it only meant I acted it out unconsciously.

5/19/90

Dream of a teenage boy who has a bad reputation but I go wandering around with him, tell him some stuff about myself, talk about how I want a cigarette, how much I want to get drunk on vodka. We are for a while in Old Jerusalem and I am swimming in deep water between rocks....
Later I tie Liz up and leave her in a room. I have told her she is locked in. When she comes to the door and finds it open, I am standing there and I march her back into the room and tie her arms behind her. I don't know why I am doing it. In some distant part of me I feel sorry for her but I am not connected with myself really. I walk out, locking the door, still uneasy, doing it anyway. Why? I wonder. Why would I do that?

In waking life too I felt disconnected, absent-minded. I ran a lot of red lights. I'd written in my journal about the memory of turning the thumbscrew, "This is the real stuff. I'm touching bedrock. This is REAL." I knew I had not made that memory up. I knew I would not inflict on myself the kind of agony I felt remembering my participation in the torture. It was a relief, in a way, to face it. But it was also too much. If this was real everything else felt unreal.

As I had done since childhood, I turned to the non-human world for reassurance. This was the spring I began to make a garden in earnest, chiseling beds out of the hillside, building retaining walls out of all the stone I unearthed, hauling manure and poring over gardening books.

In my journal I wrote out the Zen story Elsa Gidlow tells at the end of her autobiography:

> *A young woman goes from teacher to teacher absorbing more and more wisdom until one day she is "enlightened." She sees the mountains are not mountains; the rivers are not rivers. So then she sets herself up to teach, but one day a woman hears her teaching and begins to laugh. When asked why, the woman just laughs more, looking the young woman in the eye. There is a glow of light about her as she leaves. "Crazy old woman, unlearned and common," thinks the younger woman, but the look and the laugh leave a nagging doubt. She comes to doubt everything she has learned and can no longer teach.*
>
> *She turns to simple manual work as comfort in this time. In so doing she begins to feel the real ground beneath her feet. The mountains are mountains, the river is a flowing river. She becomes gentler, helps those who are weaker.*
>
> *When asked why she no longer teaches she says, "I have nothing to teach."*
>
> *One says, "Oh teacher," at which she laughs and laughs until tears spring up and she is warm.*
>
> *"Why are you laughing like that, you crazy old woman?"*
>
> *"Because I am happy. The mountains are again mountains. The river is running water. The earth is firm underfoot. There is nothing more glorious than what I do every day." (1)*

1. Elsa Gidlow, *Elsa.* p.411

Chapter Ten

5/23/90

Yesterday morning on my way to work I tuned in to WFCR to this sentence: "It is sad that children feel the need to be forgiven for crimes they were forced to commit." About children forced into the rebel army in Mozambique — massacring their own villagers — recaptured by government forces who contacted the villagers — "What shall we do with them?"

"Send them to us. They are our children. We forgive them."

They were returned to the villages, the women working with them, getting them to talk partly through traditional story-telling and dance. A treatment center [set up by the government to reintegrate the children into village life] was decentralized to the villages, recognizing the women were doing it better themselves.

I felt an ache in me, listening to this report, because I knew that the villagers' traditions of dance and story-telling were giving those children something I needed too. I needed my experiences to be heard and witnessed and accepted into the collective story of my culture. The more I integrated into myself what I had seen and done and felt the more I knew that it wasn't enough to integrate it all as an individual.

In writing this book I am making use of my own culture's version of story-telling, but there is no village to gather around and listen. I imagine that I am telling this story to people of good will, people who have undertaken their own journeys into the dark, or who are just about to. I know that I am speaking to real people, but nonetheless a book is a commodity, to be bought and sold. It comes wrapped in the anonymity of the market place. For healing one needs more than sales figures, and anyway, it took several years of mending before I could even begin to think of writing about what happened.

I tried to make a place — SIA — where I could tell my story and listen to other people's stories. I had started going to SIA meetings in New York at the end of my first year sober. SIA was a new program then, one of several which had adapted the steps and format of AA to the needs of incest survivors. When I moved to Western Massachusetts in 1986 I found there were no SIA meetings and I missed them so I started one. Soon there was a core group of regulars and a real feeling of safety developed. But when a few of us began to remember ritual abuse, and as new people with similar memories joined the group, I watched some of the original members drift away. A friend told me, "It isn't what I need to hear." She was going to other meetings now. For a while the meetings were much smaller. It upset me. I wanted SIA to be more than a place where you went to shop for whatever you needed for your own recovery right then. I wanted it to be an enclave of belonging, a place where we welcomed each other's truths, however difficult. I believed that in that welcoming and being welcomed, with all its difficulty, a place was made where healing could happen.

I still believe this but I know how hard it is to achieve. In order to afford each other such a welcome, we would have to treat each other as the Mozambiquean villagers treated their children, as if no one of us was expendable, and we would have to ask for each other's stories, however horrible, not because we were trying to be good but because we knew we needed to hear them in order ourselves to be whole.

To live from and in the knowledge that "Whatsoever you do to the least of these, you do to me," is to live the enlightened compassion of the Buddha, of Christ. Neither SIA nor any other group of human beings will do it perfectly. But some societies seem to start out a lot closer to that goal than others. Listening to the radio report, I felt impoverished as a human being beside those Mozambiquean villagers.

When I first moved to Western Massachusetts I didn't have a car and I was having trouble getting to enough AA meetings. Somebody told me that the Congregational church in Hesterton gave her the same feeling she got from meetings. So I decided to give it a try, muttering my assorted reservations about Christianity.

• CHAPTER TEN •

It was early in April and snow was falling on the village. As I walked down Main Street I felt suddenly how the villagers must have depended on each other through the long hard winters in this rocky land. I felt the ghosts of people coming on sleds from the outlying farms to go to church, and the white spired church itself as the heart of the community, where birth and marriage and death were marked. The church was plain, with long oak pews, half-empty. There were children there, and old people, and all ages of people in between, and I cried for the whole hour of the service.

The woman behind me asked if I would like to come home with her for lunch and I said no, then changed my mind. She fed me meatloaf and read my tarot cards. She commented that she didn't see any men in my cards so I told her I was a lesbian. She'd always wondered what that was like. She told me her best friend's neighbor ran away with another woman and that she herself liked to look at her son's pin-ups. She told me she'd been married for many years to an autocratic man. She married him to get away from her mother, then one day he came in and told her he'd bought a plot of land to build a house on, right next door to her mother's. When he died she had a breakdown. She thought the fridge was chasing her down the road. Then she enrolled in a literacy program and learned to read, and now she made a living cleaning houses and reading tarot cards. She talked non-stop and I laughed and marveled, my heart still raw from crying so long in the church, but happy too.

She told me she cried too when she started going to the church. She told me how the some of the old guard at the church hadn't wanted this one to become a member because he worked as a psychic, or that couple because they weren't married. I heard how Rich, the minister, had worked to make the church a place of inclusion, somewhere where everybody could belong. I said I wasn't a Christian and she said she wasn't either and Rich knew that and it was okay.

I cried every time I went to church for three straight months. Something in my chest was thawing and it hurt. I felt I could belong there. I had felt I belonged in AA, but although "the only requirement for membership" was minimal — "a desire to stop drinking" — it was still a requirement. The pure magic of that little church was that I didn't need to do or be anything. Of course individual members of that congregation had their prejudices — when, after Rich moved on, the church elected an openly lesbian minister, some homophobia showed up —

111

but as an entity, the open-hearted welcome afforded by that group of people was astonishing. All sorts of people felt it: the church kept getting certificates from head office for being the fastest growing congregation around. When I brought friends to church, they cried too.

Some of the magic came from Rich: he spoke to people's hearts about journeys he himself had taken, using the stories of the Bible to explore a rare mix of psychological and mystical reality. Familiar verses came alive. He helped us find, in those stories, a common language of the spirit and the heart. But not all the magic came from him. When I think about that first time, seeing the church in the snow, I think we were all being fed by the spirit of community involvement and interdependence embodied in the church. Many of the members had joined as children. A neighbor of mine had been a member for eighty years. Part of the power of that church for me was that it was not the sort of group I was used to belonging to. It was not a defiant band of outcasts, queers, drunks, artists, it was a medley of old and young, farmers, housewives, therapists, factory workers, professors. It was largely white because that's who lives in the hilltowns of Western Massachusetts right now, and it was obviously Christian in tradition and religious practice, but within those constraints it was an amazing mix of people.

As a teenager, the cult had used my ordinary yearning to belong in their efforts to recruit me. Feeling tainted by everything I'd seen and done, exiled from ordinary life by my guilt, I was vulnerable to their methods. In order to fight them I rejected my need to belong. In that little country church I felt the longing again and it hurt, but it was a joyful hurt. I had not known until then how much the freedom and anonymity of city life had left me thirsting for a community rooted in place, where you had to deal with each other whether you wanted to or not, where nobody was expendable.

5/27/90

After a lovely day visiting the Berkshire Garden Center I dropped L's one remaining favorite bowl from Michigan — she was sad and cross — I felt terrified and wanted to rush off alone — wondered why — only remembered scene: 11 years old, dropped something, Mum saying "Accidents will happen." — couldn't see what might be scary there — still afraid and wretched in the morning — terror at "Accidents may happen" — why? — oh, Mum switched personalities right after it. Don't know what she did.

Chapter Ten

Yes fear L. will suddenly be different.

I see now that's an old deep fear — the most basic trust is that someone is consistent and I don't have that — somewhere inside a habitual fear that people will switch.

Also realize that's a fear when someone's angry — not fear of their anger per se but fear of what will happen. Anger may have been a strong feeling which Mum couldn't deal with and which triggered switches.

Later L. talking to the tribe: Little Little, Little Hawk, Miles, Marin, Tom.

"And me" — another eleven-year-old — began to cry and cry — "horrible things happened to me" — flashback of dog burning — man behind me, holding my head, forcing me to look ("that's what we'll do to you if...") — shaking and stuttering — L. asked her name.

"Anonymous. Like Euonymous."

"Can I call you Shrub?"

"No. Names are dangerous. They can find you."

"Oh, do you not want me to come looking for you then, just wait till you want to talk?"

"I don't know." Felt scared. Needed somewhere to hide. Can hide behind Miles.

(I, adult Anna, had a flash of the two merging — the new eleven-year-old is an almost translucent presence — but thought then, no, Miles isn't ready and wouldn't want anyway to incorporate all this nightmarish information into himself. And that's OK — saw the fear of integration, the point of confederation — of bringing the eleven-year-old into the circle of the tribe at her own pace, in her own way.

Cried a bunch more.

It's exciting that she came, that I'm beginning to absorb the stories as my reality — with feeling.

Thank God for Liz my love, my sturdy darling, my sweet heart, staunch one person woman (whose complementary fear is that people will find out she's not who she appears to be.)

5/29/90

Saw Rich. Fear of being left alone very strong.... I told Granny my nightmares and she died. I killed her. I didn't say what they wanted me to and I did say what they warned me not to.

Talked of dropping bowl and terror and Mum splitting and my fear of expressing anger and he said well what if one of you broke [some-

thing...] in anger?

That stillness inside and sadness — me almost hysterical with rage hurling a teapot against the wall behind the oil furnace — blue and white tiles somewhere in there — Mum screaming back then going still — coming at me — blank eyes — hands around my throat, cold and deadly contempt in her voice — how she hated me and despised me and wished I'd never been born.

You're a worm. You're a cunt. You know what that is? A hole. I, terrified she would kill me, had no psychic screen against her hatred.

I can see Rich one two hour session a month for the four months he's on Sabbatical — and call him if I'm really in trouble — he respects my boundaries on that — I haven't been inappropriate with them. (Yuk — shrink words.)

In 1984, when I was first beginning to remember my childhood, Esther, my therapist, suggested that my mother had some form of multiple personality. She based this surmise on my descriptions of the way my mother would go blank and then be different. I had a few strange memories over the years which supported her idea. For example, I remembered seeing my mother, with that frightening empty look in her eyes, pick up a kitchen knife and, holding it like a dagger, march over to the fridge with it. She opened the door and stabbed the joint of cold roast beef with it repeatedly. And then she just stopped and walked over to the sink and put the knife in it and was ordinary again. That happened when I was ten or eleven, during the time when I now think the ritual abuse was starting.

My guess is that my mother did have some form of MPD and that she was dealing with her experiences in the cult at this time by splitting. It is possible that she developed MPD as a response to ritual abuse when she was a child, but I don't know this. From what I can put together from the stories she told about her childhood, there may have been enough trauma without ritual abuse to necessitate some kind of disintegration of her personality. Her father was killed in the Second World War when she was five. She and her mother moved to northwest Scotland to escape the blitz and lived with her grandfather. He was by all accounts a violently abusive alcoholic. My grandmother had five brothers, one older and four younger, and one sister, the youngest of all, my great-aunt Fiona. My mother told stories of the brothers bullying her, and when she and Granny were leaving, Fiona, aged fifteen at the time, begged them to take her with them, saying

Chapter Ten

(as my mother told the story) that "The old bugger couldn't keep his hands off her." It seems quite likely in that set-up that my mother could have been sexually abused. I'm fairly sure that her abuse of me when I was young was a re-enactment of something done to her.

On top of all this trauma and loss, both individual and collective, my great-grandfather was an ardent Scottish nationalist and would have no English spoken in the house. Since my mother spoke no Gaelic this must have been terrifying and confusing.

After the war Granny and my mother lived in the Lake District. Though I felt safe and happy with Granny and my mother seemed very close to her, I suspect that everything was not so rosy when my mother was growing up. Her story that Granny drank a half bottle of champagne for breakfast every morning at least hints at the possibility of alcoholism!

Most of this is conjecture. I wish I had more information. I really don't know whether my mother has full blown MPD or not, let alone why she developed it if she did. I do know that I have an habitual fear that people will suddenly become different. I want to be able to trust that people are as they appear, more or less, and that they will be consistent — but I don't. When Liz decided to give me the land to build my house on I was delighted, but I also did not know how to trust the gift. Could she be internally consistent enough to make such a decision? I asked over and over if she really felt OK giving me something so valuable with no strings attached. I wanted to be certain she would not turn around later and accuse me of having manipulated it out of her.

The fact that Liz could be angry without switching into being somebody else helped me to trust her. It is no coincidence that the eleven-year-old who carried most of the memories came into the open shortly afterwards.

Within myself I was feeling less afraid that the self who remembered would push aside my adult, conscious self entirely. I was learning from experience that this did not happen. Still I was uneasy around anything people could label as MPD in me, in part because I had never wanted to resemble my mother in any way, least of all by sharing a psychiatric diagnosis with her. Even now it feels a little weird to write about the tribe. It is difficult to convey the way in which these characters were identifiable entities and yet, at the same time, existed only within the circle of my self. I knew them to be imaginary and I allowed them to be real. I felt love for them and I found them funny, touching, sad. Little Little was two years old, a joyful child untouched by abuse; Little Hawk was about nine, intense and arrogant, a magician sure of her powers, but a child still; Miles was a boy of about eleven, kind though uneasy with expressions of emotion, taking comfort in the natural world, in the mechanics of things, with a passion for information and a strong impulse to instruct. Marin and Tom were teenagers, Marin the girl I never was, a little vain, sensitive and impulsive, Tom an angry shadowy figure who cast himself as the warrior defending the tribe. He stood watch at the entrance to the circle, half in and half out. There were two elders too, Granny and Swift Bear, an old Native American man. And then there was me, the adult, a parent of sorts, responsible for the safety and harmony of the tribe.

The tribe, more or less in this form, had been around since 1987. The characters came into being in the imaginative play that Francia, my lover before Liz, and I delighted in. We would lie in the loft of my tiny cabin and tell stories about Pan and Athena and Aunt May and Aunt Victoria (two old women who keep the world patched together) and let our various characters talk. We practiced a kind of shamanic journeying too in which we used the beat of a drum as the canoe to carry us down into other worlds populated by animals and plants and gods who took us to strange places and taught us things we needed to know. Both of us were at ease in the realm of the imagination and the unconscious, and found in the stories we brought back help in facing the wounds from two extremely abusive childhoods. Later, when Liz and I got together, she met the tribe and hung out with the kids.

I used to talk about the tribe to Rich, not as a problem but as a way of discussing complex feelings. I found that when I felt disturbed or anxious it often helped to imagine the tribe coming together for a council meeting in which everybody would have their say. As often as not the trouble I was feeling was due to one of the characters feeling excluded or unwanted.

It strikes me now that the tribe was, in a sense, my own version of the village in Mozambique, a place of inclusion and integration where nothing was too bad to be said or felt, and nobody could be expelled. Everybody belonged in my tribe. There were even the elders I lacked in my ordinary life. Granny and Swift Bear comforted me, challenged me, gave me advice sometimes. People of my parent's generation were conspicuously absent. I had to be the parent. I didn't have to be perfect but I soon learned that the harmony and serenity of the whole depended on my being consistent and trustworthy in my dealings with myself. I went to therapy and meetings whether I felt like it or not. I ate regularly. I tried to be responsible financially. I did not indulge in orgies of mental self-flagellation if I could help it. I was circumspect about the people to whom I told my memories. If I fell short in my task of being a good parent, I soon found out about it.

Treating myself as a tribe rather than as an isolated individual made it easier to be kind to myself. I might feel self-hatred and guilt and shame, but when I imagined those child selves I did not experience them as bad or tainted, I felt a deep compassion for them.

So I was pleased when the self who had been carrying the ritual abuse memories came out of the shadows and became one of the tribe. I felt very clearly that there was no point in rushing towards "integration" in the sense of merging the members of the tribe into a unitary self, and every point in maintaining a "confederation." "Bringing the eleven-year-old into the circle of the tribe at her own pace, in her own way," was one way to describe the process of integrating all this new information: "it's exciting that she came, that I'm beginning... to absorb the stories as my reality." It is through the imagination that reality comes to feel real.

6/5/90

Happy today — felt my heart open to the two newcomers when I chaired the early SIA meeting — both, as it turned out, multiples and ritual abuse survivors — felt that hot wave of love for them, hoped they could feel it. I get so much back from chairing those meetings.

A yellow moon night. I wandered with my flashlight — fed the bees who seem to be spilling over into the upper hive body, transplanted delphinium seedlings, Missouri primrose and Chinese lanterns and alyssum.

Saw Rich this afternoon — [...talked] about feeling hurt by him calculating how few times he need see me during his sabbatical and how the kids feel he's leaving, he's going away, though intellect says he's coming back.

Well, he said, it's confidential but he's 89% sure he's gotten a job at a church in inner city Springfield starting in October. I felt something relax in my chest all the while other reactions of sadness and fear and abandonment were happening — the relaxation because somewhere inside I'd picked up his turmoil and his plans. And in my guts I feel it's right for him.

The birds came back, he said, when he was driving to Provincetown and praying about this — swooping in front of his car, four at a time, and nowhere else on the road.

So we talked as adults and peers — he made reference to dealing with his feelings about leaving with the person he sees — oh I thought — felt more equal then somehow.

Later quite anxious — left a few minutes early. It's OK kids, we didn't cause him to leave — remember the birds — it's just the right time — able to be clear and firm about this one.

Growing up with so many cracks and rifts — within my mother's personality, between family appearances and realities, between what actually happened and what I knew about consciously — meant that my radar system was always on red alert. I could not trust the ground I walked on. I needed as much warning as possible about whatever I might encounter around the next corner. So, like many survivors of prolonged trauma, I am quite psychic. I start to react to situations before I know about them consciously. I've learned to take this into account as a possibility when I am responding in ways that don't seem to come from the present: most often I am reacting to the past, but sometimes I may be reacting to the future.

When Rich told me he'd been offered a job in Springfield, something relaxed in me. I hadn't, until then, been able to understand why I was feeling so strongly that he was abandoning me. I could see reacting to his taking a sabbatical, but my response had felt as if it went beyond that. It was when I was talking, in a puzzled way, about the intensity of these feelings, trying to work out what bit of the past they came from, that Rich said perhaps he had better tell me about the new job, since I seemed to be picking it up anyway.

I didn't want him to leave Hesterton I couldn't imagine the church without him. He reassured me I could go on seeing him in Springfield, and Springfield was no further for me to drive, but the thought of emerging from the bloody and desperate past into filthy streets rather than fields and trees and the river filled me with sadness. Even so, finding out what was really happening was a relief. Reality, however sad or disappointing, mostly does come as a relief to me.

• Chapter Ten •

When I'm not being told what is going on I get frightened and confused. I don't know whether to trust my radar. The ground shivers underfoot.

I was grateful to Rich for telling me when he did, and for telling me the birds had come back. He'd told me before about the first time they came, some twelve years earlier. He had been trying to decide whether to become a minister. He'd prayed and prayed to know whether it was the right thing for him to do. One day he was driving down the road, praying for a sign, and suddenly there were birds swooping all around his car. He looked to see if there were birds around the other cars but there weren't. Knowing the birds had come to him again helped me to see his decision to go to Springfield in terms of his life, instead of fastening on it as food for my own fear monsters.

Rich had been restless, wondering if he should be doing more with his gifts than ministering to a village of six hundred souls. He needed to make some more money too. These things I understood. What made me sad was when he added that the Congregational Church recommends that ministers not stay at any one church longer than about nine years. I was shocked to find the ethos of constant mobility enshrined even in church policy. So much of the spiritual power of the Hesterton church came from its rooting in cyclical rather than linear time, in the rhythms of the seasons and the seasons of human life rather than the commuter's calendar. I could accept Rich's need to move on, called by the voice in his own heart, but the notion that he *should* be moving on seemed all wrong.

I wondered uneasily whether the sense of belonging I felt in that church would survive Rich's departure. I realized a part of me would be almost relieved if it didn't. Ever since moving up into Vermont, to the town where Liz owned her house and land, I had felt odd about driving fifty miles each way on a Sunday to fill myself with a sense of belonging in a village where I no longer lived. It seemed wrong to be guzzling gas for such a purpose, and peculiar not to be making the belonging where we lived.

I wondered if, for Liz at least, and perhaps for me, it was easier to feel that belonging away from home. The desire to belong was a place of vulnerability for both of us, until recently hidden under a coat of tough dyke defiance. Though it scared me, I thought perhaps now I was ready to make my community where I lived.

The trouble was that I had married myself to the land in

Hesterton when I lived there and, try though I might, I could not seem to feel that connection with the new place. I had hoped I would grow to love it, but though I loved particular spots, the Jennison's pond, the oak woods around my house, I could not feel that deeper bond. I thought perhaps there would always be something that wasn't quite right, and in my restless search for perfection I would never stay long enough to make a real home anywhere, just as I had moved from relationship to relationship until I met Liz. I knew I was as much prey to the ethos of constant mobility as anyone, perhaps more so. Having moved from country to country every three or four years when I was growing up I have both a great longing for stability and a deep-rooted wanderlust. Having built my house, I thought I had made my choice, but every time I drove to Hesterton I felt an ache of longing. It would be a relief in a way to go there less often.

Chapter Eleven

6/25/90

Dream last night about ritual abuse — a girl angry at her mother — the mother pulls off her shirt to reveal a dark purple mass on her back — a giant scab? — and she describes how a small group of people cooked up some horrible mess of small animals and other stuff and put it on her back burning hot — except I think it was more arcane than that. The mother is a victim of the cult.

Then the girl, learning her father is a true member of the cult, decides to kill him in revenge for what was done to her. I am watching. She enlists my aid in loosely bolting together a series of planks. I am very uncertain about helping her — not sure I want to be an accessory to the murder. I realize she is bolting the planks together until they lead off a veranda/window sill in her bedroom into thin air, the idea being that he will follow this path into nothingness, blindly. He will fall and die. I decide I cannot be a part of this.

She is plain, this girl, heavier than me, a sturdy sullen face. I feel confused inside in my chest.

The angry one. 3rd person.

Was Dad involved?

Back in 1982 I remember, at the messy ending of a love affair, wanting to vent my anger by throwing something. Alone in the loft I was subletting, I took a mug from the shelf, being careful to choose one my landlady wouldn't miss too much. The walls were covered with sculptures and paintings so I went to the window. But I didn't want to throw it into the parking lot below in case it hit somebody so I hurled it at the fire escape. It clanged and bounced and lay there, unchipped, just out of reach, a mute reminder of my inability to express anger.

The girl who was angry at her mother in my dream was not me, she was "heavier than me," but at least she was the same gender. Mostly, up to this point, my anger had appeared in my dreams as a boy whom I experienced as threatening to me, like the teenage boy with a bad reputation in the dream of Jerusalem, the divided city.

I had learned, somewhere along the line, to separate myself from my anger. When I was ten and eleven I fought a lot with my brother and as we rolled about, pinching and punching and kicking, I would feel the rage hot and red in my chest and behind my eyes. But then for years I couldn't feel it at all, not consciously.

When I got sober I sat in meetings and listened to people talking about anger with bemused concern. These poor people. Anger was a feeling I seemed to have missed out on, and I wasn't sorry. It sounded very difficult.

When I did begin to feel angry it confused me: other people seemed to feel powerful when they were angry but I mostly felt helpless and despairing. I began to realize how often as a child I had been in situations which made me extremely angry, situations which I had been utterly powerless to change. Of course anger slipped quickly into a feeling of futility for me.

But that wasn't the whole reason I repressed my anger so thoroughly. When, in my eleven-year-old rage, I threw that teapot at my mother, it made her go from being her everyday self to being a blank-eyed monster spitting hatred and contempt. My anger seemed to me then something terribly powerful, a weapon to be reserved for use only in the direst circumstances. The fact that there were so few expressions of overt anger in the household reinforced this feeling. Anger was my own personal atom bomb. For all my fear of it, in myself and in other people, in some part of me I also savored it. So long as I did not use this weapon, my fantasy of its power could go untested. Precisely because I believed in its power I kept it under tight control.

It wasn't until I'd been sober a year or two that I realized I had been extremely angry in the last two years of my drinking. It was a cold anger then, a rational passion, as exhilarating as speed, an anger uncomplicated by love. When I felt it I felt detached, invulnerable, contemptuous. I felt inhuman and I liked it. I would listen to certain kinds of bitter urban music — Graham Parker was a favorite — and juggle my drugs and booze until I felt as cold as a knife blade and then I walked the streets of New York, high on my (imagined) invincibility.

Even at the time I did not like this in myself. This was the anger that would cut the throat of love rather than mire itself in the mess of pity and longing and fury which is the lot of ordinary mortals. I tried to protect other people from this brutality in me: it belonged in the box which must be kept locked. But it leaked out sometimes. I had a room-mate once, in that same loft where I tried to break the mug, who told me she was in love with me. I found it uncomfortable then to share what was, in effect, one big room with her, but I tried to be kind. One night I got drunk. I must have had a black-out. She told me later that, with icy sarcasm, I had savaged her verbally. I had no memory of it whatsoever.

In the dream of the angry girl, when the mother took her shirt off, exposing her wound, proving that she too was a victim of the cult, the girl understood that she should be directing her anger at her father who was "a true member of the cult." She saw clearly, this girl, directed her anger at the abuser not the victim, and was able to take action. No wonder she didn't feel like me.

In my life, signs of my mother's victimhood had often made me more angry with her, not less. "The nexus of hate," I wrote in my journal, "I feel I have to protect you and you say you are weak and need me but you are devouring me."

Nor did I find it so simple to distinguish the victim from the abuser. Within the family, my mother's supposed weakness gave her power. The family was set up so that she appeared to be the Empress at the center of our mechanical dance. It was purportedly for her that we sacrificed our own needs, so it was her we blamed. Later I realized that the extreme emotional repression in the household, all the strictures against upsetting Mum, were more in my father's interests than hers. I have gone back and forth in my thinking about the power structure in my family. In college, as I discovered feminism, I began to see my mother as a victim, of patriarchy in general, and in a more limited way, of my father. I saw her more as a sister, a fellow sufferer, particularly when there were several thousand miles of ocean between us. But when I started therapy, Esther commented on how much power my mother wielded in the house. I began to remember the terrifying power she exercised over my child's body, using me to masturbate herself, and then punishing me. Once again I saw her as the Empress.

But after a few months of remembering ritual abuse she was looking like a victim again. I could say she was an adult, she should have been able to stop it, to get out, but the more I learned about the power of the cult the less convincing that was.

My angry self wants to see in black and white. Who is to blame? Who should be punished? From whom should I exact retribution? But pity confuses my anger, and my own guilt makes harsh justice frightening. In the dream I swung the gun of my anger round easily so it pointed at my father, but in everyday life I found it even harder to be angry with him than with my mother. When I started remembering the incest it took me much longer to remember that he had abused me than to remember what my mother had done, and it was the same with the ritual abuse. Writing down this dream was the first time I really let myself ask whether my father had been involved.

In my family my brother was closer to my mother, and I to my father. I felt I was more like him than I was like my mother. Part of what drew me to him was that he was not a victim and he did not use his victimhood to manipulate me. But that made it harder to face his part in the ritual abuse. My mother I could excuse (though it made me furious to do so): things happened to her. She was weak, out of control, stupid. So the family story went. But my father was strong, smart, in control. If he was involved in the cult it was because he wanted to be. If he was involved, as an adult at least, it was not as a victim but strictly as an abuser.

To be angry with him was frightening, not least because I felt that I was like him. Anger I felt towards him as an abuser I also felt towards myself. He and I were responsible for our actions in a way that my mother was not. It was a fantasy this, to identify my child self with the power he had as an adult man, but it was real to me. Beginning to face his participation in the ritual abuse came hand in hand with remembering times when I was the abuser not the victim.

6/26/90

Saw Rich. He got the post in Springfield. Talked of [feeling that] belonging will cost me my soul — dark and tangled part of my mind.

Somewhere in here I began to feel weird — closed my eyes and started seeing the pentagram carved in the boy's back — with averted eyes — me in white gown — did I do it? Then looked straight at it — oh God — a knife handle there so he's dead   did I do it   am

Chapter Eleven

I a murderer?

I tried and tried to make words come and couldn't — horrible feeling — so eventually wrote in my journal.

I KEEP SEEING THE PENTAGRAM SCORED INTO THE BOY'S BACK & THEN THE HANDLE OF THE KNIFE IS THERE. I DON'T KNOW IF I DID IT. IF I'M A MURDERER. I DON'T KNOW IF IT WAS REAL. THE KNIFE. IF HE WAS DEAD. I DON'T KNOW. I CAN'T MAKE ANY WORDS COME. I'M AFRAID TO SHOW YOU THIS. I DON'T KNOW WHAT'S GOING TO HAPPEN TO ME IF I TELL. INSIDE MY HEAD FEELS SWOLLEN.

Wanted to write Pray for me at the bottom but was — embarrassed?...

I prayed for strength when I tried to talk. Later crying and crying — Rich saying "nothing will happen to you. I don't know what will happen in you if you talk about this." I prayed for help and then I was praying God help her and it wasn't me remembering anymore and I didn't feel all the stuff.

Later still I prayed for God's will for me & I heard "Then Kill Yourself" & it scared me. No. Not God's will — aware though how embedded and powerful that voice is.

My god it seems unreal — a grade B horror flick made by a fundamentalist Christian.

There's something else too I'm forgetting

Oh yes — dream of the father is a bit unnerving — is Dad involved after all?

7/2/90

Grief lurches in me through the day — swimming in Fiske pond after work — weeding at Jean and Helen's — the mind adjusting — this morning, meditating, I prayed forgive me — began to cry — "there's nothing to forgive" — Granny and Swift Bear showing me — helping me look at — my beaten, dirty three-year-old body, me at eight with Dad's penis in my mouth, at 15 with Mum watching Dad rape me, at 18 being handed a knife.

Thought I should kill myself tonight — an intent thought I intently ignore.

7/3/90

> *Saw Rich and cried and cried — sore heart — staggering under too heavy a load — too much to take in — is this my life? — is it a possibility I killed someone? And all of it. This long history of abuse.*
>
> *And [Out of Bounds] — I don't want to write about the ritual abuse.... May be the only way to lay down the load, says Rich.*
>
> *Don't want to spend any more of my writing on this — confessional stuff, weird stuff so far from ordinary experience — how could I write it and have it be believable. I don't believe it half the time.*
>
> *I'm 32 in a month and I've spent a lot of the last six years dredging up this stuff, and the first 18 living it.*
>
> *So in a way they're still running your life?*
>
> *Yes, damn them.*
>
> *Cry some more —*
>
> *Rich says, you need some conscious connection with a higher power — instead of staggering, kneel with the load on your back.*
>
> *Hah, the fucking 11th step I think and pray to no technicolor effect....*

It was beginning to be too much for me to carry, this load of knowledge and grief and guilt which grew heavier with each new memory. The frequency of my suicidal thoughts was an index of that. Some of those thoughts belonged to the past, to the time when I felt helpless to escape becoming a member of the cult in any other way, and some of the thoughts were probably residues of hypnotic suggestions that I would kill myself if I told, but I think too that I was beginning, in the present, to resurrect suicide as a possibility.

Swift Bear and Granny could tell me, "There's nothing to forgive," and show me the ways in which the eighteen-year-old holding the knife was the product of all those years of abuse; I could tune the radio in to the sentence, "It is sad that children feel the need to be forgiven for crimes they were forced to commit," and cry, but I could not let go of my guilt or the feeling that I should punish myself for what I had done and for having wanted to belong.

Chapter Twelve

7/17/90

SHAME OF WANTING TO BE SEEN.
Being seen and not being seen.
Who's doing the seeing?

Being erased — Mum and the three-year-old self.
The cult saw me in a way — they paid attention — that's what I craved.
But they were hooded. Unseen....
Can't let them see the place of light in me.

Gardening grows the seed, makes it visible.
The hurt sad seed self: three-year-old punished for trying to be seen.

On my third birthday I stood in the passage outside the room where Ma, Grandpop, my mother and my father were sitting. I took off my white dress with the red velvet sash and I walked into the room. I remember the look of horror on my grandparents' faces when they saw the bruises and burns on my body. I felt it was me they were horrified by. Then my mother was standing by the mantelpiece, her face stricken, nothing in her eyes. I knew I had made a terrible mistake but it was too late.

I wanted not to be left alone with Mum but at the end of the weekend Ma and Grandpop went back to Leicestershire and my father went to Coventry where he was involved in a research project the company was sponsoring. He lived in lodgings and came home at weekends. I imagine there was some sort of confrontation and my mother promised to stop abusing me, but I don't know.

I know that I was left alone with her again and that, to punish me, she pretended I didn't exist. She didn't talk to me, touch me, feed me, clean me. She looked right through me. I don't know how long it went on. It could have been as long as five days. I remember night falling more than once and I remember dipping my hand in the toilet bowl to get water to drink. I remember sitting on the bathroom floor, rocking, beyond crying. I felt as if I had no edges.

Eventually she picked me up and she put me on a table, or perhaps an ironing board, and she raped me with the handle of a hairbrush. It was very painful physically but the relief of being touched, of becoming visible again, was so enormous I was afraid of her stopping, afraid I would be sent back into nothingness.

Of all the memories I've had, this is the one that comes back most often. The experience of showing my bruises, and what happened to me as a result, shaped my personality. It is as if the hose through which all of my life energy has to pass had a knot tied in it then, loosely enough that the water can still get through but always there, always that extra distance the water has to travel. The shape of the knot, the pattern of fears and expectations laid down back then, is as familiar to me as breathing: the longing to be seen, the terror of being seen; the desire to reveal the truth of my life and the fear that to do so will entail utter abandonment; anxiety that to go unseen is to be annihilated; humiliated fury at my own need for touch; fear that I am not good enough to be touched; the suspicion that to need is to invite abuse; the shame of courting punishment as attention. Over the years, when I have sifted from present day experience some residue of unaccountably intense emotion, I have often found its source to be in the experiences I had when I was turning three.

Sometimes I wonder if the story doesn't make too much sense. Is it like Voltaire's God: if it hadn't happened I should have had to invent it, in order to explain myself to myself? But the memory came slowly, in fragments, the first piece present in that initial composite memory I had with Esther, when I remembered being raped with the handle of a hairbrush. I resisted each new piece as it came. Mostly I felt the feelings before I could say what happened. It took a long time to put the story together. Perhaps there are bits glued into the reconstruction that don't belong there. Did my mother really stand against the mantelpiece like a stag at bay, facing the others? It seems so melodramatic. Perhaps it is just an image, symbolizing the guilt I felt then for making her feel hunted. I don't know, but I'm sure the core of the story is true.

The feeling that it is too true to be true comes, I think, from the fact that I've told it quite often, to friends, lovers, at meetings. It's as if the edges that give me a feeling of truth have been smoothed away by much handling. But then when some situation in the present hooks into the old experience, it can feel as raw and as terrible as the first time I remembered, and I can find myself on a bathroom floor, sobbing and rocking myself at the edge of the black hole where I am annihilated.

7/19/90

Realize that for a while a large chunk of me has been in this place of nightmare, the rest of me plodding on. Out of the horror I stare at pictures of flowers, numb and desperate — some saving grace in their beauty, roses especially.

NYC 7/21/90

Visit with Sudha who says back then [in college] I was somehow like a moving statue (though also possessed of great vitality and brains), a tight oyster with a bit of grit in it. Hermetically sealed.

The Matisse in Morocco exhibit — where I was more deeply moved by color than I have ever been — without thought of content but the color itself — a sob in me — compelled, grabbed by "A la Porte de Casbah."

7/25/90

I think I have a crush on Helen ... find lust stirring in me when I look at her wide hips, narrow belly and shoulders — tallness — womanness — I looked at her today and thought, yes it is women I love.

A shit load of Evelyn Meyer transference [Evelyn was the teacher I had an affair with when I was fourteen] — Helen just read The Forest *and liked it — heard the incest in it and didn't dodge it, said it took guts to write — being seen — Evelyn reading my essays, that first one of 25 pages on* Animal Farm *— the words tumbling out onto page after page — someone at last to write to then — now the mix of longing to be seen, to be cared for and taken care of — for the good mother but with it sex....*

How I sexualize being seen by a woman.

Mum raped me when she began to "see" me again after the time of being ignored — and I couldn't bear the abandonment of her stopping.

Birthday tomorrow kicking up three-year-old stuff? also some cult stuff at 11?

It was four days after my fourteenth birthday when I did that drunken striptease in the lighted window of my bedroom in Germany while a cocktail party went on down below. Was it an echo of that earlier birthday attempt to make the truth of what was happening at home visible?

By the time I was a teenager I had learned to equate attention with sexual attention so I acted sexually to get it. But using sexual acting out to tell my truth was self-defeating. A stripper is looked at, not seen; the object of men's gaze, not the subject revealing her truth.

Perhaps I needed it to be that way. Much as I needed to tell what was happening to me, I could not afford to be believed. Acting out sexually, like madness, would allow me to tell and not be heard, to show and not be seen.

I am ashamed of my longing to be seen and heard. Growing up, if the only way to be seen was to have sex, then wanting to be seen must mean I wanted to be molested. The summer I turned fifteen, when my father was raping me while my mother watched, there was a part of me that was gratified by the attention.

I protected myself from the shame and confusion of "wanting it" by separating myself from my body and its responses, and, as far as possible, from my own feelings of need. Under this psychological apartheid, it was only in the townships of sexuality that I expressed any need, and I expressed it in the only language I had been taught for human need, the language of sex.

I fucked around a lot when I was fifteen and sixteen and I also began to fantasize. One of the key fantasies, which stayed with me for years, was about being looked at, and being turned on by being looked at, and the looker seeing I was turned on though I did not want to be, and taking my turn-on as proof that I wanted It. In these fantasies I almost always came before we got to It, to actual intercourse. The climax, the release, came when my need became visible, and that visibility gave the other permission to overcome my fiction of self-sufficiency. There was always an element of humiliation because any expression of my needs was necessarily a kind of defeat.

In the lexicon of fantasy, these needs were always sexual, but I think this was often the disguise worn by childhood needs for love and attention which were never met.

Not that there is a simple line to be drawn between sexual and

Chapter Twelve

non-sexual feelings. Though my fantasy life might deal in crude cartoons of lust and power, in everyday life the most potent aphrodisiac for me is not to be looked at as a sexual object but to feel seen. It was shortly after Helen read the manuscript of my first novel and made it clear she heard what I was saying, that I fell in lust with her.

I remember one rainy Saturday afternoon at Westwood, the young ladies' academy where I was being stored until I reached a marriageable age, I was lying on my dormitory bed in my usual state of gloom when I heard the English teacher's footsteps on the narrow stairs. This was before Evelyn and I became lovers but I already knew the swift rhythm of her feet. She knocked and came in. She'd noticed, she said, that I behaved strangely, staring at things for long periods of time, for example, and she wanted to know if I was taking drugs. I wasn't, but I wanted to say I was, just to prolong the feeling that someone was concerned about me. She was the first adult to notice something was wrong and ask me about it.

I can still hear the sound of her footsteps coming up the stairs, footsteps I recognized, coming to see me, by contrast, I realize now, to the sound, when I sat huddled on the bathroom floor, of my mother's longed for footsteps, going past me, going away.

As a teacher Evelyn made me feel that what I thought, how I responded to a poem or a book, mattered. I still remember the feeling of writing that essay on *Animal Farm,* "someone at last to write to." It was the first time writing became for me a means of discovering what I thought and felt, not simply of putting down what I already knew.

Teacher

I loved you as I could —
stood outside your window
breaking bottles
till you called me in;

I cried so you would touch my shoulder,
laughed so you would ask me why;
I read pornography in the classroom
for a minute of your punishment;

I was the hero in any play you chose;

*I would have eaten the cherry stones
you spit in the grass
the first afternoon you kissed me
on the rug by the speaker
before your husband came home,
his key in the door the first of many
alarms you almost ignored.*

*I still compare my lovers'
lips to yours,
dry as blades of grass in August,
your tongue a bee*

*that opened me
like ants that open peonies ...*

    I spent many evenings, having climbed over the school wall, standing outside Evelyn's house, longing to be invited in, ashamed to be there, confused by my yearning for something I was not entitled to. Often, through the lighted kitchen window, I watched her and her husband, David, eat dinner. Sometimes some of her children were there. I plotted ways to get her attention — breaking bottles in the street was one of the less subtle — and felt humiliated by all of them. I wanted to be lying on the rug in the living room again, kissing, our bellies pressed so close that breathing itself became a kind of touching; I wanted to sit in the study, sipping Madeira, talking about books; I wanted to sit at her kitchen table while she basted a roast of lamb with milky coffee, made salad, poured wine. I wanted to be her lover and I wanted to be one of her children. I wanted the world she and her husband inhabited, a world of art and intellect. We kissed listening to Boccarini, in the room where David's cello stood. Her two oldest children had gone to Oxford and Cambridge, her youngest was still at the progressive co-ed boarding school I longed to attend.
    After the first time we kissed, we kissed often. Sometimes we even lay together on school grounds, in the long grass at the end of the driveway. We never spoke about what we were doing. We never took our clothes off, or touched each other's genitals directly. Once we spent the night together in a hotel in London — I had told my parents that term ended a day later than it did. We went to see Peter Schaffer's *Equus,* but as far as I remember we went no further than

Chapter Twelve

usual, sexually. I think if she had made the first move I would have followed, but she didn't.

Of course it was not right for a teacher to be making out with her fourteen-year-old pupil, but, remembering the intensity of my longing for her touch when I lay in the grass the first day we kissed, how I willed her hand to my shoulder, how I held my breath when her lips touched mine so that nothing should wake her from this dream, I don't regret it. For all the confusion at the time, and all the pain that followed the discovery of our affair, I've always been grateful for it. I think it probably saved me, that knowledge of the bare possibility of love.

In the end it was less the affair itself than people's reactions to it that were damaging. I left Westwood at the end of the summer term, not knowing we had been seen, expecting to go back in the fall. Evelyn had said that when I turned sixteen and could legally leave home, I could go and live with her and her family. I wasn't sure whether to believe her but the thought that, in just over a year's time, there might be a way out helped me to face the summer vacation. (Where other girls at school crossed out the days until the end of term, I used to number the days I had to be at home in my diary: 70, 69, 68 down to D-day, lift-off, the great escape, back to school.)

In Germany with my parents I waited each day for my father to come home with the mail but no letter came from Evelyn. Three or four weeks into the holidays I made some casual reference to going back to Westwood in the fall and my mother said, "You're not going back there." I stared at her. "That woman" and I had been seen. Queers made my mother sick. She retched. Some time later my father tried to talk to me. "It is unfortunate that your first love affair should be with a woman," he said. My mother was a very conventional woman whom we must be careful not to upset.

I don't remember saying much. Whatever their different ways of handling the situation, the fact was they had the power to stop me going back to school. They had that power but I swore they would not stop me loving Evelyn and somehow seeing her again. It made no difference who you loved, man or woman, I told myself. Why should it matter? I wrote reams of poetry, some of which my mother found in my room and read, adding four lines of her own at the top of one page, asking why I couldn't love her the way I loved Evelyn. A pretty weird question to ask about your daughter's lesbian lover, I see in retrospect. At the time I felt so violated I burned the pages she had touched.

I wrote letter after letter, sending them by German mail, and waited for some word from Evelyn. Nothing came until Dan, an English kid my age who lived across the street, told me he had a letter for me. He went to school with Evelyn's daughter. We went for a walk in the park and he gave me the letter. I was so desperate to read it I barely heard him say it felt weird and he was going to tell his mother about it. Evelyn wrote that her letters had been returned with threats from a lawyer to sue her for the "alienation of a minor's affections." It was only then that I learned how we had been found out: the Italian teacher had seen us kissing in some woods ten miles from school. Evelyn said from now on she would sign herself Jeff and change her handwriting. Those letters did get through to me.

My immediate problem was where I was going to go in the fall. Perhaps I would like to go to a finishing school in Switzerland? I wanted to go to university, not a debutante's ball. My parents decided they should keep me at home for the next year, engaging the English chaplain from the nearby British army base as a tutor to get me through my 'O' Levels. I was desperate. I couldn't bear to be alone in a room with my parents, singly or together. All summer I used my brother as a shield, but in September he would be going back to boarding school. I could not tell myself consciously what was happening when I was alone with my parents — this was the summer that my father took to raping me while my mother egged him on: "Teach her not to be a bloody queer" — I only knew that I could not survive a year alone with them. I breached my wall of silence enough to tell them that, if they kept me at home, I would either run away or kill myself.

At the beginning of September I heard that my uncle, my father's brother, had found a co-ed (but not progressive) boarding school in the Midlands that might be willing to take me. We flew to England and, three days before term started, I went for an interview and was accepted. We stayed at my father's parents' house. The first evening there I walked a mile up the road to the nearest phone box and called Evelyn. I knew my parents would know where I had gone and there would be trouble, which there was, but I didn't care, it was such a relief to hear her voice again, to be in the same country once more, though an hundred and fifty miles apart.

At Elmsbury, the new school, I was visibly an outsider: it took

Chapter Twelve

a couple of weeks to get the school uniform. I quickly learned that, unlike Westwood with its divorced Society headmistress and trips to the opera, this was a school of solid middle class respectability, an old but third-rate public school which had taken the risk of going co-ed three years earlier and was at pains to reassure prospective parents that it had no radical reasons for such a move, only a bourgeois pragmatism and the unspoken hope that they would turn out less queers if the boys could experiment with girls instead of with each other.

Homophobia was rampant and constant. The boys could not seem to stop talking about who was "bent," and the dining hall echoed with cries of "Backs to the wall, boys" when some unfortunate who'd been labeled a fairy walked past. Caning and the system of fagging, where younger boys served older boys as personal servants, had only been abolished three years previously. Undoubtedly sexual abuse had been widespread, as it was in most boys' public schools in England.

Lesbianism was much less remarked upon, though at one point some boys did yell at a friend and me, "Are you dykes? Are you? Are you?" It did not take overt comments for me to get the picture that, if I was going to make it at this school, I would have to keep quiet about my love for Evelyn. On the other hand, I needed desperately to talk about what had happened. So I pretended Evelyn had been Ethan, a lecturer at Reading University. This even got me a little kudos.

As far as I knew there were no other lesbians, at least not anywhere I would find them. Secrecy bred shame. I knew the first housemaster had been given a sample of Evelyn's handwriting and instructed to stop any letters, so she was still having to disguise her handwriting. When at last she came to visit one Sunday in November, we were seen walking down some back street in the little market town where the school was, and trouble erupted all over again, with calls to my parents and grillings by the housemaster. Not long afterwards I wrote to Evelyn and said I couldn't cope with staying in touch with her, and she accepted that.

Early on, the Physics master, an evangelical Christian named John Bolton, took me aside and told me he knew why I was at the school. My housemaster had spread the news and it was the gossip of the staff room. He, John Bolton, would look out for me. Shortly afterwards, the housemaster was fired for opening the shower curtains on the wrong girl — the head of house — and Bolton replaced him as

135

housemaster of the girls' house, Bolton, his wife, and their three blonde daughters, models of Christian rectitude we were all supposed to emulate. Gone too was the old matron, with whom I used to drink gin late at night while she talked about a boy who had been at the school five years previously, a sort of English Uri Geller she suspected of being the new messiah. In her place came the headmaster's daughter, all flat shoes, print dresses and Christian patience.

Bolton did look out for me. He viewed me, I think, as a wild horse who had to be trained to the saddle slowly. He let me get away with breaking most of the rules and in general made sure I didn't get kicked out. He even offered to make me head of house if I would stop drinking and smoking — an offer I declined. In the end though he showed his hand too plainly when he told me the only way to get out of my chronic depression was to accept Christ into my life and wear more feminine clothes.

I was damned if I was going to be made into Mrs. # 534,698 (the title of the first poem I ever wrote.) That defiance remained strong in me. I had found *The Female Eunuch* and a fellow "Women's Libber" on the staff. But my certainty that it was good to love, whatever the sex of the person you loved, had crumbled.

Sometime that first term I gave up hope of going to live with Evelyn. Part of me at least realized that it would be another untenable situation, as I expect she did. My goal now was to get a scholarship to Oxford, which I did, to read English, as she had, at Lady Margaret Hall, her old college. Lady Margaret Hall was an all women's college, and it was there I finally accepted that I was a lesbian and stopped hiding it.

Those years of silence and shame were brutally difficult. I used to wake at three in the morning, sweating with fear that I would be found out. Once I stole from the school book shop (run by the Society for the Propagation of Christian Knowledge) a book called *Homosexuality* by D.J. West. I kept it under my mattress but I only read about ten pages. Enough to learn that homosexuality was a sickness. Had I read on I might eventually have come across the three references to lesbians, lesbians in prison that is.

Writing about this time I realize that I lost my innocence, not when my parents raped me when I was small, not when I first kissed a woman, but in the aftermath to Evelyn's and my affair when I discovered that love and sex did not necessarily go together. With Evelyn

Chapter Twelve

I felt the first stirrings of adult desire, and I loved her passionately. When we kissed we were making love. But that summer when my father raped me and my mother watched, I found that my body could feel aroused, just as it had with Evelyn, even though I was feeling hatred and humiliation, not love. The sexual rampage I went on when I got to Elmsbury was as much an expression of my rage and despair and fascination at this discovery as it was an attempt to prove I wasn't queer. The first boy I screwed voluntarily had another girlfriend and I didn't care. Good girls didn't have sex, but only really bad ones did it with boys they didn't love. So I was bad, and defiantly so. But all these years later I feel the ache of that first discovery, the shattered union of heart and loins, self and body, and I wonder how much it was the hurt and anger of it that drove me from bed to bed, fifty lovers in fifteen years, a long howl of yearning and outrage.

It is still painful to write about the time after Evelyn and I were discovered. I can feel again the powerlessness of being fifteen, alone and too afraid to run away. Writing this I think about the incredible power parents have over their children, even without ritual abuse in the background. When I hear talk about the need to restore traditional family values, it makes my skin crawl.

It would be so easy to look from the outside at this story of my affair with Evelyn and its aftermath and cast her as the villain while my parents were responsible, normal parents trying to make sure that ravening lesbian didn't sink her claws any deeper into their beloved daughter. They even, so my father told me several years later, went to see a psychiatrist who told them what a terrible person Evelyn was to do such a thing. It is interesting that they never sent me to talk to a psychiatrist, though hardly surprising: there was far too much they needed to keep silent.

In fact my parents found Evelyn a convenient scapegoat on whom to blame my adolescent troubles — suicide attempts, full blown alcoholism, chronic depression — and then of course my lesbianism. They ignored the fact that I had started acting out, by playing truant and stealing compulsively, three years before I met Evelyn.

Evelyn should not have been sexual with her fourteen-year-old student, but compared to not only the sadism of my parents but the smug bigotry of the school, the collective will not to know, she still looks like one of the angels to me.

I don't know all the repercussions our affair had for Evelyn. She stayed on at the school for another term — they were anxious to avoid scandal — then went on to teach at another girl's school, and later at the local university. Her marriage remained intact. But that's all from the outside.

Though we stayed in touch until 1989, we never talked about the past. Her husband had a visiting professorship at Oxford while I was there, and I used to go for lunch sometimes, always when he was out. Sometimes she asked me about boyfriends and I answered evasively, being pretty sure by then that I was a lesbian, but not wanting to cope with her blaming herself for something I felt glad of. When I did tell her I was gay, shortly after I came to America, her first response was that it hadn't been a sexual thing for her, she didn't distinguish between sexual and maternal love. A few days later a second letter arrived saying the first was a cop out, it had been a sexual passion, and that the Greeks were right, it was a form of madness. We went on writing to each other but in the end she found it hard to cope with the mess of my life as I was getting sober and spinning in and out of relationships, and I was hurt and angered by her disapproval, so we lost touch.

I'm not sure I could have taken in Evelyn's love and attention if it hadn't come in a sexual form, but what matters is that that wasn't the only form of it. She was the first person to ask me what was wrong. Not what was wrong with me, but what was wrong. She saw that I was bored out of my mind at this school, and we organized a debating club and a play reading society. She put me on the waiting list at the co-ed boarding school her children went to, a school where I would be given the education necessary to go on to university. She even, crime of crimes, wrote to my parents suggesting they should let me visit friends during the holidays rather than insisting I go straight back to Germany for the whole of the dreaded vacations. It was astonishing to feel that I had an ally, an adult who might stand up to my parents. When I think of myself back then, how desperately hungry I was for love and attention, I think what easy game I was for the cult, how astonishing it is that I did not give myself to them completely. I think the love I felt for and from Evelyn must have given me a standard, however crooked, a way to measure what was offered, a way to know that something better was possible.

Chapter Thirteen

8/11/90

Hostages fall in love with their kidnappers. I read this in a novel recently. Suddenly I get why this fact is nipping at my consciousness — then it's normal to have fallen in love with my captors. The Satanists.

Stuff about loving those with power over you — a kind of helpless welling up of love — the infant's love — I feel raw inside. Connected this suddenly to that swell of "love" for Helen — yes, like that, that powerful and warm a feeling.

It leaves the heart a mess,
this pungent swell of love
for men with hoods and knives,
women with calculated eyes.

8/16/90

Letter from Dad today — I was scared — this means Grandma or Grandad died. Went home but L. was gone — opened it and read it and cried — "Grandma Richardson died last week" [my father's mother]. A letter in which there is no acknowledgment of any conflict between us, two and a half years' silence, accusation of rape. Nothing. Fucking weird.

I wept for Grandma dead and for me not having seen her in close to ten years and more alone now but also I wept for the absence of real contact to grieve over — the great separations created by — [my family's] sickness, Mum's hate for them, whatever they were like when Dad was little.

I went for a walk to the stream on the Jennison's land, found a blue jay and a flicker feather by the running water. After all my sobbing found a ritual for our parting — the yellow feather for her birth and thanks for her part in my life — how little I know of her life — too late — the blue feather for where she's going.

Need to forgive her failure to protect me at three — I think I could.

Sadness that I didn't please her by having grandchildren, getting married, was secretive instead.

Forgive, be forgiven and finally let go the blue feather to the stream which carries it out of sight — I did feel lighter and calmer — as if I had indeed blessed her and let her go.

8/19/90

L. and I and her friend Natalie were in a crash last night — not L's fault — other car went out of control, hit a tree, bounced back and drove us off the road — L's car probably totaled. Natalie and I had been talking earlier about freezing traumatic experience — separating it into different bits — and there we all were, in shock, unable to remember exactly what happened.

8/20/90

Granny's dead, I keep thinking every time I think about Grandma being dead. And so I don't feel much about Grandma because the enormous grief about Granny — grief I'm sheltering from — blocks the path of tears. Time, time.

I've been burying myself in rose catalogues and daydreams of roses — and earlier when I thought I'd plant something in Ma's memory, I thought oh a rose, then I thought naa that's just because I want to buy roses — it's only this morning that I remember gathering rose petals from [Grandma and Grandad's] garden, trying to make rose water — so aware of the smell of them then — the pink petals in water in that little bedroom which faced onto the garden.

Later

Felt desperate and sad for much of the day — working at Jean and Helen's and worse for being there in a way — all that old longing: see me, notice that I'm sad, that I'm crying — but somehow I won't just tell you my grandmother died.

When I came home L. had brought my dirty dishes up in a bucket and washed them at her house [I had no hot water] — what a sweetie — it made me cry, a short desperate sob. She really does love me.

• CHAPTER THIRTEEN •

> *Today I thought I can only feel strong emotions when there is someone to feel to — to imagine telling the feelings to — hence how well therapy works for me — some defense mechanism against the total and devastating isolation of the three-year-old stuff and on and on from there.*
>
> *Connected some of the desperate "ask me what's wrong" with what happened when Granny died and ritual abuse was happening — the intensity of that longing [to tell].*

All through the summer of 1990, past and present wove themselves together — the letter from my father, his mother's death, Granny's death, visits to Grandma and Grandad's house when I was a child, roses then, roses now. I struggled to keep them separate but it was as if the past were the water table, the great lake which is in the earth, which, in a wet spring or fall, rises until there are sheets of water where the fields were. The past came up through the present and submerged it, though I could still look down and see the grass waving under the water.

I needed the present. I needed ground to stand on. When the car crashed, when Grandma died, I felt the tug of all my old terror at the power of the cult: if you tell, you will have a car accident; if you tell, we'll kill your grandmother, we'll kill animals, we'll kill anything you care about.

I used what I could to anchor myself: pictures of flowers, my obsession with roses — but there too the past was present. The comfort and delight I felt now was fed by the joy I'd felt as a child when we visited Grandma and Grandad and I would climb out of the kitchen window early in the morning and walk in the dew and smell the roses, gaudy Hybrid Teas mostly, not the Gallicas and Damasks I am drawn to now, but roses nonetheless which I associate with times of happiness. Times I had always remembered, and forgotten in the ordinary way of forgetting, until they drifted back into consciousness.

Memory is always present in perception, past and present entwined in every moment, but the unremembered past has an even greater power. I wanted to say goodbye to Grandma, to the particularity of her, but I soon realized that my unfelt grief for Granny's death years before was blocking the path of tears. To grieve one death, I had to grieve both, and somehow I couldn't yet.

What I could weep for was the absence of real contact. I felt the thinness of my memories of Grandma. I remembered boxes of buttons, mother of pearl and horn and tortoiseshell, and a cabinet of glass-fronted drawers, each drawer containing a different colored silk thread, the spools lined up neatly, end to end, rows of them reaching back into the depth of the cabinet, primrose yellow in one drawer, then a golden yellow, then marigold and orange and scarlet. I remembered the dusty smell of the shop but I couldn't quite summon her face behind the counter though I knew that was where she had sat. I remembered how, when she brought two sleeping bags, one pink and one blue, for my brother and me she let me take the blue one because it was my birthday. I remembered her arranging with the editor of her local newspaper for me to write an article on the position of women in North Africa when I was seventeen.

She was as an independent woman who supported my desire for a career. Outside the small intellectual world to which Evelyn Meyer belonged, such allies were few and far between for a girl in the early 1970s in England: my grandmother gave me a real gift. I remembered with sadness the way she put herself down when I was at Oxford, always asking what I was studying but telling me she was too ill-educated to understand, having left school at fourteen to go to work to help support her ten brothers and sisters.

What I couldn't remember, because it never existed, was any texture of dailiness, made by lives lived in close connection. They were noticeably lacking in intimacy, my memories, like my father's letter. It's a sad but accurate expression of the place she had in our lives that he referred to his own mother by her surname.

It was painful to look at this paucity of human intimacy with my grandmother, of whom I was fond and who did not abuse me, and at the same time to know in myself the fervid emotions, "the pungent swell of love," for my parents, and other people in the cult who did abuse me.

8/21/90

Saw Rich

Agonizing humiliation around wanting to be taken care of — sitting there half sure he's filled with disgust or pitying contempt for me — and my own brutal voices saying you can't sit around mutely waiting for someone to notice you're hurting — GROW UP

8/22/90

I feel messy inside — lacking my witness self. Grieving said Ellen, said Sharon. I guess. I don't know. I'm hearing people talking about

Chapter Thirteen

feeling taken care of by a Higher Power and thinking I don't know what the fuck you're talking about and it's a fantasy. But this morning thinking about Grandma I felt pink light and then the image of myself as a child with shit smeared around my mouth and thought I don't have to treat myself with revulsion and disgusted pity, even if that's how it was back then — imagined lovingly washing it off my face.

8/31/90

Anger with Sandy Brown who despite all her talk of wanting to be a good employer, when one job stalled and not enough new stuff was coming in left me a message saying in a garbled way no more work on Tuesday night — there is work but she doesn't want to squander it on me....

WITH NO NOTICE AND NO WARNING AT ALL. I said that felt bad several times, didn't say much else when I spoke to her and after a while she said (not very happily) she'd give me three days of work next week.

I found myself pretty angry and resentful yesterday.

Because I'd really enjoyed feeling taken care of as an employee....

All the rage of all the times I felt not taken care of.

Cathy at the meeting talking about her rage and how it's like the pressure cooker her mother let cook too long exploding, pot roast stuck to the ceiling.

In the literature of AA I read that anger was a luxury that alcoholics could not afford: it would lead us back to drinking. For years I had argued with this viewpoint, saying it might be fine for men but women were more likely to go out and get drunk if they couldn't feel angry. But now, for the first time aware of the cauldron of old fury bubbling away in me, I realized it was not something I wanted to hold onto for ever and ever.

It was all too apparent to me that the anger I felt at not having been taken care of as a child was exactly the anger that is passed down from generation to generation in abusive families. This was surely the anger my mother felt, on her own five days a week, taking care of me when I was two and three, a kind of incredulity I found it easy to imagine: "You want me to take care of you?"

That old anger in me, I saw, was like a monster with many arms, only one pointing at the people who had actually harmed me, the rest aimed at myself for ever having needed anything from anyone, at friends and lovers who asked me to give them the love and attention I had not been given, at people I barely knew who somehow reminded me of my parents, at anyone who believed god was in control. At meetings I heard people talk about "an attitude of gratitude" as an antidote to anger. Focusing on the ways in which they had been taken care of, some people felt their rage lift. When I looked back on my childhood I could see that my mother did not just abuse and ignore me, she walked me, told me stories, fed me. There were people who were kind, and their kindness mattered. I got many of the physical necessities of life.

But at this point in the recitation I balked. I still do. What was lacking was too fundamental. When I remember the happiness of visits to Grandma and Grandad's house it makes me sad too: I was so happy because I felt safe there. Even remembering the things I can be grateful for involves remembering the absence of basic necessities.

I can't tell myself with any conviction to lower my expectations. Children are entitled to parents who protect them, not parents from whom they need to be protected. But that's a theoretical entitlement. In practice I did not get that from the parents who raised me, and nor in all probability did they get it from their parents. I can say they were grown-ups, they should have been able to look after a child. But they weren't. In AA I'd heard people say their parents had done the best they could and that knowing that had opened the door to forgiveness. Somehow forgiveness was the real, the spiritually grown-up answer to my rage. But what did it mean to say my parents had done the best they could? What about choice, intention, accountability? How could rape and torture be the best somebody could do? And how much difference did it make anyway, to say someone couldn't help hurting you? You were still hurt.

In the fall of 1987, I dreamed a letter in which I confronted my parents with the incest I'd been remembering. I wrote as much of the letter down as I could when I woke up, knowing I was going to have to send it. I showed it to Rich who said, "Well, if you can write a letter like that to them, you must be ready to send it." It was a much more open-hearted letter than I would have thought myself capable of. I told them what I knew, saying I could no longer play the everything-is-fine-we-just-happen-not-to-have-seen-each-other-in-six-years game. I told them I loved them, that I wanted a real relationship with them but that that had to include some kind of acknowledgment of what had happened, though I did not expect our versions to agree exactly.

In waking life I wasn't entirely sure I did want a relationship with them. What if they did come clean? It was unlikely but suppose it happened? Would I really be able to forgive them and go on?

I needn't have worried. I have never heard another word from my mother, from that day on. My father wrote and told me what a happy childhood I had, that my problems only started when I met Evelyn Meyer, and that I was jumping on a bandwagon. He said we had never been close but it would be unfortunate if we lost touch altogether. He offered to forget I had ever said any of this. It was the answer I expected. I opened his letter in the bathroom at work and I watched myself begin to think, "Oh, see, I made it all up. None of it happened, I'm making it up," but I felt detached from the voice of my denial. Of course I was going to feel this, I thought, it was inevitable, but in the end I had a choice: I could believe my father's version of reality, or I could trust my own. It was freeing, though painful, to face that choice.

The hardest part was my father's indifference. Writing that letter I had given voice to my longing for real connection with my family and this was what it came down to: it would be unfortunate if we lost touch altogether.

All that was before I remembered the ritual abuse. I would not consider writing such a letter now. It would be foolhardy and dangerous. But occasionally I have wondered what I would do if, by some miracle, I got a letter from one or both of my parents admitting what they had done, taking responsibility for the places where they felt they had choices, mourning the places where they didn't, asking my forgiveness for the hurt they caused. It would be terrifying, I think, because I would have to take in at a yet deeper level that the horror I remember really happened. I expect I would feel new depths of rage and grief but I can also imagine a loosening in my heart, gladness and willingness to acknowledge my part, a profound relief at not being alone in my knowing. I might even feel joy that the love I've harbored for them in spite of everything could at last have a chance to spread its wings.

When the rage was finally surfacing in me, the best I could do was to accept that I felt what I felt and that what happened to me happened. Not that it was right, or for the best, or that really I was being taken care of after all, but just that it happened. Above all I had somehow to accept the shameful intensity of my longing to be taken care of, and simultaneously accept that it was nobody's job to fulfill that longing.

I will never have another childhood, another mother, no human being can satisfy the hunger in me. I need a relationship with a spiritual power. For all my doubts and angers, I do have access to a source of help — a pink light comes and helps me accept and love my own shit smeared child self — but I don't know how to think about it. People talk about feeling taken care of by their Higher Power, and I can see that there are ways I have been too. I'm sober, and not by my own will-power. I survived the abuse in part because, in extremis, relief came mysteriously, as a light, a cross. But that is also part of my difficulty. Many of my clearest spiritual experiences came at moments of acute pain and powerlessness: if such agony is the price of coming close to god, I'd rather not.

It feels dangerous to write that, and it's only partly true. The other truth is that, reared on such intensities, I crave ecstasy, annihilation, union. They are part of what I have sought in sex. I might envy others their cozy filial relationship to god, but in the end I'd rather a wilder power, a more dangerous, passionate, difficult god than the fantasies of paternalistic piety can offer.

Writing this, it occurs to me that my conception of god is no less a mirror image of my experience of my parents than the conventional Christian formulation of "our Father" is a reflection of the patriarchal family. Unbounded, dangerous, difficult gods my parents were, and my love and fear of them informs every relationship, including my relationship to god.

It has mostly been easier for me to find spiritual succour in the non-human world, in color and smell, water on rock, feathers, roses, but there have been times when I have felt the spirit inside me and I have felt beloved. Though it is what I crave, it is terribly painful to feel loved. Once I went to a Sufi temple and on the wall there was a poem in which god was longing for each human soul as a lover longs. The thought of god longing for me made my heart ache and my throat swell. Why it should hurt so much, to feel beloved, I don't know, except that perhaps, at the moment when a longing is fulfilled, one also experiences all the times it wasn't, and grieves for those.

Chapter Fourteen

9/1/90

Emma [my dog] gone — missing for over twenty-four hours now — I don't know how to believe it — keep thinking I hear the clink of her collar.

The kids almost hysterical — must be the cult, first the car accident, now the dog gone, so I'm playing sane Mom a lot.

I dreamt of a broken collar, so did L.

9/2/90

It drags on — I hear the clinking of her collar, expect to look up and see her coming around the corner of the house, come out to meet us when we come home, see her in the shadows by the roadside.

9/10/90

I feel lonely — need to overhaul some friendships. I barely talk about Ritual Abuse — who wants to hear it? But people love me enough to listen.

Don't they?

Sink into that pit.

I wish there was a right place to talk about it other than with Rich.

9/11/90

Tonight, ambivalent about sleeping with L, I had a flash of looking up to see Dad watching — part of the ring of watchers — cult times.

9/12/90

I felt SO MUCH BETTER *after the newcomers' [SIA] meet-*

ing — having waded through sludge to get there — and shared honestly on the topic of "we don't have to do it alone" instead of taking cover as an SIA old timer — I drank in other people's belief in the program — Lillian's amazing opening up in less than two months — the HONESTY — God I love us for our courage and hurt and hope — the strong fire — Mist with her 24 hospitalizations, Lillian modeling now, crying when she takes the make-up off the scars where her stepfather stabbed her in the face — tears of happiness for her life now, and sadness too.

Keep thinking of Millie jazz singing her truth Tuesday [at the women's AA meeting] impeccable honesty — oh the marvelous courage of women to be frightened and sure and angry and kind all at once — to have such a heart as she has — talking about how all you need is willingness. Just a little willingness.

9/14/90

Despair.
I'm back on wanting the writing to justify my existence, to weigh in the scales against that nagging sense of futility I've had always — I have to do something great. If I don't, how can I bear the daily grind of existence — not that exactly, not grind, but the whole sense of meaninglessness.

So back comes insecurity and fear and jealousy around writers — and my own poor craft or talent or whatever staggers under this high burden of proof — a child forced to feed and clean and look after the whole family when all she wants is to play in the meadow.

And beyond it all — Dad watching — just got very sleepy as I wrote this

North Truro   9/15/90

The sea breathing and breathing — I feel like a person on holiday — a week in a cottage right by the sea. No work, no desk, no garden — the wind and Milky Way and milling queers in Provincetown. Happy and relaxed. It's such fun, says L. next to me in the soggy bed.

9/17/90

Realized how unsettled I am for lack of my morning prayer — the need to find the place of connection on this earth — began my prayers in the porch and moved out — at last to round the corner of the cottage where it is sheltered by a small slope and there in the corner of the

Chapter Fourteen

house [were] sprays of small white asters, the buds yellow points of hope, and around them branches of a kind of goldenrod — waxy leaves and thicker buds — lovely lovely — fell to my knees, spurt of delight, of faith, of here is the place, of the world is lovely.

Wed. 9/19/90

Monday I wished for an SIA meeting — feeling turbulent — I went instead to AA, there being no SIA yet out here — and there on the wall was a series of captioned photographs — the one I looked at first — a woman standing on a fragment of a vast ice floe on the beach — said something to the effect that "I was mute, alone. When at last I began to tell the truth of my experience, the very people who should have supported me, abandoned me, left me isolated."

When I looked to the left I saw the title — "Healing from Sexual Abuse" — the captions from the words of the different women [who had been photographed] — just like a meeting....

"The universe arches over what is without home," says Rilke. (13th letter to Erika Mitterer.)

Later in the dark of the night and wild night surf roaring I realize how furious I've been ... the spluttering incoherent rage at all the silence, all the denial, all the women called crazy, all the years lost, all the children, all the free perpetrators, all of them, the rage relentless as the pounding ocean, keening and howling and beating at the screens of this cottage. I feel afire, driven, ran up the road in the night and back.

9/21/90

So sad and mad — I'm seeing, admitting, how the years of rape have scarred me — I'd held myself somehow inviolable — a smaller and smaller part of myself, and now I say — I was vulnerable, a creature of need, of desire and longing, I was wounded as deep as you can get. Damn. Damn them. And out of it all I am the one who has to convince other people these are not my own diabolical fantasies. Shit shit shit. And those who believe can't bear to hear.

And my grandmother's dead and my dog's gone....

9/30/90

I feel thin and high-wired with feeling.
As though I cannot tolerate another loss. What am I thinking about? Last night I made peach jam, tonight L. and I bottled seven

quarts, golden in honey syrup.

I'm medicating the bees against Nosema.

Sat on a rock by my asters in the wind, under a grey sky, my hands grimy with old manure.

God help me. Help us all.

We inch toward war with Iraq.

A policeman at the National Children's Rights Alliance conference's RA panel (which I didn't attend) said he didn't know of a town in Berkshire county where there was no satanic ritual abuse activity.

Oh God.

My newest primrose is chocolate brown.

My heart hurts.

10/1/90

Praying I am prey and prayer. Without faith I lie in the dirt and sob and wait.

Rereading my journals for August and September 1990 three and a half years later, I can see the knowledge of my father's participation in Satanic cult activity shouldering its way into consciousness. I knew and I didn't know what was coming: I felt I could not bear another loss but I couldn't say what the loss was. I had become familiar enough with the process of remembering to recognize the presence of new information, like a package of bees arrived through the mail, waiting in the barn for me to hive them, the box humming, palpably alive. I wasn't ready to open it.

The loss I couldn't bear was the loss of a fantasy, that my father would have protected me if he had known, that he wasn't the sort of person who would be involved in ritual abuse. My stupid, hysterical mother might get caught up in such mumbo jumbo but it was inconceivable that a rational, scientific, detached man like my father could be performing rites of human sacrifice and cannibalism.

In August I dreamed about a watching man and in the dream I was furious with the man for pretending that the act of looking is a neutral and innocent activity, having no effect, bringing no obligation. At the beginning of September I dreamt I went to see a psychoanalyst.

I told her being looked at made me frantic sometimes — about Dad watching me and Mum (Oh, I've said it again — I mean Mum watching my father and me. I did this in the dream too.)

Chapter Fourteen

Two days later I had a flash of my father being in the ring of watchers at a ritual.

My father watching, aloof, an observer, keeping his hands clean. In ordinary life he was like that too. The quintessential scientist. If watching was what he was doing, it was not so impossible that the man I knew could be involved in ritual abuse. It even seemed likely that, if he were, he would be a member of the elite, those who held the real power, while someone like my mother would be in the lower ranks, among the unstable, the erratic, those who acted from their emotions.

But it was not likely, it was impossible.

10/2/90

Such despair in me — awake since 6.

I believe the grief I am feeling is beyond personal grief — that the tears which come when I see a roadkill (moved a dead raccoon the other day), or listen to the news is grief for the planet, for the All of Us as well as for the dark and terrible twistings of my abusers.

I am not sure the earth has the power to shrug us off — to heal from humanity ...

I think about a war with Iraq for oil. For our fix. Is this a bottom yet?...

Saw Rich — Hallelujah — what a relief (and I like his new room, blue and cream and light, high up and private. Solid.)

Re eco-despair — my environment was polluted — doubts about whether I can heal from that (I started to cry when he said that.)

Despair re the writing followed the flash three weeks ago of Dad watching — with a look of interest — I in a hole? very low on the ground. Crawling, that is? The feeling that I have to achieve, do something great (be recognized as important?): the dam I built to hold back all this grief and anger.

Talked of the N.C.R.A. panel on ritual abuse — Rich liked the Chicago cop who's been tracking this stuff for two years on his own time — police department wouldn't pay for it. Fax machine in his own house. Recently flew to England as a consultant — a lot is being uncovered now — there in particular.

Their need for information.

[Good idea] for us to have our names at [the] D.A.'s office in case anything happens.

Common theme: heavy suggestion — "If you begin to reveal, you

will have a car accident."
WOW. Not just me.
The most untraceable kind of death.
I want justice.
I want to begin to feed information into the map they are making of the centers of activity.
How the Chicago man got involved — one therapist had been talking about her off-the-wall client to another who flipped, said but those are the same details my crazy client is bringing up.

Later
Writing group exercise:
I am bigger than a clam. Or an oyster. A squid or a barracuda. But smaller than a shark. And whales are islands with bad breath to me. Every day I do this exercise. My right size exercise. There are great mammals on this earth who might carry me in their bellies, birth me over and treat me like a young animal, feed me and laugh at me, teach me to dive and how to breathe out well enough to breath in enough to dive for an hour into the deep where fish carry flashlights on feelers and squid sparkle. I can swim in the dark.

It is not Satan's kingdom. Not for me. I am the child of something much bigger and warmer and nicer than human. Something with old eyes which see me and smile quietly at my follies. I am not amenable to torture or teachings of evil.

And when I come to the surface I too send up a blast of stale and fishy air, I expel everything old and used and I make room for fresh air.

10/5/90
I feel SO MUCH BETTER. Since seeing Rich and touching the nerve of the despair, the roots of that craving for recognition, I've been able to start work on Out.

It was a huge relief to see Rich in his new church and to know I could see him once a week again, having been meeting with him once a month while he was between jobs. But I also hungered for a group where I would feel welcome to talk about what I was remembering and feeling. I needed people to bear witness and to respond. I always needed that, but I needed it especially now, as I began to face the fact that my father had watched my humiliation and suffering in the cult and done nothing.

• CHAPTER FOURTEEN •

I went to SIA meetings once a week but I didn't feel OK talking about my memories in detail there. Rich and I tried to put together a small closed group, but it quickly dwindled, one woman feeling so on the edge that she could not afford to invite more memories, another, who had been abused in a neighboring town, needing a level of confidentiality the rest of us felt we couldn't provide.

What I did have was the writing group I had been in since 1987 which had, at this point, two other members, Tina and Leslie, both of whom were also ritual abuse survivors. (None of us knew about the ritual abuse when we started meeting together, though I expect that unconsciously we had registered a connection.)

When I confronted my parents with the incest, part of my father's denial was that I had simply jumped on the bandwagon, getting nasty ideas about my lovely family from other people's stories. There seems to be a general idea that groups of women get together and egg each other on to make up all sorts of terrible abuse so they can blame their parents for their problems. When I think about the realities of Tina and Leslie and I meeting, they couldn't be further from that version. Individually we struggled so hard not to believe what we were remembering. Though I hadn't seen my parents since 1981, and did not expect to ever again, I was still trying to keep my father out of the ritual abuse picture. Leslie too refused to believe in her father's involvement. Tina and I worried for her because she kept going to visit her family, even though she almost always returned dissociated and wanting to hurt herself physically. The father she was so busy protecting was the man who, when Leslie was a child, forced her to keep hiking all afternoon after she had injured her hip and was in tremendous pain, causing so much damage that, as a direct result, she now spends part of her time in a wheelchair. It is much easier to see through somebody else's denial than one's own, but though we sometimes poked a little fun, we didn't push. Acceptance comes slowly.

Far from wanting to imitate one another, we each tended to view any pressure to conform to a norm, overt or otherwise, with almost comical alarm. We also, clearly, differed from each other in the ways we had coped with the abuse and were coping with recovery. Tina had a headache for the first four years of her ritual abuse recovery. X Rays, CAT scans and other tests revealed no biological basis for it. Eventually, when she came out the other side of the memories, it went away. Leslie buried herself in her studies — she was getting an

M.A. in Japanese art and history — tried not to cut herself and periodically had to check into a psych ward. I made a garden, weeding by flashlight, hacking out roots and rocks, working often to a state of trembling exhaustion. Far from merging into generic survivors, the more we faced our pasts, the clearer our individual identities became.

As a writing group Leslie and Tina and I kept to a pretty firm format so that our meetings did not turn into therapy sessions, but inevitably we wrote about our experiences. All of us suffered from excessive stoicism so we set aside time for whining which we developed into an art form. I offered to bake Leslie a cake the day she managed some genuine self-pity. Mostly we made bad jokes and exercised our irony. Semi-consciously we were finding ways to make it possible to meet and acknowledge the realities of our lives without being overwhelmed.

Though we were not specifically a Ritual Abuse support group, some of the same issues came up. Sometimes I was afraid that I would not be able to trust my own memories and hunches if I listened to theirs. What if I were just being suggestible? When one day at my gardening job I felt frantic because the feeling of soil caking on my hands reminded me of blood drying, I wondered if I were just mimicking similar feelings Leslie had described the previous night. It was both a disappointment and a relief to remember that, although not given to excessive cleanliness in general, I had felt anxious if my hands were dirty, particularly if something were drying on them, long before I ever met Leslie.

Balancing my fear that the dye from their memories might run onto my cloth was the painful relief when, independently, we remembered very similar rituals. However grotesque, they became more credible and we felt less crazy. (Just as the two therapists in Chicago found out their clients were less off the wall than they'd thought when they began to compare notes.)

In any group the shared experiences of that particular collection of human beings become normal while the group is together, however abnormal they may be in the general population. For us, grotesque cruelty was a given and it was a relief not to have to deal, when telling a memory, with the usual incredulity. But to be blasé for long about the blood and horror felt in a way like being submerged all over again in the world of ritual abuse. Instead it was necessary for us to pitch our tents in the no-man's land between the worlds. Together we could say, it exists, this no place is where we live, this place between two countries, only one of which appears on the map.

Chapter Fifteen

10/20/90

Flashback time with Rich (after we sat outside waiting for Triple A to retrieve my car keys) — the other voice spoke — W_____ garden, a stone bench, an enclosed garden "room" with high yew hedges, a girl on the bench — naked — me — a silver knife, a roaring, the ground is roaring. I am watching from high above. Cramps. I am on belladonna. The silver knife at my belly button. It draws a pentagram of blood in the air. The knife is trailing blood in the air.... Something is on the tip of the knife, like a crab. Fetus? Who is there? Is my father there? They are in brown hoods. I get further and further, higher and higher. The body is a pentagram. There are 10,000 yew berries, red eyes in the hedge watching. The ground roars like a train rumbling by underground.

Time for Anna to come back.
I felt terribly ashamed (of this voice speaking.)
Watching/ being seen — the 10,000 eyes, the yew berries I collected the night before trying to kill myself.
My father watching — the impassive, the implacable observer.

10/22/90

Acres of happiness with Liz, bright October Sunday, pulling brambles, mulching pear trees.

10/23/90

Saw Rich.
Talk of W_____ — could perhaps find photographs of the garden — then somebody is running interference.
Coffin being lowered — open, a white dress — oh, must be me

seeing myself from above — oh — no — six- or seven-year-old girl's body, head cut off, goat's head there — a camera going, small spotlight on the girl. My father is running the camera I think — someone fishes her head out of the cauldron (somewhere a little ways away) — blond hair — bleached skin and cloudy white eyes.

My father, cameraman at a snuff movie.

10/27/90

I've cried a lot this week — Tuesday night just sobbing for an hour when I got home [from seeing Rich] and again (but not for so long) on Wednesday night — and at moments at work in South Hadley too — crying on my knees in the bathroom, in the basement beside the wine rack, stacking tiles.

The final (?) releasing of my father, the end of my attempt to uphold his innocence, to find excuses for him.

This. This was my father. Even swearing at him — that evil bastard — brings him too close.

My head does not fully believe it but I keep crying in a most suspicious way and not with anything in my head even, just the breaking forth of a great swollen hurt inside me.

10/30/90

Saw Rich.

Hands, gruesome hands, white, plumpish, soft, slightly hairy, severed hands everywhere on my body, between my legs. Cold rubbery hands. And my father, my urbane father, laughing as if in his strong warm hands he is holding a cigarette, a whisky soda, as if it is light and dry and warm here, he laughs.

I shiver. My body shivers as I sink into memory.

Mostly we look at the lengths I have gone to to protect my image of him. Layers and layers.

He meant the world to me. He was the world.

If you had had no hope, no out, you would have gone hopelessly mad or killed yourself.

Yes.

He was the world.

And so in RA recovery, first I stare at the world, say how can it be so evil.

Then I worry about the planet — it has been so poisoned.

And slowly I look at my father. Could he have been so evil? No

Chapter Fifteen

excuses left (that I am aware of?) This is the man in the green sweater pushing a wheelbarrow full of leaf mold from the spinney.
 The man I built dams with.
 Who taught me to swim.
 But saying all that I realize I do not have a sense of him as a continuous kindly presence. Instead there are these moments made into icons, constructed to represent his necessary qualities. Necessary if I were to survive and have hope enough of a world out there worth escaping to.
 Despair — can I bear the world if this is true — of my father.
 MY FATHER IS NOT THE WORLD.
 Hands — Remember the dream, said Rich, from a while back, of a dead baby and hands reaching up above the ground.
 Yes and an embankment damming water.
 That dream the beginning of RA recovery.
 Damn. I'm sad and tired.
 And shook and cried and was back there with dead hands and Dad watching and I really felt it, the desperate, sad, sick feeling of it
 And also them turning me on my belly, raping me with something I feared was the severed penis.

10/31/90

Horrible dream
 I am being executed for a crime I didn't take seriously enough to appeal — sitting in at a shopping mall? construed as terrorism.
 I am walked out between two men. I'm in a town square and it's fall. I pick up a couple of pieces of newspaper and put them down on the wet pavement. They tell me to lie down. I know one of them is going to shoot me. Nobody seems to notice. I don't feel I can do anything to stop them. I am about to die. I look around, at the blue sky, the red maple, wonder what happens when I die, think how my friends will be shocked. I'm waiting. When he pulls the trigger nothing happens — out of bullets. Then again and it fires but I don't die. And again. And perhaps a third time.
 Then the third man shows up. He has a short silver knife. Very sharp. He says he'll do it with this, no problem. I am terrified. No, I say, no, you can't do it with a knife. No. I'm good at it, he says, it will be over. No, I say, I appeal. It's against the law. So we walk to a town office, like tourist information. I say suddenly, passionately, to the dark haired woman at the desk, "Do you know what's happening to me?

I'm being put to death. I'm going to be killed." She shrugs. It's not her problem — no big deal.

I am thinking now how I didn't appeal. I never thought it would come to this. I look at the beautiful world and at people's faces. I think, I could fight, I could struggle, but I can't bear the idea of being overpowered. It is easier to just let it happen. I lie down again and again one of them holds a gun to my head and pulls the trigger and again nothing happens. I think there may be a law that after a certain number of times they have to set me free. I am lying there waiting for them to pull the trigger again when the alarm goes off.

I wake up shaken and very frightened.

YIKES

Fear after really naming my father — fear I'll be killed — Rich saying some serious programming against remembering him.

In late September and October I had a series of dreams, five in all, featuring murder threats and actual attacks. In all the dreams I was very frightened, in none of them was I harmed. They seemed to be both expressions of my terror at remembering my father's involvement and reassurances from my psyche that nothing bad was in fact going to befall me now.

Starting to type out one of the dreams, in which a friend's father hired an assassin to kill me, I became terribly sleepy, just as I did when I tried to write about Granny's death, as I did when I made reference in my journal to my father watching a ritual.

It was this same instant sleepiness which would come over me sometimes when I was driving, usually to or from either an SIA meeting or seeing Rich. I was tired a lot during this period but the sleepiness happened so much more at those times that there must have been something other than plain exhaustion at work. When I was first remembering I also used to hear a voice in myself saying, "Drive off the road. Drive into that tree." These may have been ordinary fantasies of escape, but they didn't feel quite like that. It was a jolt to hear from Rich that many ritual abuse survivors had found implanted in their psyches the suggestion, "If you begin to reveal, you will have a car accident."

11/6/90

Saw Rich.

The will to fight.... The dream of being executed — not fighting because nobody notices or responds....

Chapter Fifteen

Left Rich's... felt panicky that I hadn't remembered anything — got down near reception — Rich suggesting I put some protection thing in the car — and was suddenly TERRIFIED — walked back up to where he was and said so and we went back up — me in flashback — shaking and jerking my head and crying — They cut up a boy alive with a silver knife (and a saw?) because he'd tried to tell and they made us (not sure who else) watch.

That's when I thought I would go blind? I could see his dark hair, pale face thrown sideways, mouth open in a scream — but I heard no scream, only perhaps a kind of whimpering — did they cut out his voice box? I thought — but surely he'd die quickly then.

Or his tongue I think now.

Christ what a nightmare — can't make the face go away (boy, white, 11 or 12?) — don't try, says Rich.

11/8/90

I go to work and I perform well. I am a good carpenter. I tell stories of my outrageous but amusing past. My work is careful, precise, swift. If I have to go in the truck to the lumber yard despair clutches at me.

Sometimes it comes as doubt. What am I doing as a manual laborer, I who thought I would be a don at Oxford — sharp envy of academics in the deli. More often fear and grief at what is happening in the world — at approaching war in the Gulf, the killing and counter killing in Israel, the battles between Hindus and Muslims in India. And sometimes I see the boy's face — think I glimpse him in a boy by the wayside, his dark hair and white face twisted away, trying to escape the pain.

I am exhausted by this balancing act — glad sometimes I can escape into work, torn other times that here I am, also in a way living the double life I find so terrifying to contemplate — the ordinary bank clerk who at night cuts up a living child and in the morning smiles at each customer.

I am exhausted by this living, given to gales of tears and desperation, to falling to my knees and praying.

I am strong

Yes, I think, and sad.

Tried to call Clair just now — feeling her able to understand — someone to reach to in this — who's been through her own version of hell, a hell which goes on and on.

11/8/90

"I just swam the river of grief. There is no other way. You have to jump in and swim to the other side, otherwise you don't make it." Helen Caldicott on the radio tonight. Yes.

So I called Clair (amazing the mending that happened between us the other weekend — the power of choosing vulnerability?) and cried some and talked some and it helped a bit. She says the children of Nazi war criminals were torn apart most by the fact that their fathers came home from committing atrocities and played chess or worked in the garden.

Then I picked the rest of the beets and Swiss chard from the vegetable garden...

Less despair, more cheer.

11/13

Saw Rich. Knew it would be a rough one — grief grabbing at my heart by mid morning...

Blathered a bit then said I don't want to do what I did last time — not deal during the session — closed my eyes and bingo the boy's face — they're going to cut off his arm with a saw. He can't scream — they already cut out his tongue — they see tears running down my face — hand me a very long thin knife — here, then put him out of his suffering. I stare at him, trying to see in his eyes, what he wants me to do. I can't see. They're going to start. I try to do it. The point goes in an inch. I can't do it. They start sawing. I pass out.

They revived him when he passed out.

When I come to there is something in my mouth. It is round. An eyeball. One of his eyes.

I am on the verge of hysteria telling this to Rich — the words straining, stuttering — my body jerky, I gagging, hands stretched out — no — horror

then suddenly all I can think of is

> Thou art a soul in bliss; but I am bound
> Upon a wheel of fire, that mine own tears
> Do scald like molten lead. [Lear]

The blinding of Gloucester is the connection.
The boy is dead.

Chapter Fifteen

And then I am floating, full of warm feelings for the tormentors. Everything is all right. I surrendered.
In the remembering I am floating, filled with well-being, warmth.
Rich suggests — was I shot up with drugs?
Don't have to care — free of all responsibility.
And they took me to that place, step by step — moved me into an utterly untenable position for the will — then applied more pressure — collapse — the relief of giving in.
I think — yes, SM people talked about this experience — the "love" of the bottom for the top. Related it to spiritual/ religious experience.
Endorphins.
Rich said — wow, yes — Conversion experience — experience of God as vengeful, hating you, backed into a corner of self-hatred — no way out — then suddenly the release, the relief — at-one-ment with the tormentor.
YES!
Absolute surrender of the locus of authority within oneself.
No wonder that's such a sore point for me.
Still felt floaty as we talked more intellectually.
I of how the warm feelings I'd had for Helen resurfaced for Sandy — the warm feeling of total dependence — loss of autonomy, of self.
Before the memory I was talking about feeling torn apart — the everyday world and what happened alongside it.
That's exactly the tearing that leads to dissociation said Rich — it is the bringing together of those experiences which is the work of becoming WHOLE.

It was no accident that I began to remember the torture and dismemberment of the boy just as I was beginning to talk about my father's involvement. The boy's murder was exemplary, a lesson in the consequences of trying to tell.

Who was the boy? Wasn't he reported missing? How was his death accounted for? I don't know the answers to these questions. I don't know his name, or where or how his body was disposed of. I only know what I saw and felt. The experience lives in my bone, muscles, nerves, so strongly that when I remembered I felt as if it were happening there, in Rich's room.

And the girl whose decapitated body I saw being buried with

a goat's head where her head should have been, what about her? Was she a drug-induced hallucination? Did they really boil her head in a cauldron? Both these children were white. Were they British citizens? If so, wouldn't they exist officially, on paper, in school records?

It is possible, I suppose, that I may know more identifying details but be too scared to remember them. I imagine that the cult guarded possibly corroborative evidence carefully. Between terror, shock and mind-altering drugs it is difficult enough to comb out the sequence of events in a memory. I do have a name in my mind for the garden where I remember the snuff film being made, but I am not sure enough to risk maligning the place in print. I don't even know if I have the names of the drugs right: belladonna was a hunch, weird enough to mention. Belladonna is another name for Deadly Nightshade (Solanum dulcamara) which is supposedly an hallucinogen if administered in the right dosage.

In the memory of the tortured boy, when I slipped abruptly from horror to a warm floaty feeling, Rich wondered if I had been shot up with some drug. I had as an adult twice taken opium and the feelings in the memory resembled the effects of that drug, but I wasn't sure I had been drugged this particular time. The surrender of the locus of authority in myself to the cult may have been enough to produce that feeling. Descriptions of religious conversion experiences do show that such a dramatic switch from torment to peace is psychologically possible.

But how could I be full of warm feelings for people I had just witnessed cutting a child into pieces? I felt monstrous and alone. I was afraid that the extreme situations concocted in the rituals had taken me beyond the realm of ordinary human emotions. I needed every reminder Rich could give me that, however abstruse the vocabulary, the alphabet of human feelings is the same.

11/14/90

An odd, exultant happiness today, especially in the SIA meeting — my heart opening — loving — especially Mist who chaired the newcomers' meeting, who talked of her childhood faith in Mary and Jesus and her anger now — were you just watching, God? Her strength and frailty and HONESTY. Being able to love like this is the best high.

I don't know how this happiness is related to the surrender experience of yesterday's memory.

It reminds me of something — yes, it's like the feeling in the morning after being drunk and having puked it all out — a kind of clean emptiness, a starting over.

All day I was consumed with lust for Sandy.... I think she must be attracted to me too — a mutual charge. Perhaps not.

Anyway I kind of enjoyed having sexual feelings again — I want to lay her down and make love to her and feel her passion ... don't want the vulnerability of being made love to, that exposure — just want to be the occasion and the guest of a woman's passion. This woman and her sexy frank face, her short determined body.

These unglamorous, unfemmy women. These very American — and very kind women.

She asked to read Harvest *and I said yes (oh my God)*

11/15/90

I have nothing left in me with which to live. Last night I think I dreamt I screamed and screamed until there was nothing left, no voice, only rasping breath....

I have nothing.

I think about telling Sandy what I am going through. I don't know my motives — using my suffering as seduction? or is it that telling is eroticized? Would it be a relief, to break the wall down, the divide.

Sometimes I feel I can't bear that divide. But I can't bear anything. And there is relief in going to work and being a carpenter and not an abused person.

Bla bla
I have a sore heart
CHOOSE VULNERABILITY
God help me.

I lean into the oak tree, press down into the fallen leaves, sob and pray. God help me. Give me the strength to live through the healing.

Looking back, I don't know how I got through these months: I suppose one can do anything one day at a time. I diverted myself with the garden, with lust, I cried, I prayed. Sometimes I avoided feeling what I was remembering by having complicated thoughts about it, but that trick only worked for short stretches of time. I learned to take pleasure as it came, to find "acres of happiness" on a bright October Sunday, mulching pear trees when, two days before, I had been remembering, through a haze of drug-induced hallucination, some weird ritual involving knives and blood and pentagrams. I jettisoned any expectation that I should feel "appropriate" feelings consistently. I could not afford the weight of most of my ideas of how things should be.

My heart, breaking, broke me open to love. I found I could love fiercely, impersonally, and that loving sustained me as nothing else did. I felt not so much that I loved but that, stripped to my bones, love could love through me. I felt afire with it, utterly alive. It was all I'd ever looked for in booze and drugs and sex, that feeling of loving.

I felt it most often in SIA meetings but around this same time I had another odd experience of it. I had done some carpentry work for an elderly couple, Violet and Robert Williams. When I heard that Robert had died, I stopped in to see Violet. I felt awkward in the usual ways at first, trying to think what to say, but after a while I just sat with her on the couch. We held hands and she talked about Bob and her childhood and her fear that she would have to leave her home. I wasn't afraid of her grief. Love for her poured through me. She felt it too I think. It helped me to sit with Violet in the terrible ordinariness of her pain. However weird the details of my memories — and they seemed to be getting weirder all the time — my feelings were not so different from hers, my grief an ordinary grief, at loss, mortality, irreversibility, my anger the ordinary anger at cruelty, injustice, indifference, hypocrisy, fate.

One of the bonds between Violet and I was that neither of the available mythologies of our culture, Science and Christianity, worked for us. We couldn't bring to either of them life and death and suffering as we knew them and make meaning out of our experiences.

But whether or not there is a collective myth that works, the individual psyche goes on needing and making stories in dreams and in waking life. When I look now at my carefully preserved image of my father, "the man in the green sweater pushing a wheelbarrow full of leaf mold from the spinney," I see how, unconsciously, I clothed him in the archetype of the Green Man, a figure embodying the violent, beautiful, untamed power of nature. Elsewhere I have found myself casting my mother as a vast and shadowy figure who holds in her hands the power of life and death.

I've had to struggle to topple my parents from their thrones in my psyche. It was a shock to realize how deeply my father had represented the whole world to me, to see how my conflict-ridden, despairing desire to win approval in the world had everything to do with my longing to win his approval and my fear of what I would have to do and be to succeed in that.

My father is not the world, I told myself. He is certainly not Green Man. He is a single, twisted human being. But the way in which he is twisted does feel in some way representative rather than aberrant.

As a child my father carried for me the splendor and power of science, and its promise of predictability and control. When I began to remember ritual abuse I couldn't believe he was involved because ritual abuse seemed so primitive, so irrational, so — unscientific. But my father was involved and the more I remembered about the way he was involved the more I felt that in looking at him and the form of ritual abuse he practiced I was also looking into the shadow face of science. Science, meaning science in the widest sense as the view of the world central to Western society since the seventeenth century, science which glorifies objectivity and seeks to exclude empathy from its operations.

In a number of memories I'd had a feeling of having been experimented on. There was an investigative element in many of the rituals: What images come to a child locked in a coffin? What sequence of terror best silences a child? What happens to the human mind when it is faced with impossible choices? Will a child kill a child to save that child from suffering?

It's fairly clear from my memories that my father liked the stance of the detached observer. He liked to watch. Gradually I realized he liked to watch things suffer, especially he liked to watch vulnerable creatures suffer, children, animals. This was his passion. It feels horrible to write this but I think it's true and I wonder, is this what is also at the heart of the scientific mythos, not merely an indifference to connection but a contempt for it, a frenzy even to violate it?

When I was first remembering ritual abuse, my experiences seemed so weird, so utterly aberrant, that I was mainly aware of the chasm separating ritual abuse from ordinary life, and afraid that I was stranded on the far side of it. But then I began to have another equally horrifying thought: that it is not so aberrant, not so separate from ordinary life at all. Perhaps ritual abuse, far from being the opposite of the scientific mindset, is its natural, if monstrous, offspring, the fruit of the ethos of domination and disconnection which governs my culture.

Chapter Sixteen

12/7/90

Reading Simon Wiesenthal's The Murderers Among Us — *he was crammed into a railway car with other Jews and Poles and Ukrainians. It was widely believed the Nazis were going to gas the carriage in the night but just before the train left the door opened and an S.S. man put in a little black dog and a canary in a cage and Wiesenthal knew they would not be gassed. The S.S. men loved their animals....*

At Mauthausen, after many journeys to the edge, Wiesenthal lay in "the death block", in Room A — prisoners too weak to work, expected to die shortly. Room B was even worse. The S.S. wouldn't come in, just open the door and ask, "How many died last night?"

He ascribes his survival to willpower and to the help of a Polish trusty named Edward Staniszewski, a coffee merchant Wiesenthal had known in Poznan. S. would bring him a small piece of bread once in a while and talk about what they would do when the war was over. They knew it couldn't last much longer — they could hear the American planes. S. said he wanted to go back to Poland and open a beautiful coffee house, and suggested that Wiesenthal, the well-known architect, should draw up the plans for the establishment.

"He brought me paper and pencils and I began to draw. It helped me to forget where I was and took my mind off the dead and dying people around me. I made detailed drawings for the coffee house. I even designed costumes for the waiters. Lying on my bunk I drew so many plans they made up quite a book. Staniszewski was very happy and brought me more bread. We talked for hours about the colors of the rugs and the shape of the tables. He took the plans with him. I met him several years ago, and he told me he still had them. Unfortunately things

didn't work out for him, and the coffee house was never built." (p. 44)

I was drawn during this time to books about the Holocaust even though I could scarcely bear to read them. Wiesenthal's use of irony felt familiar. It was not a mannerism but a description of the world. Sometimes it was the bitter irony of the S.S. men loving their animals, sometimes the tender irony of the prisoner and his guard making plans for a coffee house, but always it said, the world is cracked, disjunctive, do not pretend otherwise. I found strength in Wiesenthal's refusal to collaborate in collective forgetfulness, and in his difficult passion for justice. I was beginning to discover too that his quest for "the murderers among us," the Nazis who lived on in Germany and elsewhere, had some personal relevance for me.

12/14/90

Saw Rich. Flash of being raped by the men in a circle in the woods — of one beating a swastika shape on my back with a riding crop perhaps.

I went into immediate denial — no body or emotional reactions to the memory therefore I'm making it up — pushed it all the way away — a fantasy — said "Oh well, no memory today, I can't get to anything" then caught myself — "Well, yes, this flash."

In 1989 I had remembered being raped by a group of men connected with the riding stables in Germany where my mother and I kept a horse. I had remembered my mother delivering me to them, and how I had gotten into the car and gone meekly with her, even though, in some part of me, I must have known where I was being taken. Now I was remembering more about that group of men. I remembered that swastika shape being beaten on my back. I remembered a group of people, including both my parents, watching while a German Shepherd was supposed to be having intercourse with me. I remembered a riding crop being pushed into my vagina and laughter and a voice saying "Hund," the German word for dog. More memories crowded in, more about dogs, and then one about being shut in a box, perhaps a coffin again, with snakes. I realized that I had experienced ritual abuse in Germany as well as in England.

We were sent to Germany when I was thirteen. My parents lived there for three and a half years, Bill and I visiting in the school vacations. We lived just outside Wiesbaden in a large spiritless box of

Chapter Sixteen

a house built just after the Second World War on a street lined with similar houses. I hated that house and, without being able to say why, I hated Germany. I had been bilingual in German and English the time we lived in Austria, from when I was three until I was seven, but as a teenager I flatly refused to relearn the language.

In the first abuse memory, back in 1984, I had remembered a voice speaking in German. I couldn't translate what the voice was saying. I didn't want to. I thought perhaps the voice belonged to the *au pair* who, so the family story ran, had been nasty to me, but later I learned that the *au pair* had been a New Zealander and it had been my mother who was abusing me, so I wasn't sure where the voice speaking German came in. That first memory was a composite of memories from different times: I think now that the voice probably belonged to the time we lived in Germany, not Austria.

The first layer of abuse I remember happening in Germany had as its center the riding stables. These stables, a few miles outside Wiesbaden, catered mainly to wealthy German businessmen and women. I assume that the circle of men in the woods used riding as a convenient cover for their activities.

This group of abusers showed a marked bent towards bestiality and there was a new Nazi overtone. At a minimum, imagery from the Third Reich was being incorporated, but I think it was more than that. There had been anti-Semitism in the English ritual abuse but this was more focused. My guess is that, after the war and the suppression of the Nazi party, there were Nazis who were drawn into the secretive and violent circles of ritual abuse. They would have felt at home there. (There may have been links before 1945 too: there is ample evidence of an association between Nazism and occult practices.)

There was also, in the abuse I remember taking place in Germany, a virulent homophobia at work, but that is hardly the exclusive property of the Nazis.

12/8/90

Yesterday I felt obsessed with Sandy, and L. and I going out on our anniversary dinner and me scarcely present and feeling very tense and silent and my voice high, sitting in the restaurant, mad at myself for not being present. Everywhere my mind turned I found the word Sandy. I thought, this is ridiculous — it's an attempt to block something out just as once I thought Evelyn, Evelyn, Evelyn, to block out everything, to refuse to give my mind to anything else.

I was afraid I was going to go into a flashback.

I could feel L. nervous too. "Would it help if I talked about other things?"

No, then I just feel far away and distant. Does this aggravate you? "Yes," she says, "but it's not with you."

Can't finish my lamb chops — baby ribs, sweet meat....

I felt a bit better having talked .... less far away.

Said let's go to the dance (the lesbian Home Show) — not sure if my motivation was that I might see Sandy there or whether it was that I wanted to dance out some of this sexual energy among crowded sweaty lesbian bodies.

12/17/90

Saw Rich — fit of revulsion on the way down there — thought of a cunt, fat and folded, smothering — uh oh — aversion therapy for lesbians. Rats.

Hold off flashback while driving down 91.

Fear when I get there — want to run away....

Naked foot, a rat squeaking.

Picture of a real cunt right up against my face. Electric shocks to my genitals — don't really feel the acute pain. My mother has organized this, is directing it. She is the one who says when to give me the electric shock. She is in a frenzy of hatred, of loathing for my queerness (for Evelyn taking me away/challenging her authority too?)

Then I am on my back in a cage? a sack of rats near me, squeaking? But the cage is soft, plastic mesh, a woman sits down on my face, sits down and down. I am suffocating. I vomit and start to choke on my vomit. It was my mother I think.

Then men stimulate my clit and rape me. Something — bare feet — a man standing over my face — his erect penis. I am supposed to get turned on. I'm not sure how. I don't know what to do to stop this — to stop them.

Writing this I get turned on.

I don't feel this is my body really.

Solstice 12/21

Desperate this morning — didn't know where to put myself. Eventually began to cry and ended up seeing and feeling myself in excruciating pain, my mother looking, pressing a button in a box connected to electrodes in my cunt — I reduced to a nameless, hopeless,

Chapter Sixteen

desperate scream by the pain, all boundaries I had built against her gone — and writing this it occurs to me that's what she wanted — a version of orgasm, of complete vulnerability, of taking her in, of being possessed — that that is what she was watching for and enjoying.

I was hoping to go and live with Evelyn at 16. This I think happened Christmas time when I was 15, after Bolton saw Evelyn and I together in the street in Elmsbury. It was in January I think that I wrote to Evelyn and said I couldn't handle staying in touch.

Christmas Day
In Sandy's presence the sexual draw is so strong I find myself flirting slightly, making unnecessarily long eye contact, seeking out her eyes, drawn to be near — even though I do not want to be lovers with her, even though I love and trust Liz as I have never loved and trusted anyone before, even though I shiver at the consequences in pain and suffering of acting on this desire — despite all that I fantasize about sex with her and masturbate. And then walk down into my real life, into the real relationship I am so grateful for, us hosting twelve people for lunch and talk and later cards. A kind of solidity I've never known.

I wonder how Sandy is handling this. Is it purely my fantasy that it is reciprocal?

1/1/91 by half an hour
What a year it's been — in my own house, remembering ritual abuse, with Liz, Grandma dead, Esau arrived, Emma gone, nothing much published.

Am feeling very skittish around L. Is it because of ongoing lust for Sandy and not being ready — or willing? — to open up sexual relations with L. again?

Or because the latest memories do not make it a serene and simple thing to be a lesbian?

Somehow I feel as if I am losing some connection with L., not being honest enough? Not taking risks?

I want to push her away.

And she is herself needier than usual — out of work and scared and not sure how to decide what she wants to do.

1/2/91
A shaky day — close to the hysterical scream, the complete panic and loss of control I fear so much.... Glad when Linda P. called tonight

saying, "Are you having a rough day? All the RAs are, Tina thinks there's a [satanic] holiday on the 2nd."

That helped. I'd felt terribly bleak but had cried a bit and cleaned and read some and felt much better.

1/5/91

If I glimpse my pubic hair/cunt in the mirror when I'm dressing I feel a sort of horrified fascination and separation from it.

I continue to masturbate to the fantasies of sex with Sandy which are about touching deeply each other's selves, opening and surrendering boundaries and wanting that from the other.

I need to be able to want this with Liz and yet that terrifies me — to have that loss of boundaries with somebody who is — family. I feel desperate inside just writing about it.

1/6/91

L. and I did have sex this morning — me praying to walk through my fears and I did and it was nice actually and truly and I felt close to her afterwards (even if the kids were nervous) and she was relieved she remembered how.

Sex is a mouth, it takes into itself otherness. Sex is a gap in the boundary of the self: whatever comes in through that opening ceases to be entirely other, but neither is it entirely self. It is volatile, difficult, necessary, what happens in the place of opening.

One does not have to have sexual intercourse to be open in this way, sexual hunger can be fed by flowers, conversation, music, all sorts of things. What matters is that one must hunger.

My parents and the other abusers tried to kill the hunger that came naturally to me, out of my deepest self. Looking at what I have remembered, I think of those peoples in Africa who perform clitorodectomy and enfibulation on young girls. They cut out the clitoris, stitch shut the labia, making an opening only when the girl marries, the opening an artifice now. What size would the husband like? The girl can be fitted to him. To control another's sexuality is to lay hands on her soul. My mother wanted possession of me. The cult wanted possession of me. They tried to take it by restructuring my desires.

It was not my rational mind that faced the abusers' efforts at "aversion therapy," it was my sexual self. I swallowed what was put in

Chapter Sixteen

my mouth. I became aroused by what I was taught to find arousing. They tilted me towards the shadow side of sexuality. I desired sujugation to their will, the relinquishment of responsibility. Their images hung on my walls, the anonymous men of my fantasies.

But they could not force my sexuality without loosening its connection to my deepest self. So though I learned to desire what I was taught to desire, the desire and its gratification was superficial, junk food which could not satisfy my real hunger. The sneeze release of masturbation to the old fantasies was a kind of tax I paid, a rendering unto Caesar. My heart was not in it.

It amazes me still that the real hunger survived, the hunger for connection in which the boundaries within the self dissolve, and that old apartheid which keeps sexuality separate from the longings of the spirit, the heart, the mind, is overthrown.

In lusting after Sandy I lusted after the sexual self I felt separated from. When I imagined our joining I felt it in my body as a deep and joyful union, very different to the get-it-over-with-quickly orgasms of my obedient fantasies.

But a colonized country does not shed the imprint of its rulers the moment independence is declared. In lusting after Sandy I was lusting after somebody I could not have. It was still safer to keep my sexual self over there, just out of reach, than to share a bed with her.

For Liz I felt love, affection, a physical liking, but little desire. The first two months of our relationship were as wildly lustful a time as I'd ever had and then, almost overnight, I found myself repulsed, afraid. I tried to be clear with her and with myself that these feelings were not about her. They were feelings from another time, but that made them no less potent.

We made love very sporadically that first year and scarcely at all after that. I had had altogether too much unwanted sex in my life to have sex now for any reason other than that I felt like it, and I didn't feel like it.

Those first two months had been something of a sexual awakening for Liz so it was doubly hard to have me slam the door so abruptly, but she was marvelously kind and understanding, and quick to acknowledge her own ambivalences. My lack of desire was probably a mixture of needing to prove to myself, after an overly sexually active life, that I could be loved without putting out; terror at having sex with someone who felt like family, and the stress of remembering first incest then ritual abuse.

Whatever the different factors, it became clear to me that mending my relationship to my own sexuality would be a long and difficult process. There were rules I didn't know about, eruptions of rush and anxiety when I tried to learn a new way of being with myself. And in my body was stored knowledge of maddening terror, panic, physical agony, which I could not tolerate feeling and releasing, so I continued to need to separate myself from my body. I noticed too, without being able to account for it fully, that in my dreams I associated my sexuality with a powerful guilt. Specifically I felt that it had made me a killer, though I couldn't say how.

Sexually and in other ways I was not able to be much of a partner during this time. I did my best, but the inner requirements of recovery over-rode everything else for a while, and often the best I could do was to keep Liz informed about what was going on.

Liz had listened and held me and listened some more, and left me alone when that was what I needed. I tried to make sure her emotional needs did not go completely unattended, and we were very affectionate physically. Still a year of ritual abuse recovery had left its mark on her, not only because of the ways it affected me but also because she was facing information most people prefer to dodge.

In the first two years of our relationship, Liz had begun to open up, to play more. The frightened and withdrawn child self in her was beginning to trust that the world was a safer place than she had believed. And then I began to remember atrocity after atrocity taking place in the woods thirty miles from where she herself grew up. Gradually Liz withdrew into herself again. I felt it before I could grasp what was happening. I was lonely for her, for a connection with her spirit.

It often seemed to both of us that the less drastic abuse in her family had wounded her more deeply than all mine had wounded me. There was a dimming of her vitality, a fundamental depression, which had its roots in coldness and neglect more than in overt abuse. Loving her, I had a vision of her in my heart, alight with laughter, golden and free. I think love gives one that, a glimpse of the other's undiminished spirit, and the task in a way is to hold to that vision even when the other cannot see herself in that light. Robert Bly says that lovers hold the leash of each other's nethermost beast. The complementary truth is that lovers keep faith with

Chapter Sixteen

each other's angels. It became one of the more painful aspects of recovery, seeing that the kindness and courage which made it impossible for Liz to leave me alone with my nightmarish memories, cost her dearly. It was as if a young and tender plant were thrust out into the searing sun, or so it seemed to me.

I am not God, I cannot know the requirements of Liz's soul. She must in some part of her have known what she was getting into, given how much we all know about each other below the level of consciousness. Still I wish the ritual abuse hadn't affected her too. I might angrily demand that the world look ritual abuse in the face, but I wanted Liz to feel the world was safe enough to come out and play. Sometimes, as they were for Wiesenthal and the Polish trusty talking for hours about the colors of the rugs, the shapes of the tables in their coffee house, dreams are more necessary than reality.

Chapter Seventeen

1/16/91

Saw Rich — mostly talk about the war to come — entering the world of double speak — war for peace etc. — I feeling energized — abuse in the outside world to face and fight.
Went to Westover Airforce Base to demonstrate.
War broke out in the Gulf at 7 this evening — I heard during the S.I.A. meeting.
I think about the people in Baghdad being bombed. About the radio report yesterday — schools in Baghdad were open — parents were reluctant to take their kids out as they would miss the midyear exams and therefore be held back a whole year.*

1/17/91

Feel as if I'm coming back to myself again, have found my ground after this desperately hard year, sunk in the ritual abuse memories, the sore-hearted grief and rage, the shock. Now — these last two weeks — I'm writing again, able to meditate, feel I have some energy to spare.

1/20/91

Crush on Sandy largely evaporated when L. and I had sex the other day. Week. Whatever. Part of me wanting greater closeness, the rest terrified — and terrorized.
A yearning in my stomach for England, my England. I look at how quickly and easily L. and I and Peggy [another Brit] fall into a kind of intimacy.
Part of homesickness I think is beginning to feel the losses the ritual abuse and my efforts to survive it involved. Radical discontinuity, fugitive living.

1/24/91

Terror at what's happening in the world — that all the rich white men are getting to do what they want and use their toys of destruction and set the terms of perception (which is why I must ACT, be part of the opposition, speak from my heart and see it and say it my way) so some people and deaths and destructions don't count, aren't seen. I know about that and it scares me.

1/26/91

Fun at Peggy's birthday party tonight — I want to be close to her... to be in her life — drawn by her — a kind of warmth and humor and depth of humanness to her. She told me tonight she once broke both of someone's knee caps with a crow bar for not paying up on a drug debt. She was the heavy, the one who collected — once pulled a knife on someone on a bus and walked them off the bus with the tip of the knife at their throat — under the chin.

I saw a genuine horror in her at what she'd done, and a kind of disbelief or shock — the sense she'd had even then that this was not her doing these things. Yet acknowledging too that she got a sense of power and invulnerability out of this — "No one would fucking dare touch me."

I recognize that from the pleasure I've felt when people say, "I used to be afraid of you."

When Peggy told me about her brutal behavior as a drug dealer I was not repulsed, even though I am usually very squeamish about violence. Partly it was because she talked about it truthfully and with feeling, but also I found it a relief to talk to somebody who had blood on her hands. Most of my support came from other survivors — other victims — and from friends who had not themselves been violent. Without any conscious knowledge of Peggy's past I had felt I needed to get to know this person. The memories that were surfacing made her entrance into my life feel providential.

The Gulf War, in a way, helped me to face my own violence too. I was deeply disturbed by the war, but I think it also brought me a sort of freedom. Public discourse about violence shifted abruptly: from being a crime, killing became a legitimate means to gain "freedom" and "democracy," a righteous vengeance to wreak on a tyrant, a moral duty even. However much I disagreed, this was nonetheless a new context for remembering.

• CHAPTER SEVENTEEN •

1/29/91

Saw Rich.

Talked about [a] dream of killing a woman ... then a tugging inside... a girl's face, pock-marked and pale, long lank brown hair. She lay naked, at least all I saw of her down to her hips — her eyes had been gouged out. Around her neck was a silver chain with a Star of David on it. An upside down cross had been carved down her chest to her pubic area and across her belly. I didn't know, couldn't see how she'd been killed —maybe the handle of a knife plunged between her breasts, at the centerpoint of the cross.

I was standing not very far away. I felt thick and immobile, numb with horror. They burned her body on the fire to get rid of her. The smoke was thick and greasy. At the end somebody touched the tip of a knife under my left(?) eye and said my eyes would be gouged out the way hers had been if I told. Something at my throat too?

I think an image of her face appeared somewhere — a paper or on TV.— reported missing. I didn't say anything. Not sure how old I was. Assume 15/16 in Germany then not sure, could be 11. (Less likely. Think I want it to be younger, less guilt for doing nothing to save her.)

1/31/91

The war, the war goes on — I read about roses — see the face of the girl, her eyes gouged out, her slit belly — think of the soldiers and bombs the size of tennis balls which kill anything which moves them, any curious rabbit blown apart — and bombs and mines which are designed to cut a person in half at the waist.... Somebody designed that bomb and tested it and figured out how to improve it.

2/5/90

Saw Rich. — driving down I just wanted to drive and drive, north or west or south, go nowhere, listening to the radio. Drink and smoke.

Bombs cutting people in half — the girl cut in half — I'm naked, arms held behind my back — they've cut off her legs and cut them at the knee too — on a stone/wood altar/platform — they put the pieces of leg in a fire in a tall round hearth. The man behind/to my right hits my face with his hand, a silver spike ring, a peaked black shiny cap — He says, "That's what we do to Jews and perverts" — puts me on the altar amid the debris of bone and flesh and skin and blood, legs spread. He holds a lighted cigar over my clitoris. I am terrified, feel myself on

179

the verge of hysterical fear and then I'm floating, feeling nothing, reached the shut down point.

2/18/91

Grief and despair about this war — the army official who said of the upcoming ground war: "It'll be fast. It'll be violent. It'll be massive. It'll be everything you ever wanted from war but never got." (Quoted in "The Sunday Republican.")

The pro-war demonstrators at Westover yesterday yelling "Faggots" at us.

2/20/91

To live as though what happens to you happens to me is all but unbearable in a country cheering on the "softening up" of the Iraqi ground forces, gloating over the bomb counts, quoting the statistics of devastation.

I look out of my window at the oak and beech and hemlock trees, the ridge visible through the bare branches, the lightening sky, and think we're bombing the earth. One bomb of the kind which is being dropped on the Iraqi troops night and day can make a hole a mile wide.

But to try to live knowing you and I are one is the only antidote to the evil of war, genocide, torture.

Last night there was an open forum on the war at the Town Hall. I talked about planned evil, about the Holocaust, and how in order to perform such acts you had to dehumanize the victim. That is what terrifies me about this war. The media and so many people seem complicit in this: the video game war.

The techno babble, the manufacturers rubbing their hands, the pride in technological superiority are no different to the Nazi's corresponding with manufacturers of the gas vans to "improve" their design.

2/21/91

Saw Rich. A sense of circling around a big pile of shit.

What came — image of me stabbing and stabbing into a body — me covered in blood — then glimpse of woman, brown-skinned — Filipina? Indian? The left upper quarter of torso no skin — skinned. And me stabbing her belly and genitals, covered in blood. Someone had cut off her arms (on one — left — a silver bracelet), had skinned her upper body — a waistcoat of skin they put on me. Some kind of initiation. "Your first woman" said somebody perhaps. I started saying

• CHAPTER SEVENTEEN •

over and over, don't think don't think don't think.
Then they raped me, some of the men.
I stabbed her as if I was stabbing my mother.
Brown skin girl stay home and mind baby.
I think I might have murdered her.
(Talk to Peggy on phone about towing Jeanine's car while writing this.)
I mean I think I probably did.
Odd memory though — usually the line from me to memory stays tight, this kept going slack — my body limp suddenly — less sure of it therefore.
But possibly because I was so split to do this stuff?
Or that this time I managed to stay with rage and hysteria past the shut-off point — and here is the rage which is not powerless and which terrifies me. No wonder I've had a hard time getting in here.
The skin stiffening, my hands caked with blood.
Oh god
Help me.
Hung out with P. the rest of the day — towed Jeanine's car until the tow rope snapped — talked about violence — the violence she did, the violence I did and had done to me — felt good to talk to her and not try to justify or exonerate myself. The feeling I had when I did my first fourth step in AA that I'd murdered someone and forgot to mention it.
Went to a meeting.

2/24/91
Want to cry just sitting still and quiet — first time in days, so it feels — I keep thinking I'm drowning in a sea of violence — the ground war started about 9 or 10pm yesterday evening.
A week or so ago on Amherst Common Gregory Levy burned himself to death, a small sign saying "peace" resting near his body.
I want to cry and cry — the blood on my own hands and the vaster violence around me.
The fear of murderous rage in me.
In Liz too who tried to strangle a girl when she was thirteen or fourteen and it took three people to pull her off. No wonder we have such trouble fighting.
I don't want to believe this memory — I wonder if I'm being melodramatic — but I don't think so. I mean the way I'm reacting to

the memory is pretty strong — sure was Friday night but also since then — not being alone....

What else would get me to five meetings in a week?

2/25/91

Walking in the woods today I came across a ring of blue material — it took a moment to register — dog collar — Emma's — a bone — shoulder blade — and then I saw the skull and jaw bones — some feet from that the rest of the skeleton and then to my left a circle of dark fur sinking into the ground. It smelt of decay, sweet stink of death.... I didn't cry. In a way I was relieved to know — she died here, three minutes from my house ... probably from her stomach twisting on itself [the way it had twice before.]...

I didn't want to talk to anyone, dug holes for roses in the half-frozen ground, but I felt better after Liz hugged me and made me tea. She cried when I told her about Emma. I felt monstrous. I thought I would go to a meeting tonight but I stayed home and cleaned and read and watched TV. Cathy called but I didn't talk to her either. I wonder how I will account for myself to Rich. How should a person react when they remember they have killed someone (I try to refuse the word murderer and am right to refuse the name I think.) I don't have much to say. Have retreated within myself. Well, that's OK for a day.

It's 1:30am and I'm wide awake. Chocolate sauce and decaf? Or this other — feeling? I don't have words for it.

2/26/91

Saw Rich. Recounted the last few days.... Said I need to go into that memory again and did: the woman was naked on her back, arms tied out, a spot made on the point where I should stab. I couldn't see her face clearly though she was looking at me (but not struggling) — dark hair and brown skin — saw somehow a violet haze of rage and my mother. I stabbed and then I stabbed over and over in a kind of hysterical rage and then began to laugh, covered in blood. One of the men slapped me. Then I thought don't think, don't think, don't think.

Glimpse of skinned flesh.

Rich said perhaps — a shadowy sense — initiation — the skin being put on me — snake skin — image of death and rebirth — killing her was killing the victim and being reborn as the perpetrator.

He said perhaps my thinking this is my mother was a kind of mind game to keep control of my thoughts.

• CHAPTER SEVENTEEN •

Could be both. I saw my mother as victim.

2/27/91

Bush declared victory tonight, offered a cease-fire at midnight — thank God — but it scares me that America got off so lightly.

2/28/91

If I really stop and think, think I took away somebody's life, I feel desperate and as if it is a bad dream I have to wake from. I think tonight was the first night I let the knowledge enter me.

I spoke at the Hesterton AA meeting — felt invulnerable, making jokes. Earlier when I told it to Sue I cried but not really.

It's not even about blame or how much to blame myself, it's just the bare facts: this hand, the knife, that heart, breath, life.

She didn't fight.

Too gone? or drugged? or do I not remember?

I am avoiding Liz like the plague — want to anyway.

Mix of shame and fear.

Fear of the fear.

I won't get more today than I can handle with help.

Look at the intricate workings of the last few years — there is something which draws me onwards, a direction to my tide.

3/1/91

It's different, feeling like an abuser.

I don't want to talk about it, I want to forget it, deny it, not feel it. 'So? We all have to die.'

3/3/91

Serene today — open chest — a sunlit room, the dust having settled — nothing held back or guarded somehow — could feel more love for L.

3/4/91

Not feeling it except for moments and then unbearable — how on earth can I take in this information about myself — have it be part of who I am? I am either in that story or I am in normal life.

That rift again.

3/5/91

I go to meetings and think I should be in the company of thieves and murderers.

I'm not sure where I stopped being powerless and had a choice. It didn't feel like I had any choices. When I was at home I felt numb and unable to fight back. Could the girl who went with her mother to get gang raped, who went obediently, slipping into a child self who said "This is my mummy, she wouldn't hurt me," could she have said, "No, I won't kill this woman?"

3/5/91

But it wasn't the little girl self who killed, it was the angry boy/man who killed in a rage, stabbing his mother over and over in the belly and genitals.

I'm not writing this to exonerate myself but to try to see whether I could have changed anything.

As far as I know I didn't do it again.

I know there was a long process of intentional mind-fuck abuse which led to this "initiation."

I know I was brainwashed and tortured to the point of complete collapse of self.

I know there was no voice telling me I didn't have to do this, that I could leave....

It's a miracle that I'm here, I'm alive and in all the time since I came to America — and probably from the age of 18 on — the only person I have done violence to has been myself. I still feel like shit about it.

I killed an innocent woman with the rage I felt for my mother.

3/7/91

A happy day — walking the woods with Esau, work on the novel without too much despair, lunch and a walk with Liz, time spent watching the bulbs — the first orange crocus opening — the sedum and columbine with their underwater colors, purple and turquoise and pink, rich as a coral reef.

Great blustering winds and I dug out holes for the arch I made of copper plumbing pipe and two New Dawn roses and two blackcurrant bushes when they come — rocks and roots and dark rich leaf mold... later I drank tea and finished May Sarton's Plant Dreaming Deep *and began* To the Lighthouse...

It is still difficult for me to go to the AA meeting I went to the

• CHAPTER SEVENTEEN •

day I remembered killing the woman. When I am in that particular church basement I remember in my body how frantic I felt, like a bird without legs who must fly till she drops. I could not imagine a place of rest, of stillness.

I had remembered times when my hand was held to the handle of the knife as it went in, times when I stood by and did nothing while a child was murdered, and those were hard enough to face, but this new memory was different and worse. I had killed a woman by myself. Nobody's hand but mine was on the knife. I had killed, not because I was told to but because, for those few minutes, I wanted to. The rage boiled over in me and I stabbed, the physical action a release, a relief.

I thought the woman I was stabbing was my mother. Whether I was purposely led to believe that, whether I was given some kind of hallucinogen, or whether the delusion was all of my own making, I don't know. I believed she was my mother and I can feel in my stomach as I write the shock and the horror I felt when her hair slipped back from her face and I realized I was wrong. I had killed an innocent woman. Despair overwhelmed me. The cult had won, they had made me one of them. Yes, they had set up the situation, procured the victim, perhaps tricked me into believing she was my mother, but the violence had come from inside me. I knew it in my arms and chest and stomach.

Who was this woman? I knew nothing about her other than that I had killed her. I didn't even know her name. Who would notice she was missing? Who would mourn her? Was she a Gastarbeite, a "Guestworker," sending her wages home to the Philippines? Did she have children there? These were questions I could scarcely bear to ask myself.

Did I know subconsciously that the woman I was killing was not my mother? Would I really have killed my own mother? I don't know. When I saw Rich the week before the memory surfaced, what came up were more fragments of abuse at the hands of that circle of men in Germany. I think perhaps my mother's orchestrated attack on my sexuality was the detonator to the powder keg of childhood hurt and fury I carried around.

I had been able to deny and excuse my mother's abuse of me when I was younger: even at the time I felt instinctively that she wasn't really doing it to *me*. When she got involved in the ritual abuse I

185

told myself she was a victim too. When she and my father abused me together it was more difficult. I had gained some feeling of power from thinking I was the keeper of the secrets in the family and then that illusion was gone: they each knew the other was abusing me after all. But it was when my mother gave me to other men that something snapped in me. Perhaps by pitying her I had leashed my anger. But now she exercised her power over me openly, in front of other people. And with her box of electric shocks she tried to tear out of me something essential to my being.

In theory, at 16 or 17, I could have run away. Evelyn would probably have taken me in. But the worse the abuse became, the harder it was to leave. The torture had made it frightening even to think about Evelyn. I believed more and more deeply in the power of the cult, so escape seemed impossible. And, unable to cope with what my mother was doing to me, the split in me between a passive little girl and an angry boy/man deepened. To run away would have meant abandoning the fantasy of my kind Mummy. This, it seems, I could not afford to do, even though holding onto the fantasy threatened my physical survival.

While the obedient and trusting little girl went on getting into the car with her Mummy, another part of myself had to carry all my instinctive aggression, all the animal urge towards self-preservation. An integrated person capable of feeling both anger and love, trust and fear, might have been able to act to get away, but in my divided self I could not do so

When I first remembered the stabbing I thought a lot about "the line," the line I feared I had crossed. I felt separate and different. I remembered Peggy telling me how she had been unable to face her own violence without the anesthesia of drink and drugs. But I knew too that the steps of AA were formulated precisely to help people face their past actions *and* stay sober. I was not so different: in AA meetings I had indeed sat in the company of thieves and murderers. I listened when Liz told me about her own eruption of uncontrollable rage when she was a teenager. Other people told me similar stories. People told me that I would not have crossed the line into active violence in any other circumstances, and I thought they were probably right. I recognized the distinction between premeditated and unpremeditated killing. I tried myself and found I had been of unsound mind. But all this felt like an excuse in the face of the fact that I had taken someone's life, not in self-defense but in anger.

Chapter Seventeen

I see now how my disintegration into passive girl and aggressive boy contributed to my eruption into violence. I see too how the split within me mirrors society's casting of men and women into separate roles, and how that split also gives rise to violence.

My personal task is not to eradicate violent impulses in myself but to integrate them. It's odd, looking back, to see that during the Gulf War small steps were being taken towards a parallel social reintegration: women were officially given combat roles for the first time. The heat of the debate surrounding that move reflects the importance of such a shift for the collective psyche: if women are aggressive and capable of violence then the whole nature and role of the army is challenged, and with it one of the essential distinctions between men and women.

Aggression is so identified with heterosexual masculinity that many people are genuinely afraid that an army composed in part of gay men will mysteriously find itself unable to fight. Must a body of men, in order to fight, be united in their desire to fuck women? Fuck and fuck over. Do desire and anger have a common root in the mix of longing and hatred for our mother's bodies? I don't know the answers to these questions, but I know that they are relevant to my own life. The boy/man in me attacked a woman with a knife thinking she was his mother. How many women have been killed by men in just such a way?

Do women traditionally renounce aggression when they renounce desire for their mother's body? My mother tried to force me to renounce my sexuality and that, somehow, was the detonator for my rage. It can't be an accident that, in the months before the memory of killing the woman surfaced, the two major issues for me were sex and anger. I dreamed about both, and in waking life I felt desire again for the first time in a couple of years. I even noticed, out of the corner of my eye, that I seemed to be being drawn to women like Sandy and Peggy who were able to get angry easily. If, in lusting after Sandy I was longing for my own sexual self, then the self I longed for was one capable of both anger and desire. The tide that carries me towards wholeness was taking me to the place where I would have to face my aggression, its connection to my sexuality, and the necessity of owning and integrating both.

Chapter Eighteen

3/12/91

Saw Rich.
  Talk of the gathering [he attended in Connecticut] of people working with ritual abuse survivors — a big haul of videos of satanic rites etc. was seized coming down from Maine — the police will try to match faces to missing children.
  Eye doctor, I said — need to get to why I feel hysterical when I try to call one. Immediately I am in B_____? [the opticians I went to as a child in Surrey]. Balding white-haired man, pale blue eyes peering into mine — a slowly flashing bright light — I catch in consciousness a few words coming from my left: Grandmother, dying, blind perhaps. The man is holding a scalpel or other thin sharp blade in front of my right eye — I'm terrified — have to keep looking — he comes closer, goes further away — I can't pay attention to blocking whatever else is coming into my brain — sense of words going in but I can't hear them. I can't shut my eyes to block out the light for fear of the blade being pushed into my eye — remembering it, I'm frantic, can't bear the nothing happening — keep waiting — what comes next — don't realize for a long time that all this is probably creating optimum stress conditions for brainwashing/programming.
  At some point realize I can't move my hands — tied to arms of the chair...feet locked into metal stirrups? — perhaps gagged.

3/18/91

  Good talk with Clair about, amongst other things, beginning to remember programming, saying I have no idea how to access that stuff and a voice in me saying, "Yes you do" — shamanic journeying, especially the cave of records I went to once and couldn't read.

3/19/91

Saw Rich yesterday. My hunch about finding ways into the programming and how I suspect there are blocks like the blocks used to secure computer programs. Chat, chat, then I said, I think I need to get in [to whatever was programmed into me] — maybe use the journeying — scary — OK, need some anchor — image of a mandala endlessly folding in on itself — green candle, a rope of light tied around my waist — down the hollow tree where the forget-me-nots grew, down, down, dropping through some layer into the cave of records.

A sort of stone font — bathe my face — water became milk when I dipped my hands, became fire when I brought them out and touched them to my eyes — I looked at the rock walls — could sort of read/hear: your grandmother died because of you (don't remember the wording), you killed her — repeated and repeated

and killer kill, killer kill

and something else — you will be blinded if you tell?

then looking at a sort of dark rose on the rock — folding in and in — go inside it

Through the rose — at the end of a tunnel I see for a moment the radiant child — yes, yes, you, I welcome you but then I see she is mutilated and burned, her skin bubbled, her tongue cut out, eyes gouged out — horror — but also I am already moving toward her, I embrace her, wrap the rope of light around us both and come back up. When I get back up she is within me

But then I'm in the [optician's] chair again, tossing around, can't really talk... don't hear anything only see an image of jaws — boney jaws with dog teeth opening wide — the burnt dog I think — horror and fear — see this image to the left while the man holds the knife to my right eye and feel him saying, you can't hold anything back, not anything, until all that is left inside me is the image of the tongueless, eyeless face trying to scream, the darkness of her empty mouth and eyes.

Took a long time to come back [to the present] and I felt confused, stressed out.

Rich says he thinks that image is indeed a block — meant to stop me, to divert me.

Maybe.

It's so weird.

They didn't get all of me — they didn't get my ability to love and accept that wounded girl.

Chapter Eighteen

This was one of the few times I used the technique of shamanic journeying during the years when the ritual abuse memories were surfacing. Mostly in the past, when I was journeying regularly, I did it with friends, each of us taking turns beating a drum in a steady, quite rapid rhythm. I would picture myself in an actual place where there was some kind of entrance into the earth and then I would find myself crawling or falling down a tunnel to the "lower world." The entrance place I imagined most often was a hollow tree which grew on the bank of the river below the Mill House. In spring it was surrounded by forget-me-nots. I spent a lot of time there when I was ten and eleven, dreaming of setting up house in the tree. Picturing that hollow tree, sitting in Rich's office, I found I was able to slip into the trance state without needing the beat of the drum.

It was strange, going down into the "lower world" again. The surrealism indigenous to the unconscious mind, which I usually enjoyed, knowing it was truth speaking the language of dreams, was coming uncomfortably close to the actualities of ritual abuse. In the past, before I started to remember, if I had encountered, during a journey, a tongueless, eyeless, mutilated girl I would have taken her as an image of my own wounded child self. I expect I would have wrapped her in light and taken her into myself, just as I did in this journey. But now I had a kind of double reaction because I couldn't be sure: was she a child I had actually seen? Was she an image I was forced to look at during the brainwashing?

Ordinarily when I journeyed I didn't expect literal truth. I suspended my incredulity. If I bathed my face from a stone font and the water became first milk then fire, I didn't think, "Oh that's stupid, that wouldn't ever happen." I had, so to speak, followed Alice down the rabbit hole, and what happened happened. But I did expect that, when I came back up, I would find a world where water remained water and the earth was firm underfoot. This time, when I surfaced, I found myself not in Massachusetts in 1991 but in Surrey in 1968. I surfaced straight into the optician's chair where the cult was trying, through stress and terror, to induce exactly the sort of unshielded psychic openness I had chosen when I slipped into the journeying state. No wonder I felt confused. It took a long time to make it back to the green candle on the table in Rich's study. I had crossed too many frontiers too quickly.

However disorienting, this experiment with journeying helped me untangle another strand of my denial. The two states, journeying and remembering, are not dissimilar. Both involve opening a channel to the unconscious, and to do that one has to suspend the skeptical voice, but when I am journeying there is a part of me that knows, "This is a dream," whereas when I am remembering, I am thinking, "Oh my God this might have happened."

Still, there is no way to divide fantasy from memory absolutely — the psyche, in its labor of integrating experience, takes what happens, selects, shapes, makes a story of it, and so mingles memory and myth.

I kept hoping that the way my memories were weaving themselves into patterns, recurrent themes, was an indication, not that they really happened but that my psyche was exceptionally good at making stories — making them up, that is. In journeying, over the years, I had given my psyche free rein, and the stories it told me were intricate, archetypal, surprising. But the jolt of going from journey to memory showed me the inescapable difference between the two. In the journey, when I touched my face with fire I didn't feel the burn of it in my skin. But when I found myself sitting in the optician's chair again, I felt the thrum of terror in every muscle. I felt the memory in my body, not as a passing response to an image but as sensation released, the psyche having at last found a way to tell the body's story.

When my hold on reality feels sturdy, I can afford excursions into other realms unbound by probability and logic. Remembering ritual abuse robbed me of my desire to travel in the country of the imagination. I went there still in dreams of course, but awake I clung to the literal world, the way I used to when I was ten and eleven, staring down my microscope at the skin of an onion, learning the orderly progression of the periodic tables from my chemistry book.

But I missed the play of imagination even while I feared it. Without that interchange between self and world, life feels flat and lonely. In the garden I found I could harness fantasy to rock and root and muck, realities so tangible it became safe to play again. And although it felt like a deprivation at the time, the restriction taught me new delight. Looking at flowers so opened my eyes to color that, when I went to see the Matisse in Morocco exhibit in New York, the paintings entered me in a whole new way and I was caught up in the sort of ecstasy that enters one's cells and is never forgotten.

• CHAPTER EIGHTEEN •

During the spring of 1991 various friends got sick. Peggy was diagnosed with a potentially fatal liver disease and Liz had discovered a lump in her breast. I found myself in hospitals and they stirred memories of Granny's last months when she was dying of cancer. I began to see how deeply I had absorbed the cult's message that I was to blame for her death. I noticed that I was afraid in the present that I was causing people I cared about to get ill.

During this time I also remembered a ritual, at which my father was present, in which I raped my mother with the handle of a knife.

3/28/91

Wooey, weird reversal — that's what was done to me at the very beginning of the ritual abuse, the knife handle in my vagina.

My mother left behind [among the victims] when I graduated in the cult. Complicity and bond between my father and I — him being proud of me, contempt for her, her out of controlness, displays of emotion.

4/2/91

Saw Rich. He asked me to speak to a group of therapists etc. working with RA survivors.

Talked of feeling I harm people I care about.

A propos [he says] when I'm remembering harming people.

Anxiety when talking about programming.

Finally was quiet, closed my eyes. Instantly I'm there with the knife handle up my mother's vagina, jabbing it — I am full of rage. I look down at the blade and then she and I are the two wings of a big black bird flying up and up — grainy, entrapping hallucination.

Stuck after this, no feelings, say to Rich I need you to tell me I can still be angry at her even if I did things to her that she did to me.

Yes, he said, began to talk — I began to cry and then a flash of the terror [I felt back then] — They're getting me, they're making me like them and I can't stop them. Utter horror. My own emotions — rage at my mother, wanting to belong, to be picked by my father.

Suicide was my only option, my hidden ace.

And the note which said this is the only way to prove free will was no more nor less than true.

4/4/91

Scared myself last night — driving to the SIA meeting my heart started pounding and for a moment my vision narrowed — I held my breath and the pounding stopped.

193

No more decaf than usual — anxiety — from agreeing to talk in front of RA support people.

Black snow fell in the Himalayas — a result of the oil wells on fire in Kuwait.

4/9/91

Cult threatening to hurt Granny — my terror and confusion and helplessness — no one to turn to to protect her — she's too frail herself and I can't do it. Grief grief.

Rich asks about her death. I still don't remember when or how she died, if there was a funeral, if I went — nothing.

Someone wants to speak: They killed her. I couldn't stop them. They put her in the fire in the box. They burned her alive.

I cry and cry and cry.

It's what I believed happened — because it really did? Doubtful. Because it's what they told me? Probably. Because it's what I thought, knowing she was cremated? Possibly.

4/11/91

Said at the meeting tonight — I did to my mother some of the things that had been done to me and I can't find it in me to be sorry for that, not after eighteen years of savage abuse by her.

I feel nervous having said that as clearly as I did: now I know I'm bad and I'm going to get zapped by a lightening bolt.

But it's true. It rang true when I said it and it rings true now.

4/21/91

After Granny died ... I refused to sing hymns [at school], said I didn't believe in God.

4/23/91

At the meeting I didn't plan to but I talked about dealing with having killed somebody — broke into a sweat saying it too.

Hard hard hard

But Alison D, pregnant and due any day, hugged me and I thought she thinks I'm all right. She wouldn't have done that if she thought I was evil.

4/24/91

To the tune of "I'm a wanderer" — I'm a murderer murderer

194

• CHAPTER EIGHTEEN •

murderer.
Jolts of unreality — can this be my life? This?!
Tina on the fire escape during the break: "You look different." Oh? "This being a murderer must be suiting you."
I felt that sick tug in my belly.
Me. And we're laughing, a little hysterically....
Angry that this happened to me — that I did this stuff. That these are the terms of my life.
Angry when I'm not disbelieving.
I don't have a shred of evidence to hold against me yet I believe myself.
Oh God or something help me.

4/26/91

Something clicked, praying this morning, about grace and I cried — felt it — you don't earn grace. In fact, feeling you deserve grace stands in the way (as does hating yourself and feeling you don't deserve anything.)
Grace is an unearned gift. I didn't earn sobriety or Liz or this house or incest recovery.
I don't have to earn God's love, I don't have to be good enough.
I felt that and cried and for a moment something relaxed in me — then I thought, Oh this is great, can't wait to write it down in my journal.
This is what I was trying to say to Rich — I'm exhausted from trying to be good enough.
And then I hit the murderer business and I feel my god, I'll never be good enough now — there's no way to "forgive" this — wipe it off the score card so I can get on with the competition/ordeal/trial.
It's good that the recognition of that — sin — stalled out the Good Enough machine — left me empty and in need of grace. In a position of humility which, just as the steps [of AA] say, turns out to be the key.
Somehow humility and grace transform the rules — good enough and too bad become IRRELEVANT. Not wrong, just unnecessary.
I know in my gut this is how changes happen — you shed the old pattern of thought.
Let my heart feel it — what it is to be without the armor of deserving, of earning, to be at the mercy of love, god, grace
    is to be lighter
    and nervous!

195

This glimpse I had of the nature of grace could have saved me — could still save me — a lot of thrashing about. It surprises me, how clearly I saw for those few moments. But understanding is not the same as doing. Really to live without the armor of deserving, relying on grace — I couldn't do it for more than a minute. I always had to shoulder my guilt again, carry it a little further, always looking for someone to take it from me, somewhere to leave it, always picking it up again.

Relying on grace would have spared me my anxious accounting, trying to keep the balance sheets of blame though the lines between the columns blurred and sometimes disappeared. But to put myself at the mercy of God required the very trust I lost when Granny died.

"When you are lost, go deeper into the woods" says Sophia, my poet friend. There was no way out but through, no way through but down. Below the layer of guilt at the murder was guilt at the ways I had abused my mother when my chance came, and below that the responsibility I felt for Granny's death. It is strange, from an adult's perspective, that this last should have been the hardest guilt to reach. My culpability is obviously greater in the first two instances, but as a ten-year-old I believed it was indeed my fault that she died the way she did.

The memory of her death took a long time to piece together. It began to surface at the beginning of March and it didn't come into focus at all until mid-May. While it was surfacing I felt bad most of the time, morally bad and physically ill.

Chapter Nineteen

4/28/91
he edges of everything are somehow dislocated — I keep thinking that, the greenness outside crowding into my bones.

5/4/91
L. told me of goings on in town — accusations that N'gara and Zeus were a satanic cult, that N'gara aborted her own fetus and ate it — the selectmen had met in executive session, members of a commission on satanic cult abuse were called in and said no, this isn't a cult. Even the police chief spent an hour at Zeus's — "one of the most instructive hours of his life" — very impressed at all the work done there. Rod Brown actually apologized to N'gara for his part in spreading this rumor.

Another rumor — that Rupert Smythe was planning to give his 13-14-year-old daughter as a satanic sacrifice. The police chief went and talked to Rupert, and, once convinced that Rupert wasn't in a satanic cult either, began to ask in a lot of different ways, OK then who are the lesbian witches in town?

It was unsettling, to say the least, to face the possibility that ritual abuse was going on here, in my village — my village in America now, not my village in England. But Zeus wasn't anything like the sorts of people I remembered being involved in the cults either in England or in Germany. They were respectable middle to upper-middle class people whereas Zeus was a long-haired hippy war tax-resister whose house in the center of town had "Love" and "Peace" painted on the gates.

I couldn't be sure but it felt much more likely to me that the accusations had sprung from the rifts in town life revealed by the Gulf War than that they were based in fact. During the war pro-war citizens felt invisible. They organized a group to counter the widespread image of the town as pacifist. The tension between that group and the mostly radical lesbians and hippies in town was palpable. Rumor, fueled by the impulse to persecute, would travel quickly. I saw how easily accusations of satanic cult activity could be used against dykes and other outsiders, and how pernicious the difficulty of disproving such involvement would be.

The witch hunts in England and Europe and Massachusetts came to mind and hooked into the emerging memory of my grandmother's death. Long before, in my first novel, I had cast Granny as a benign witch. Now, horribly, the pieces came together.

5/4/91

What happens to witches?
They get burned.
I cried and cried, a loud, desperate, howling cry.

Planning to go to church the next Sunday I felt suddenly terrified. I remembered that I knew the shape of the vicar who presided over Granny's funeral: I'd seen him in the cult. I thought, he knows her body is not in the coffin.

5/7/91

Saw Rich — no major feelings — close to the pain but not in it.
Wasn't Mum fond of Granny? Yes but that doesn't make abusing her — or murdering her? — impossible. Somehow her rage, hatred of queerness, wish to be protected, have become quite palpable.
My fury at religion — refusing to sing hymns makes more sense if the vicar deal is true — otherwise seems unlikely I should have felt so betrayed by something I didn't believe in anyway.
Possibly funeral in chapel attached to crematorium? The coffin cremated? Not our village vicar then?...
Story of Harry Johnson, furnace repairman whose wife Lucy died of cancer at 42. She was cremated and Rich officiated at the commitment of the box into the ground. Some time later Harry approached him and confessed that before the funeral he'd had a dream that Lucy wanted her ashes spread in the garden she'd made so he'd done that but he hadn't told Rich. Only later he got to know Rich and felt bad about

Chapter Nineteen

having put one over on him.

5/8/91
Liz has to have a biopsy done on the lump in her breast — scary.

5/10/91
Evil not as a source but as an accumulation — of twists and kinks, fear and anger and need to control, failure of empathy, refusal of empathy.

5/13/91
I saw my grandmother burned to death. Her hair caught fire and her face contorted. I saw it as if I was a cartoon character from outer space — or an astronaut — a glass bubble around my head.

First I saw stone, porous, white, like an old tomb stone. I knew what they were going to do.

Driving down to see Rich I heard on the radio Winnie Mandela giving a speech in Soweto: "With our necklaces we will free this land." "Necklaces" are the punishment for police informers: burning rubber tires put around the informer's neck.

If I told Granny what was happening and she tried to talk to someone — her doctor perhaps
and then they burnt her to death
and told me it was my fault.

Could my grandmother — Granny — my mother's mother — really have been burned to death in front of me? I can't believe it. I want to leave this bit out of the book. Nobody would know except Rich and a few friends. If I tell this part of it, everybody will dismiss the entire story. I don't even believe it.

Why is this memory so much less credible to me than the others? Because I knew Granny in the everyday world? The women and children I saw murdered, the woman I killed — they existed in somebody's daily life, just not mine. Because Granny was officially a person, a citizen, she had a legal existence? But she had no other children, only one sister she was in touch with, who lived in another part of the country. She came to die in a village where she knew no-one, all her friends were in the Lake District. My parents too had few social connections in the village, having only recently arrived from East Africa. How many people's complicity would have been required to make her death look ordinary? She was expected to die. That wasn't the issue. A doctor then, to issue a death certificate, an undertaker, perhaps the vicar. She had asked to be cremated so there wasn't supposed to be a body buried under her gravestone anyway.

I can tell myself all this and still I don't believe it. How could my mother have let such a thing happen to her own mother? An only child, her father killed in the war, they were very close. So she always said. But when I looked at what I had written about their relationship in *The Forest,* my first novel, I found my grandmother portrayed as a woman who was afraid of her daughter's rage and unable to stand up for herself. When I was writing about them I gave myself full permission to invent, but what came out of my pen felt unexpectedly accurate. It wasn't what I would have said at all, if someone had asked me about their relationship, but it rang true.

And after all, look at what I had done to my own mother. I had tried to kill her. I had raped her. She was afraid of me. If Granny had been involved in ritual abuse when my mother was a child, perhaps their relationship had evolved in the same way.

I didn't want even to entertain the possibility that Granny had been in the cult too. She was my safety, the most consistently kind presence in my childhood. But I couldn't rule it out, and the memory of her death made a lot more sense if she had been.

I don't know if the story I told myself, that she was being punished because I had told her about the abuse and she had confided in the doctor (who turned out to be involved in the cult himself), is true or not. It is comforting to think that, though she might once have been involved, age and sickness and perhaps love for her grandchild, had wrought a change in her and she did try to help after all. But is horrible to think that telling her my "nightmares" led to her death.

5/13/91

When Granny was killed, any hope of being taken care of was killed — she represented religion to me ... No wonder I was — am — angry at religions promising a god who'll look after his own.

5/17/91

I've been thinking about what to say to the RA therapists etc. Facing malice. Formal, intentional cruelty.

Seeing/being seen: incest left me feeling annihilated, invisible. I knew somehow it wasn't me they were doing it to — I was irrelevant — but the ritual abuse was targeted at me and my responses were watched.

• CHAPTER NINETEEN •

What I need from a therapist — a human being willing to listen, believe, respond some — to go with me into a terrifying world of cruelty — not to try to reassure me with pat answers or explanations but to be present — a tall order — how grateful I am for Rich.

5/18/91

Still felt shaky this morning — started to cry — afraid of why the sound of L. eating chocolate sauce freaked me out so much last night — anger and panic — afraid they ate her. Doesn't figure — thought they burned her.
 Pray for strength.
 Image of dark red rubbery blood — gelatinous on white.
Did they stab her first? Better [if she was killed before being burned.] Was the face contorting just the physical effect of fire? Maybe the eating sounds are like the sounds a body makes when it is burning.
 Pray.
 It was her heart on the white stone, or what was left of it — they ate it — (did I too?) — it was crimson like the anemones in the rock pools we watched open and close, the rock pools on the beach where she lived.
 Oh God.
 It terrifies me, this stuff, it's so crazy and yet — I believe it.

5/19/91

I keep thinking of the story Hazel told me and then NPR reported it — the Tibetan monks at a museum in San Francisco making a sacred sand painting, one grain at a time. They'd worked on it for two months already — a woman came and danced on it, destroying it, screaming that Tibetan Buddhism was a demonic cult. The monks stood aside, smiling and talking, laughing a little.
 They demonstrated their dedication to love and compassion, said another monk on the radio.
 Feel tired and sad and fucked up.
 The lump in Liz's breast isn't cancerous thank god but it turns out she does have a hormonal imbalance, and the medication for that has a frightening enough list of possible side effects. This afternoon Helen and I were talking town politics — the rumors about N'gara and Zeus being part of a satanic cult have not died down after all. I showed some knowledge of the issue and Helen asked how I knew about it and I said because it happened to me. Then a kid knocked on the door for a

bucket to catch tadpoles.

I felt scared and embarrassed — went back to weeding.

Helen came out and said she hadn't meant to pry into personal matters.

Later I apologized for having landed a confidence on her unasked, but also said it needs to be confidential....

Helen said it helped because she tended to dismiss the charge out of hand — helped too to learn that stuff had happened in A_____ [a nearby town] recently. Penny [another neighbor] had told her this stuff happens all over the country.

So maybe it wasn't such a bad impulse, to break silence — motivated partly by fear of another summer's gardening like last year's — making nice and being a stalwart gardener and then weeping behind the raspberry bushes.

5/23/91

Spoke at the SIA meeting last night — talked of myself as a highly cultured manual laborer which brought a laugh. Barely talked about the ritual abuse or the sense of being torn apart, the crack between the worlds.

5/24/91

Hived a swarm of bees today — my bees swarmed into a hemlock 15 feet off the ground and at the end of a branch. I was serene — flowing with, not working against — and so enjoyed it. A moment walking down the path I'd cleared through the swamp maple and beech, holding a 6-foot branch with several thousand bees hanging from it, when I felt ALIVE and happy for it. Shook the bees off onto the plywood ramp I'd laid so it led into an empty hive body and watched them begin to walk up it, several stopping to signal to the rest, waving their abdomens in the air.

5/25/91

God of beauty, of green leaves and wind in leaves and rain in the night, help me say yes yes living yes
    whatever the terrible cruelties of it.

I think of Joseph Campbell saying we have to look at all this evil and say yes life is good, all of it, yes.

Maybe.

Chapter Nineteen

5/28/91

Saw Rich who was playing therapist more. Each time I talked about being taken care of — or not being — I could feel the swell of pain in my chest.

Help, I need looking after. Don't come near me, I go it alone.

Talked to Clair last night who has been wonderful about the ritual abuse — honest and present — has been broken herself.

Wrote to Laura tonight about her bloody woodshed [which I was going to build] and then this:

"I've been having a lousy time with the ritual abuse. I'm angry and sad and lonely. It's the hardest stuff I've ever dealt with and it pisses me off that I have to. But I keep showing up. Faith is at a low ebb, I'm just waiting for someone to tell me 'There are no mistakes in God's universe' so I can quote Elie Wiesel at them....

I feel cut off by the sheer continuous cruelty of this abuse, the endlessly inventive malice, the human capacity for evil. I'm sick of feeling I have to protect other people from the truth of what happened to me (and to a lot of other kids).

I'm sick of jumping back and forth across the crevice, the chasm between everyday life (pleasant in my case) and the other truth, the other reality of what happened. I feel torn apart often. Mostly.

There's no end in sight.

One day at a time.

I don't want cheering up. I want people to listen, to imagine, to risk believing what we all know from history and the news. Hitler and Idi Amin and the CIA. Planned cruelty and mass complicity. Not somewhere out there. Not 40 years ago. But now. Here. All over the place....

I feel I said none of this on the phone the other week so I felt unheard and alone — I know I find it hard to insist, to say LISTEN to what's really going on.

It's easier for me too to talk about the dogs.

Only it leaves me feeling desperate and mad and sad.

Under it all I'm afraid to tell, to ask that anyone listen because I told my grandmother when I was ten and the cult burned her to death."

I didn't mince words and I feel stirred up, enlivened by speaking my anger.

6/5/91

Managed not to come up with new memories seeing Rich yesterday — have been feeling better — cooler weather and practicing the second step and the click about my beef with God — that I want to believe in an all-powerful caring God who will protect me from harm — wanted to back then anyhow.

With some of that anger released I am left with the belief that
            THERE IS HELP
a vast regenerative power which, I felt strongly tonight driving home from the SIA meeting, I can rely on, lean on, trust. Sense of not being alone — seeing how powerfully I have been helped, sense of being woven into this vast mesh.

Then a fox kit crossed the road. I stopped the car, watched him cross back and then a second one appeared — such big ears and gangly legs and fuzz.

I had been thinking that when one is woven in, connected, magic happens — or is it that we notice it?

6/9/91

Talking to Rich's gathering of RA therapists went well. Rich said he's worked a little with two other RAs — both with upper class, British connections, and all of us with parents working abroad, in their cases in the diplomatic service.

6/11/91

Saw Rich — went better than I feared from the crying on Sunday night — followed the "I can't" in — I can't watch/see/stand it. Man's voice telling me Granny is one of us. She belongs to the devil. Look. The devil's mark will appear. I unable to bear it but looking. Her white robe caught fire and as it burned there remained a dark circle with a sort of Y in it — Satan's horned head — like the road sign [for a fork]. Don't tell or you die....

Perhaps it wasn't a real body I saw burning. The cult used illusion and sleight of hand when it suited them. Perhaps they were just using Granny's death by natural causes to grind the terror of telling deep into my psyche. I would have been easy to fool. So much that was incredible had already happened, nothing felt quite real anymore. Even at school, which had always been a place of refuge and reliable accomplishment, I was losing my grip. I lurched from one discrete chunk of time to another without much certainty as to how the

Chapter Nineteen

pieces connected. So perhaps they did trick me into believing I saw my grandmother being burned to death. Perhaps it didn't really happen. I go on hoping, though reason tells me that if the other barbarities I've remembered really happened, this one probably did too. Not necessarily, says my heart, not necessarily.

Chapter Twenty

6/16/91

To go or not to go to the Adirondacks on Thursday — is this idea of solo camping just an endurance test — especially since (as Clair pointed out) it will be summer solstice — or is there a more useful purpose to it?

I'm afraid of my fear, afraid of panicking in the woods at night alone.

Try to turn it over, the decision.

6/18/91

James Baldwin: "Any real change implies the break-up of the world as one has always known it, the loss of all that gave one an identity, the end of safety." (Quoted in Adrienne Rich, Blood, Bread and Poetry p.176)

Saw Rich. My indecision re Adirondacks trip — what began to come clear was that I want to do this trip, to confront that fear alone in order to avoid my greater fear of facing it with someone else around.

A fear-driven attempt to "conquer" fear.

I still want to go but I think I'll err on the side of caution.

6/19/91

The magnetic pull to go to the Adirondacks this solstice weekend is so strong I'm going to go and, trusting that pull, I feel safe — really, strangely, safe — plugged in and full of energy. Some sense that this is a point when I can let magic back into my life, the magic I turned away from as the ritual abuse began to surface.

I felt full of love tonight, and loved.

Still a little nervous — can I really trust this instinct in me?

Solstice 6/21/91

Sitting on Weston Mountain in the Adirondacks, the High Peaks spread out before me, the shadows of clouds floating over the shifting tree tops....

I've sat here much of the afternoon reading Anne Scott-James on the making of Sissinghurst, wandering on the rocks, watching the wind whiffle the surface of Lost Pond. In a little while I'll do a sort of solstice ritual, the shape made by Sophia and Clair who will be doing it too.

Emptiness and fullness.

It feels very good to be here — I feel still inside, like the clear mountain pool where I swam this morning.... I slept in my truck just off the road — badly — not at all until the sky was lightening — nerves? The passing cars, the roar of water over rock.

Already yesterday I was dropping into stillness — visited Clair at Yaddo [the artist's colony] and words came more slowly than usual.

Wind on the great breathing pelt of the earth. The whole green world. My ally. My greater power.

Wind in the spruce trees, the mountain ash.

Wind which keeps the blackfly and the biting fly bearable — the flies stupider here than at home, far easier to crush — can't afford the afternoon-long dance of the deerfly.

Fretting as usual about not getting work published, the twists of jealousy looking at the anthologies [Clair edited].

C. said again, I have complete confidence in you as a writer. It will come. It's not good necessarily to be in the public eye before you've made yourself — it can freeze a person in a gesture. And also you're on a path. It goes straight ahead from here. It's a very hard and sometimes boring, sometimes scary path, but my god you're on it.

It's as if you're putting yourself through university. You know. You're doing it and somehow you agreed to it.

(That rang true.)

Cloud of blackfly descended despite the wind.

Time to do the ritual.

I feel — safe
    empty
    quiet
    still
    calm
    enough

• Chapter Twenty •

The magic is back. Not the high moments but the anchor root which goes down below the humus, below what's living and what's dead to the rock, the soil, where the minerals come from.

Dark clouds blow across the sun. I'm done with my solstice ritual — simple, not looking for extravagance.

I am sitting on rock looking out over the dancing twisting sighing trees to the great simple mountains and the movement of light and shadow.

The flies I've been killing don't bite (the ones I called stupid.) They vacuum the surface of my skin.

How small and big I am. A whole square foot of earth. Perhaps not quite as big as that....

Sophia, Clair, I wish you health, fruition on our turning day, the earth turning... tilting back toward winter and sluggishly the green and water world follows...

I love change, the turning seasons.

I don't need anything just now. Enough. Rare.

Think of loss, of emptiness, said Clair, said Sophia, but I felt full, even of emptiness — full of the wind blowing through my empty room.

Later

How differently time moves alone and in the woods — I've eaten my supper, walked around Lost Pond, made and drunk coffee, almost finished Sissinghurst *and it's not even dusk yet.*

I have a fire burning to keep away the blackfly and mosquito and it feels OK.

I'm nervous — night will come so early and I will lie awake sleepless — but more to the point, night shows few signs of coming, only the birds at their dusk chorus and earlier some frogs.

6/22/91

I eat lunch on a rocky ledge, small gray birds scolding from the one sided spruces, clouds holding over the mountains, around me wirey gray lichen and sunbursts of orange and yellow over plain green leaves. Indian paintbrush. A shrub with deep veined leaves and small green cones, a few patches of powdery pale green lichen among the silver gray, a curl of chalky white shit. Coyote, perhaps.

I'm happy, hardly talking in my mind, looking at leaves, rivers of arrow shaped rich soft green down the north side of this outcrop, ladys-

lipper and bunchberry, bunchberry and Indian paintbrush, shadow and birch, birch dancers, old girls with swollen knees and bright eyes, aspen rustling, a narrow vein of moss, meadow rue rising out of it, floating its blue green leaves in the shadowy air, opening white downy flowers four feet up, such smooth stalks. Thalictrum. A good name.

Lovely lovely lovely. How can I praise you?

Look.

A man and a woman walk by. He has a great ugly blue tattoo of a marijuana leaf on his upper arm, a burly brass belt buckle. The first people I've seen in 24 hours.

I read "Fern Hill" to the wind and the birds who would rather I just leave. Not so the flies who nip at my skin.

To come into harmony with what is.

To accept it, to nod and look and see.

I feel there is nothing within me to fear anymore. (This can't be true!) (Can it?)

6/23/91

God in beauty (go in beauty), not of but in. A carpet of bunchberry, hemlock seedlings low to the ground, ladyslipper rising above and here and there tiny pairs of deep pink funnel shaped flowers over alternate dark green round leaves, the ones closest to the ground divided at their tips like tiny paw prints. Silver gray dew on the arching grass and far away a great white cobweb by the beaver lodge.

And the birds singing and singing, now and then a contrapuntal croak from the frogs.

God in beauty

In a world of death, suffering, cold, old age, the wearing away of things, hunger — the monsters the Hero Twins did not kill, the necessary monsters.

Better this — to see and accept their necessity than to hold out for the vision of a time when there will be no death and the lion shall lie down with the lamb....

To love the world and embrace it — recognizing within it Coyote — chaos — the impulse of malice, the breaking of taboos, the dedication of a person to evil, to opposition to harmony and right living — but also to see and to work towards harmony in one's own living.

The steps really! Things one needs to feel serene:

> *to feel a part of something larger than oneself*
> *to feel useful*

CHAPTER TWENTY

to try to be true to oneself
to accept the past
to love
to be aware

And then bang, the issue: *isn't our whole industrial capitalist way of life opposed to beauty, to harmony, dyed in every fiber with the impulse to conquest and domination.*

Still somehow you have to live with a Yes?

The Hero twins in the Navajo creation story had almost finished their long labor of freeing the earth of all the monsters who preyed on their people. Each time they had gone in search of a new monster they had come first to their mother, Changing Woman, and she had given them directions. But now, with only the monsters of Hunger, Cold, Old Age and the Wearing Away of Things remaining, she refused to help them. When the Twins went anyway, she told them to listen to what these monsters had to say before killing them. The Twins listened and they let the monsters live.

In Western culture the impulse is to eradicate every last monster. This is progress, to dispose of whatever brings suffering or inconvenience to human beings. We are only just beginning to learn to look beyond our immediate interests to the interests of the ecosystem in which we live, to ask the earth what is necessary to the harmonious working of the whole.

I come back and back to the Navajo story because it offers a middle path between the assumption of unlimited license to change the world to suit our needs and desires, on the one hand, and on the other, passive acceptance of things as they are.

I need the middle path not only in my dealings with the world but in my dealings with myself. I don't want to let old fear rule my life but when I treat it like a dragon whose head I must chop off, I find a hydra sprouting new ones wherever I look: it was fear of my fear that put the sword in my hand.

I am not good at middle paths. I want either or. Yes or No. Either I fight or I surrender. The way of the middle path is to ask, to listen, to pay attention. Perhaps it is the way of middle age too. Life begins to seem less like the last battle and more like a long marriage. We jostle along together, sometimes I yield, sometimes resist. There are things I won't budge on, pockets of resentment, but places of mutual contentment too. And ecstasy. I'll probably always need a little ecstasy. Perhaps this is the first level of acceptance, to accept the untidiness of life — and of my own self.

A part of me is always looking at the world and myself with an eye to improvements. When I can drop this critical separation and feel instead that I am woven into the whole, I find a quiet (and sometimes not so quiet), sustaining joy. I go from awe to cosmic mirth, a sort of divine giggle passes through me when I can just sit, without thought or resistance, paying attention to what is.

This is much easier to do when what is, is lichen and leaves, not the knowledge in my body of torture and rape. But I cannot be fully open to the one without being willing to be open to the other. For the first year and a half of ritual abuse memories, I was too frightened and overwhelmed, but in the spring and summer of 1991 I felt myself unclenching. I was beginning to accept both the memories themselves and my feelings about them. So then, somehow, I could spend three days alone in the woods without it being a military offensive mounted by my will against my emotions.

That first night in the woods with the fire burning — a sight I had been afraid would trigger terror — I was able to acknowledge my nervousness and then draw my attention back to the present, to the birds and frogs. Somehow, having walked gently through that fear, neither trying to avoid nor to beat it, I found myself for a little while in harmony with what is, in the inner as well as the outer world. "There is nothing within me to fear anymore." When the weight of that fear was lifted, I felt how heavy it had been.

Facing and accepting both my fear of being in the woods alone and my fear of being with other people, I was able to hear, beyond my own ideas about what I should do, a voice calling to me to make the trip anyway. Following that voice, I was given an unexpected gift when Clair suggested I participate in the solstice ritual she and Sophia had planned. Performing the ritual alone in the woods, I felt as if Sophia and Clair and I were the three legs of a tripod, holding the pot steady. I didn't reclaim the solstice as a holy day from the cult by myself but in the company of the two people my receptive, intuitive self feels most at home with.

I had been lovers with both women at different times, and had run scared from the depth of recognition and intimacy possible between us, hurting them in my flight. When I visited Clair at Yaddo on my way to the Adirondacks, I felt a new openness with her. She

Chapter Twenty

remembers that visit as the time when I cried in front of her for the first time in years, and she began to trust me again.

I'm grateful I followed the pull in my gut. When I start worrying at a decision with my mind I get into trouble. It's as if I put my foot down hard on the gas but I don't let the clutch out: there is a lot of noise but no movement. I can feel when my thoughts are disengaged from the rest of me: my voice goes flat and I feel uneasily aware of the arbitrariness of everything. It is usually then that I think I must make up my mind right this instant about whatever it is. When I was newly sober, an opera singer from Florida said to me, setting aside the gas mask she wore to protect her throat from the cigarette smoke which hung over the lesbian AA meeting, "Honey, if you find yourself driving up an unknown mountain road and the fog comes down, what do you do? You pull over and wait for it to clear." I think of her often. My impulse is always to drive faster.

When I'm frightened I think I should trust in reason, but when I follow the small promptings of my heart, leaving my mind to fret and wrestle with itself, I find my life unfolding in ways I couldn't have planned. I feel part of a pattern which is being made in each moment, the way the village weavers of Iran and Afghanistan make their rugs, not, as in the cities, with a man shouting out each line, but from memory, with room for innovation. The weave is a little irregular, the colors uneven, but a pattern emerges, one that feels both unexpected and right. Sometimes I think the pattern exists only in the eye of the beholder, sometimes I am sure it is there always, and I can see it whenever I look the way I look at lichen and rock, a smear of coyote shit, wind in the trees.

Still enough inside to see the pattern, I know for a moment or two that there is no necessary opposition between spirituality and activism, serenity and change. The human urge to alter, to improve upon, is as ordinary and as essential as the frost which crumbles the soil to a fine tilth. Winter prepares the spring. The whole is whole and always changing. The necessary monsters are those which keep the ball rolling: hunger demands another meal, the worn out tool a replacement, perhaps more effective, perhaps more beautiful. Old age makes room for children.

6/26/91
The damn grief is back — wading through it all day.... grief at

all the endless violation of me, of other people. The brutality and hatred and contempt.

As if I had to order every fucking dish on the abuse menu. When the pu-pu platter would have been enough, said Tina.

7/2/91

Dad how could you do these things to me? Why?
Crying into the asparagus bed I was weeding.
Then I think this is it — this is what it is to recover from this horrendous abuse — just this — to walk through days of joy and grief, despair, loneliness, detachment, contentment.
It's not so complicated but it takes courage.

Today I read through and sifted out more poems, shingled more of the south side of the house, chased our errant dogs, fed the bees, planted the second Eglantine rose, went to Green Hill Farm and bought three plants, went to the chiropractor and to the AA meeting and then out to supper with Jen and Cathy, after picking up some pallets in Florence for Cathy. And so home to talk to Sandy about work plans on the phone and to read my mail and then up to Liz's house for chat and tea and bed.

7/7/91

Yesterday I sensed for a moment the terrible physical pain of all the rapes and how I've tried to conceal that from myself with rape fantasies — fantasies in which being roughly fucked by groups of men turns me on.
I shudder at the reality of the wrenching tearing agony.
My body my poor poor body.

7/25/91

Saw Rich.
Some major patches of stuttering. Fear that on my 33rd birthday I will be burned to death or ccccrucified — or return to them. They'll come and take me back.
They can't really, can they?
[Dream from 1987 that] when I've run 33 miles I'll outdistance the lions.
All my feelings somehow fuzzy, not the usual sharpness. A ticking, tick, tick — they must have put a clock near me. A bomb going to

go off. My ticking heart. They put a bomb in my heart, they said.

Rich concerned for me tomorrow — my birthday — make plans so you won't be alone. He offered for me to stay in his house — maybe even use one of their cars [my transmission had gone] which made me cry — so sweet.

I care about you, he said.

Sweet man.

When I started to let kindly magic back into my life, relinquishing some of the dogged literalism I had retreated into, I had also to face the misuses of "magic." At a distance, as an adult, I can say of course they didn't really plant a bomb in my heart which would explode if I told, of course they couldn't make me come back to them, on my thirty-third birthday or on any other day.

But the more I experienced the cult's power to perform actual, outlandish, incredible acts, the harder it became to sort out what they had literally done from what they pretended to do. It felt as if they could do anything, and there was nothing they wouldn't do.

Even as an adult I don't always find it so easy to draw the line between the improbable and the impossible. It is a judgment call, often, the sort of complex act of calibration I became acutely aware of at the end of my drinking, when I began to see the world as a skyscraper propped up on girders of ordinariness, normality, commonsense, girders flimsy as toothpicks.

It is one of the legacies of my experiences of ritual abuse, this fundamental uncertainty, this uneasy sense that the ordinary world is a tiny circle not unlike the fenced compound in which my grandmother lived when she was in Africa in the 1920s. The lions are roaring outside and the jungle seethes with life and death but inside in a circle of light four people are playing bridge, following the rules, observing the amenities.

The people inside the circle believe in their world, believe it is essentially different to the "dark continent" surrounding them. They believe in their civilization, its habits, its common-sense. They know what is possible, what impossible.

When I began to believe my memories of ritual abuse, of cannibalism and infanticide taking place in Surrey, I stepped outside the circle of my culture. Often I want to step back inside, to say, "But that's unthinkable," and relax. The unthinkable doesn't happen. Only I can't shake the feeling that it might, that it has, that it does. And what then?

All this colonial imagery is no accident. It was Sudha, my Indian friend and professor from Oxford, who, of all the people I told about Ritual Abuse, expressed the least surprise. It wasn't just because she had grown up with a culturally different set of ideas about what was normal and probable. Living as an Indian woman in England, as a don at a Oxford college, living, that is, both inside and outside, she had come to see through the illusion of the British sitting in their circle of light, on their island of civilization. She knew, or so it felt to me, better than anybody, the unmapped place where I found myself.

Sudha told me, when I saw her in New York in July of 1991, that in order to heal I would have to go to the depths of the personal unconscious where my mother's and my unconscious touched. She told me I must not take on the guilt of the murder personally. It was a ritualized sacrifice and I must become one with the sacrificer, the victim, the act of sacrifice.

"I know this intuitively," I wrote in my journal:

> *don't resist it, become it. The "conversion" experience.*
>
> *Is that why I didn't crack completely, because I had some facility for flooding my own boundaries, letting them dissolve?*
>
> *But I wanted to feel separate, to keep my own mind, and it was a source of agony that I couldn't, that under torture they could get what they wanted.*
>
> *But they didn't get me — so I am not my ego?*

Sudha was telling me that I needed my fluidity, my many-ness. An irritable reaching after fact and reason, a grasping for boundaries, for certainties and distinctions would do me no good. The lines which offered definition, identity, easy meanings, were of little use to me anymore. I had somehow to let go of my longing to say, "I am not this. I am not what I have done. I am not like them." Instead I had to find a way to be all of it.

I found myself thinking of a handful of experiences I'd had when I was fifteen and sixteen, moments when I felt at one with the fields and the stars, when I knew beyond question that I was simply a particular, temporary patterning of the energy which was everything. These were experiences I had never forgotten. They had come unbidden and I had felt their power. "These are saving me," I said to myself back then. I couldn't have said what from but I knew it was true.

Chapter Twenty-One

Just before the memories of German ritual abuse began to surface in December 1990 I had an unsettling experience driving home one night. I was following behind Liz's car, the road being unfamiliar to me. I found myself feeling trapped and frantic. I couldn't overtake her because I didn't know the road, but the feeling of having to go where she went was suddenly unbearable. I screamed as I drove until I was hoarse, and still I felt desperate.

Having to follow behind Liz had triggered a memory of being driven somewhere, blindfolded, by my father. Somewhere in Germany. One of the "lies" I told as a teenager was that my father used to drive my brother and I, blindfolded, to places a few miles away from where we lived in Germany and drop us off so we could hike home. I told the story as if it had all been in good fun, but I used to wonder why I was telling such a lie when I knew he'd only dropped Bill and I and two friends off in that way once, and we certainly hadn't been blindfolded. I began to wonder if this hadn't been another fragment of memory masquerading as a lie. Had I in fact been blindfolded and driven by my father to some place where ritual abuse happened?

I knew about going to the riding stables but that was mainly with my mother and in the day time. I'm not sure where the blindfold comes in but I did remember, seven months later, being driven by my father to a different place, an old Schloss near the Rhine.

7/29/91

Image of being at home in Germany and my father saying You Belong to Us — weird because cult stuff at home — usually a separa-

tion maintained. Image of the drawing room in Germany and feeling terror — my father — get dressed — as if we were going out to dinner, but I knew somehow we weren't.

We drove and I didn't think. The road was a thick green braid. I plaited it with my eyes.

Beige stuccoish walls, a tall gate, a grill in it, someone opening it. A castle — everyone dressed up in medieval/16thC costume — down wide stairs to a huge dungeon? — men dressed as executioners with the masks on — fires and babies roasting on spits. (Stutter — remember anxiety at Taylor Rental the other week — a cotton pig on a spit.) At the door I was given something bitter to drink. Some hallucinogen — everything close up but me watching. In one corner some men are raping a woman. Girl.

People laughing, like a party.

There is a king in a crown sitting at a high table. Is that really his face? Bulbous nose, ugly. Silence is called. A man is brought forward, bound. The executioners cut off his head with a sword in front of the king.

Then I and other young people are drawn to one side. We are to get dressed — in white and red robes — gowns — but I am to be a boy — dressed in a doublet and a sort of short robe. First a man rapes me. It is the last time. Does he say that in German? Perhaps. In turn we kneel in front of the king. We are given our secret name. (I don't know/remember mine.) When the ceremony is over a crowd of young girls enters the room. They are in white robes. They are like butterflies. Men rape them and tear the white cloth when there is blood on it to keep as trophies. A man puts my hand on the rounded bony handle of the knife that hangs at my side. My father. I am to rape one of the girls and I do. I don't look at her face.

Remembering this I feel an agony of shame.

In my memory the scene in the castle resembles a painting by Hieronymous Bosch, writhing with grotesque activity. Could it have been just a bad acid trip? The bitter drink I was given at the door probably was a hallucinogen of some kind (ergot of rye?). But that was at the door, so the castle at least existed. Besides, the memory of leaving home and driving to it with my father is very clear.

I don't in fact find it so hard to believe in the existence of that castle. A few months spent on the fringes of the lesbian SM scene in New York, and a night at "The Hellhole," a sex club catering to

Chapter Twenty-one

everybody from transexuals in leather G-strings to polyester suited tourists from New Jersey to an elderly man in boxer shorts carrying a sign saying "Spank Me," gave me convincing evidence of the fantastic made actual. That club was only a few steps down from the street where people walked their dogs, bought newspapers, hurried off to work. Knowing that a group of lesbians who were into SM could, and did, rent a mansion on the banks of the Hudson for weekend-long fancy sex parties, makes it easier for me to believe that the cult could use a convenient castle for their theater of blood. And it was theatrical: the scene I saw happening in that castle could have been a tourist trap re-enactment of life in a medieval court, execution and all, except that the blood was real and girls were being raped.

What I was remembering, I think, was one of the high points of the ritual abuse calendar: the induction of initiates into the cult. There was a festive air to the scene, and far more people were involved than in any other memory I have had. The lavish expenditure of sacrificial victims supports my sense that this was a rare and important occasion — there can't have been an unlimited supply of babies to murder.

Initiation into the cult as a perpetrator: this was the culmination of six years of effort on the part of the abusers. I was sixteen or perhaps just turned seventeen. I had been raped innumerable times, told that I had caused my grandmother's death, forced to eat human flesh, watch murder and torture, make impossible choices. I had been drugged, brainwashed, buried alive.

My hand had been held to the handle of a knife as it went into a baby's heart, I had watched another child being tortured to death, I had killed a woman myself. I was confused, desperate, numb, split. I was afraid, I hated myself and, though I had friends at school, I felt completely alone. I craved attention, I was full of inarticulate rage, I longed to belong to something, anything. The cult must have considered me ripe for the picking.

Just as they used my rage at my mother, they used my yearning for my father's approval and my unease at being a girl. When was it decided, and by whom, and why, that I would be initiated into the cult as my father's son? Was it because my brother clearly wasn't going to make the grade as a monster? Were any other girls treated the same way? Was it the way they incorporated lesbians? (Everybody except me probably knew that's what I was by then.)

I know that, when I was sixteen turning seventeen, my father began to take my education and career prospects far more seriously than he had before. Perhaps this was just because he was willing to believe estimates of my talents when they came from the headmaster of Elmsbury, predominantly a boys' school, whereas he had dismissed reports from the young ladies' academy. Or perhaps his increased interest followed the initiation which turned me into his "son." But I have a hunch that my imagined career prospects — the headmaster said I was one of the six most intelligent students he had ever taught, I should get a scholarship to Oxford or Cambridge etc. — stirred a new level of interest in my future role and usefulness in the cult. My father started urging me to take P.P.E. — Politics, Philosophy and Economics — a stepping stone degree for a career in politics, journalism or the Foreign Office. He introduced me to one of the few women career diplomats. He even came to Elmsbury to talk the headmaster into dissuading me from applying to read English at Oxford. This was a far cry from his earlier disregard: my first boarding school had been chosen for it's convenient proximity to my brother's prep school, rather than for any academic credentials.

Perhaps the reason I was being initiated into the cult as a man was that I was intended to have a career, to exert influence in the public world, and, in the cult's eyes, only men did that.

In deciding to initiate me as a man, the cult, skilled as ever at manipulating reality, led me down a fantasy path I was already primed to follow emotionally. Long before the ritual abuse started, I knew I did not want to grow up and be like my mother, forever dieting and yearning for complements. Impatient with the constraints on girls' intelligence, strength and curiosity, I wanted to be a boy. I had a best friend and her secret name was Dave. Mine was Jack, my father's name. We were sailors and spies. We collected pin-ups. We despised Dave's twin sister, who liked to cook with her mother and play house.

Being a tomboy wasn't too unacceptable when I was eight and nine and ten but then puberty came, and with it all the pressure to shape up. At school I was endlessly in trouble for behaviors which would have been praised or at least accepted in a boy. I resisted as best I could but the feeling that there was something wrong with me for not wanting to be a girl in the normal way crept in.

I knew too, in my heart, though I could not say it aloud to myself, that it was women I desired and fell in love with, and it was only

Chapter Twenty-one

men who were supposed to feel that way. The upshot of all these factors, and no doubt other less conscious ones, since the sense of ourselves as gendered beings goes very deep, was that, at sixteen, I was quite willing to be treated as if I were a man, if I could get away with it.

So initiation as a man was not merely an idea forced on me by the cult, it incorporated some of my own desires. This left me terribly vulnerable: even while I was donning the costume of invulnerability, and acting my part — raping a girl with the handle of my knife — I was laying myself open, emotionally, to the cult.

Gender identity, my father, success in the world: these things got tangled up in me as a teenager and they stayed that way long after I got away from the cult.

In 1982, when I was at Yale for a year, I began to fall apart. I was having anxiety attacks which made my vision swim; a professor told me I could get a paper published if I finished it, but I couldn't write the last paragraph; I couldn't do much of anything except drink and have affairs with straight girls. Through the women's center I found a therapist. I wondered if I should talk about the problem I thought I might possibly be having with booze, but I decided instead to talk about my father and how I was afraid I was really a transsexual even though I didn't actually want to be a man and by then I was a feminist and glad to be a lesbian but still, somehow, something was wrong with me and gender. We didn't make much headway — not surprisingly since I always drank a beer right before going in to see her.

Once I got sober I used to cite this worry as an example of the sort of elaborate distraction an alcoholic will devise to avoid looking at her drinking, but, writing this chapter, I thought of it again and realized it was probably another fragment of the wreck floating to the surface.

It seems no accident to me now that feelings about my father and the sense that I was somehow really a man came up when I was at Yale on a scholarship intended to allow "future leaders of our country" to develop a rapport with the future ruling caste of the US. Unconsciously I set about sabotaging my chances of the sort of success which my father, and the cult, would like. Instead of making "useful" contacts at Yale I hung out in the ghetto and the gay bars and the battered women's shelter. And in the end, instead of going back to England, I went to New York and started writing and have stayed safely on this side of the Atlantic ever since.

I did take my place in the male world, I suppose, but I became a carpenter, not a diplomat. Like many women, my main reason for entering a traditionally male field was the pay. (And as a writer I was drawn by the possibility of self-employment.) But the choice also had to do with my relationship to gender. I didn't even entertain the thought of office work because, in female office worker garb, I would feel uncomfortable, humiliated, sure people were looking at me. I would feel, in fact, rather like a boy dressed in girl's clothes.

Quite how much this has to do with the ritual abuse I'm not sure. I know plenty of women who feel the same way who weren't initiated into weird cults as their fathers' sons. And I know that many women who look feminine share the uneasy feeling that they are not "real women" — the unease simply marks the gap between the assumption that femininity is innate and the actuality, which is that it is largely learned behavior. I don't think the abuse, ritual or otherwise, made me "butch" anymore than it made me a lesbian, but it certainly left me confused.

8/28/91

What made me more liable to cooperate with the cult?
   Low self-esteem from abuse
   Need to feel special
   Desire for invulnerability
   Lust for intense experience
What helped me not to become one of them?
   Compassion and empathy
   Existing in the world of books
   Ability to feel connected, at one with — sustaining mystical experiences

The more I remembered of my induction into the cult, the more I wondered, how did I get away? It wasn't only a matter of physical escape. There were parts of me that had wanted to belong and inexorably the cult had strengthened those parts. Still, I had escaped. In September 1991 it would be ten years since I left England, over ten years since I'd seen anyone in my family except my brother. I hadn't been back and I was sure I had not been part of any ritual abuse in America. I suspected that my involvement with ritual abuse had ended earlier than that. I had had the feeling for a while that my cult involvement ended with the suicide attempt I made

Chapter Twenty-one

when I was eighteen.

On the eighth of September, (ten years to the day since my arrival in America), I had a confused memory of some men telling me, "If you die, it will be because we kill you." They were jeering at my failed suicide attempt.

It was in the fall of 1976, during my last term at boarding school, that I finally decided to kill myself. I'd stayed on to take the Oxbridge entrance exams. My friends had already left school. It was a Sunday and I collected yew berries in a milk bottle. I knew they were poisonous but I wasn't sure how many would be enough so I thought I'd better wait until the shops opened in the morning and do it properly. I put the milk bottle full of yew berries on the windowsill of my room. I hoped someone would see it, that they would be able to read my signal and come to my aid. It was all I could do.

At nine the next morning I was waiting outside Boots, the chemists, but they had chosen that day to open late (for staff training.) I waited, looking around me, testing my resolve. The street looked wide and flat and gray. Wind caught at an awning. There was sunlight in the branches of a tree.

When I got back to my room I ground up the pills (was it one hundred or two?) and mixed them with water. I wasn't good at swallowing pills whole. I wrote my note, put on a Mozart clarinet concerto, swallowed the foul-tasting paste and lay down. I felt calm about dying. It was a relief to have decided.

When I came to, lying on my bed in my little room at school, I was filled with self-loathing. I had failed. I couldn't even get this right. And I was terrified. I had to make sure no-one knew I had tried. If the school found out they would tell my parents. I looked at the clock. Five past two and I was supposed to be at a tutorial at two. I had to get there, then nobody would know. I crumpled up the suicide note and shoved the two powder encrusted glasses under the bed.

Outside I realized my legs were shakier than I'd expected but it wasn't that far to walk. The tutorial was at Mr. O'Connor, the English master's house. He'd hurt his back so it would be up in his bedroom. His wife opened the door. She was the Games mistress and we didn't get along. I grasped the newel post and looked at the stairs despairingly. A wave of nausea rushed towards me. "What's the matter? You look dreadful."

I threw up, on and off, for the next twelve hours. I'm not sure when or how I told Mrs. O'Connor what I had done. I know I begged her not to tell my housemaster. I was almost hysterical, pleading with her, and in the end they let me stay in their spare room until the next morning.

Mrs. O'Connor had been a nurse. She must have known that, once I was throwing up, the paracetemol I'd taken wouldn't do me any more harm. I had chosen paracetemol because somebody had told me they couldn't be stomach pumped.

I learned later that it is not uncommon for someone who has taken a lot of paracetemol to wake up briefly before lapsing into a coma. The fact that I got up and moved around and so made myself vomit may have saved my life.

The night after the attempt, lying on the O'Connor's spare bed, a bucket beside me, I heard a voice. It was in the room, not in my head. It told me that I would not succeed in killing myself. It was not in my power to take my own life so I might as well stop trying. I believed that voice absolutely. I trusted it. It was the voice of my body, I knew, and its presence filled the room. It was strange and comforting, to trust something, anything, so completely. And it was terrifying to have lost the only weapon I thought I had.

In the morning the O'Connors told me they had had to tell Bolton, my housemaster, but they had asked him, on my behalf, not to contact my parents immediately. When I talked to him he told me he would not tell them so long as he had my assurance that I would not try again.

I was sent to see the psychiatrist at the local hospital. I was glad of that. I had been reading books about mental illness for a while, trying to find a name for what was wrong with me. After I'd slashed at my wrists the year before, the school doctor told me I had an inferiority complex but that only told me what I already knew, that I hated myself.

As I stood outside the hospital I felt as if I were stepping out of the world of school and home into a new world where there might really be help. But the psychiatrist had a waiting room full of patients and I was, I suppose, just one in the multitude of adolescent girls trying to off themselves. He asked me why I was trying to hurt my mother and how I felt about my father, questions I took for the crassest kind of Freudianism. He hadn't grasped the idea that I didn't want either of my parents to know. I saw him four times. He said the only way he could help me was to admit me to the mental hospital for

• CHAPTER TWENTY-ONE •

three months. The fifth time another doctor was standing in for him. I smiled sweetly and said I was feeling much better, I'd been a silly girl and I wouldn't do it again, and that was that.

So I lost suicide as an out and I lost the hope that the doctors could help me. Or perhaps I should say I was liberated from the illusion that establishment psychiatry would help me. I also lost the fantasy of escape into madness when I looked at the doctor's blue, measuring eyes across the metal desk. I did not want to be in that man's power. The cult claimed that I had failed to kill myself because my life was theirs, not mine, to dispose of. I don't know how much I believed them. It didn't matter really, I believed the voice of my body more. Suicide was no longer an option. And nobody was going to rescue me. Somehow I was going to have to do it myself. I was going to have to get out.

Where was there to get out to? For a child, the world beyond the family is a nebulous place. Moving from country to country every three years made it perhaps even harder to picture a place to go to, a place where I might survive. As a child my fantasies were mostly about islands, the sort where, with enough skill, you could feed and shelter yourself without needing anything from anyone. I collected information which might come in handy, from how to cook sea cucumbers to the best techniques for weaving a roof out of willow wands.

At fourteen I discovered Kerouac's *On The Road*. I sat on my windowsill in Germany and thought about saxophones in the hot Louisiana night, about highways and headlights and being on my own. But I knew I had no idea how to get a job, a place to live. Crippled by shyness and self-hatred I could barely look anyone in the eye. Who would hire me, and to do what? I'd never had a job.

I had few friends when I was at home, but at boarding school I had several. Katarina came to Elmsbury the year after I did, when we were both sixteen. We quickly became friends. I was set about with thorns and wire and crocodile-infested moat. Laughingly she took my defenses as a challenge and teased a way though. She had a wholly unEnglish innocence of spirit. Wounded and confused by the repressive glares not only of the grown-ups but of her peers, she kept singing and dancing and getting in close to people anyway. I hungered for her warmth even more than I feared it. And though it made me uncomfortable and I mocked her, I think I understood that vulnerability was her strength, that it took strength to stay that open. She didn't even drink. We fell in love with each other, which terrified me. It didn't seem to worry her. She was impatient with categories. We gave each other endless backrubs and I suffered torments of unnamed jealousy when she went out with anybody else but we didn't make love until I went to visit her my last term at school, a few weeks after the suicide attempt, and then I leapt off the bed saying "This Must Never Happen Again." A few months later we became lovers, and have been friends ever since. (She came to visit in 1992, and it was odd and lovely to find that, for all the changes in each of our lives, there was no strangeness. We have each only become more like ourselves, and utterly familiar.)

Katarina not only gave me love and attention, which I scarcely knew how to receive, she gave me a possible world to escape to and, in a small way, she was a bridge between the worlds. Because we lived abroad throughout my adolescence and because my parents didn't encourage Bill and me to invite friends to visit, almost nobody I knew at school had seen my home. One friend had visited in Germany and then Katarina came to stay in North Africa the summer I turned eighteen. My parents made sure both she and I understood that her presence was a great inconvenience. When she got back to England she wrote and told them how rude they had been. I was shocked and delighted that she could speak her mind to them. It put a hairline crack in my belief in their power.

It helped just to have a witness. One night at a dinner party my mother leaned across to a diplomat who had been flirting with Katarina and, moistening her lips, told him girls were a bore, he should be interested in older women who'd had a roll or two in the hay. There was a pause and then conversation went on as usual. I don't think I would have registered more than passing unease if Katarina hadn't commented on it afterwards. Bill and I didn't talk much so we didn't help confirm each other's perceptions, and besides it was all ordinary to him too though I do remember him writing to me in America asking if I had ever had trouble bringing friends home. Mum and Dad, he said, had been so rude to some of his that they had left.

Boarding school helped by giving me another place to be, and I'm grateful that it was assumed that upper- and upper-middle-class Brits living abroad would send their children to England to be schooled, but school was a world unto itself, offering little grounds for

• CHAPTER TWENTY-ONE •

comparing the insides of my family with anyone else's. Nor did it offer an image of a world to go to, being much more like a railway station than a house. More than any kind of therapy I needed to know in my bones and nerves that another world existed. I needed to see it, not just read it.

Spending half-terms with Katarina and the occasional day here and there, I came to know her family a little. She lived in south London, her father English, mother Swedish, both mildly intellectual, and kind and friendly to me. Katarina and her family had a circle of oddball friends of all ages and nationalities, from Frieda, a forty year old American who dressed as a king and sang medieval ballads, to Isabella who was ninety-one, who had gone to Newnham when Rupert Brooke was at Cambridge, and walked the sacred valley to Delphi with her Russian lover when there were still bandits in the Greek mountains, and driven an ambulance in the Spanish Civil War. There was Henry, the gay man who looked after Isabella and periodically asked her to marry him, and Tom the hermit who used to be an architect and lived in a packing crate on the beach in Suffolk until the authorities evicted him and Isabella offered him her shed and he designed her cottage and slept on reed mats and wove his clothes from the tufts of wool he found on barbed wire fences.

The open-ended multiplicity of this world was the best possible antidote I could have had to that house of mirrors in the dark I grew up in. This was a world I could imagine myself belonging in, a world I wanted to belong to, even if I did feel boring and shy and uncultured.

I stayed on at Elmsbury after the suicide attempt and took my entrance exam to Oxford and went home for the Christmas holidays. My parents wanted me to stay at home until I went to university the next fall but I refused. It was the first time I remember saying no to them, directly and simply. I arrived in London with twenty pounds ($30) in my pocket. It was a difficult, frightening, euphoric, drunken, wonderful time. I slept on the floor of Frieda's bed-sit (studio apartment) until a friend of hers heard of a room for rent. It was on the edge of Hampstead Heath in a house owned by an elderly Viennese Jewish couple. On Sundays I drank tea with Victor and listened to Mahler. Rachel, his wife was a painter, a lesbian feminist, as it turned out, who took me to an exhibit of Monica Sjoo's work. I got a job as a waitress, bought a cookbook, hung out with Frieda and her friends, drank single malt whisky with Henry while he played 78s of Victoria de Los Angeles. In March Katarina left university and came down to London and we made love and saved money and for three months in the summer we hitch-hiked through France and Italy and Greece and Ireland.

I remember everything about those nine months, the smell of London streets when it rained, where I bought cigarettes, eating Jerusalem artichokes for the first time, the route I walked to the cafe, the smell of Daphne, the woman I worked with there, the color of her eye shadow, the plays I saw standing by myself at the back of the National Theatre. I remember Katarina in Greece, playing her tin whistle on the plains of Sparta while we waited and waited for a car to pass, the putty colored dust, the mulberry tree we sat in and ate until our lips turned purple; in Ireland the Blaskets black across a silver sea, and prehistoric huts beside the road.

Ordinary tales of an eighteen year old out on her own for the first time; a teenage lesbian discovering she is not the only one; two girls setting off to see the world. For the first time my experiences could be extraordinary in an ordinary sort of way. Part of the vividness of my memory of this time is that this was the only world I was inhabiting: there was no secret world I had to forget as it was happening.

Chapter Twenty-Two

9/23/91
Cape Cod

E*quinox*
By the sea I need you Sophia, Clair, hands held out to you. At the center of our triangle, belly button, place of connection, separation, birth and death. Poets, harvesters, I need you, the year tipping from ripeness to decay, for a full moon moment balanced, a moment observed through all centuries.

This year's harvest — of grief, of doubt, of knowledge, of progress with Out, of Common Bone [a manuscript of poems,] of my garden, of daily kindness with Liz, trees planted, vegetables grown, doubt again, sobriety and recovery and the ability to face and accept the truth of my life.

9/24/91

Violent, tangled dreams last night — captured or capturer — the long need for alertness, keeping a man captive, aware the tables could turn....

At the AA meeting last night some again of that feeling of looking in from outside, watching people warm themselves in front of their fire of certainty.

I want to destroy their faith, to snatch it from them, to scream, Look at me, whatever you say about God, say it before my body twitching to the wires carrying the current of my mother's hatred, her sick joy. Say it to my bloody hands, to the woman whose belly I stabbed over and over....

Say it, say what you believe and I will laugh in your face, I will cackle and gasp and spit my venom in your face.

This is what I feel: hatred for the insiders, for Evelyn in her kitchen with her children and husband, for Bolton and his blonde children, for all the comfortable, I hate you, I blame you for my loneliness, for my suffering, for your innocence which must surely be blindness.

I DON'T BELIEVE IN INNOCENCE

Not yours, not mine

I hate you, you have what I want, what I am exiled from, what I have always yearned for.

Don't tell me I can have it. Tell me the cost. No, I'll tell you, the cost is forgetting is denial is complicity.

Everything that happens is God's will and I love God.

Make me puke.

Say it over the pit of burning babies.

Say it to Tina, to Leslie, to Carol, to Kate, to Jan, say it to Celia, to Erica, say it to me.

Go on, say it, and for once I will reply. I will not slink off, shamed by my knowledge, my absence of innocence. I will not pretend humility, forbearance, tolerance, I will tell you I hate your smugness, your intentional innocence. I will tell you grow up, there is no great parent in control, able to guarantee whatever happens to you. Your blindness has cost me too much. I will not pay your price any more.

I wanted to go blind in one eye. In my left eye. In the eye that saw the world of torture, of hatred, of domination, of annihilation. I wanted the eye who looked through the window to die, the one who, seeing Mum and Dad drinking by the fire, said they fuck me, they rape me, they burned Granny alive. They are the ones with the power. No god is strong enough to stand up to them. I have prayed to that god from my child's heart and my grandmother burned in the flames of their fire, to death she burned when I prayed.

No I do not believe there is a god who could have stopped them but didn't.

I hate your god, you smug disgusting bastards, you passive innocent assholes

I HATE YOU

I blame you

I judge you

I will no longer tolerate you

and I have been one of you. One of my eyes belonged to you. But the other one, the other one which refused to go blind, has always seen

Chapter Twenty-two

and in the space between I am torn by bitter night, by the unmapped void.

Only the plants, the animals who do not pretend to know, who struggle with every ounce of their being to survive
only among their fierceness can I rest.
I need fierce friends. I need friends who open their mouths and tongues of fire flick and singe.
Among the comfortable I am an alien without rights.
Look look here, you with your two good eyes, look at this, look at it damn it, smell the blood on my hands, on my belly, smell the charred flesh, smell the poisoned juices, smell my sex, smell my breath, smell the stones, the ground, the blade, smell my hair, look through my eyes, see what I have seen
Damn you
because you cannot
however hard you try
and some of you do try
I will be alone always with what I have seen
I wish I could thank you for trying but right now the acid aloneness burns in my belly
The aloneness we all share.
Our words so far from true telling always everything always becomes a story when it's told.
A story to touch you with pity and terror and that's the best hope — imagination — as long as we have imagination we cannot be rid of the hurt of the color of blood.(1)

And then the other side of it all:
This is mine
I won't share it
It belongs to me
Nobody can take it from me

My experience.

Thank God for Rich, for Liz.
I don't even want to write that, want to hold to the new clarity of this anger.

> *I am allowed to hate.*
> *It does not make me one of them.*

Rage carried me like a river in torrent to the mouth of the cave, the dark opening beyond which there was only the void, the place of nothingness in which I had to face, over and over, my absolute aloneness. This is what I could not, cannot, tolerate, the thought that "I will be alone always with what I have seen." At the root of my fear of my anger is fear of feeling this aloneness. But there is a part of me that has clung to the aloneness. It is where I know myself. I don't mean only that I derive my identity from what was done to me, and cling to the particularity of it, though I expect there's some truth in that. Nor do I mean only that my sense of self is so fragile, and my fear of people so great, that I have to be alone in order to feel myself, though again there's some truth to that. It's something more elemental: that black hole I fear as nothingness, the death of the self, is also the place where I come into being, where I am always coming into being, the place where creation and destruction interweave.

That place, both dangerous and fruitful, has always drawn me as well as frightened me. But it is one thing to come as a tourist, armed with camera and notebook, a ticket home, another to come as a refugee. The more I faced what had happened to me, the more homeless I felt. The deep dark forest became less glamorous, the lighted kitchen ever more desirable.

9/25/91

> *I am beginning to value more what seem to be purely human constructs, constructs which do not derive from nature directly but are things we must consciously make and maintain: ethics, law, fairness, a sense of justice, compassion for the weak and the broken....*
>
> *In the interplay between nature and culture, staying with the edge, the interface.... Art, the intermediate ground — the relationship of ego to unconscious, of the island to the ocean — the shoreline is always the most interesting place. Language itself is that shoreline. It comes damp and tangled with seaweed, smelling of fish, but it breathes air, is happy on the hilltop.*

10/1/91

> *Saw Rich.*
> *Mostly I read my rage pages.... It felt good as well as frightening*

• Chapter Twenty-two •

to read them.

White hot, said Rich — good — powerful — give me a copy. Maybe.

What to do with my anger — at some point I need to act on it, to go into the world in a way that will make ritual abuse more visible — In the meantime — live with it, let it be there — it does feel like a potbelly stove alight inside me, a power source.

I felt calm and relieved after this session — I'd expressed my rage and been accepted.

10/2/91

Driving I thought yes, I will write a RA detective story — that's how to make it bearable to read and how to give myself that hope — the dream of uncovering, of people finding out.

I feel calm and strong.

I know this is only the beginning with anger — when will I be angry with the perpetrators?

When I'm ready. Yawn.

1. From Wilfred Owen, "Insensibility"

> Happy are these who lose imagination:
> They have enough to carry with ammunition.
> Their spirit drags no pack,
> Their old wounds, save with cold, can not more ache.
> Having seen all things red,
> Their eyes are rid
> Of the hurt of the color of blood for ever.

Chapter Twenty-three

I went on being angry — with Liz, with myself, with the world. (This last was easy as Senate hearings on the Clarence Thomas nomination had started.) I noticed that when I felt angry I often felt worthless and that my fury was frequently touched off by the feeling that I had to take care of someone.

I began to wonder about my brother. Where was he in the German memories which were surfacing? I knew Bill had been abused by the cult in England when I was ten and eleven and he was six and seven but I only remembered one time when he was abused in Germany. I suspected that my mother had somehow kept Bill safe, that she had protected him but not me. Why? This was a question I'd asked when the abuse was happening and my answer had been that I wasn't being protected because I was worth less. It was a short step to believing I was being hurt because I was worthless.

This idea is a splinter lodged deep in my spirit. It hurts the way a septic wound hurts. The thought throbs: I was hurt because I wasn't worth protecting. Anything that puts pressure on that place makes me want to scream with pain. The whole area is infected. I am jealous of anyone who was protected, and angry at them, and ashamed, not only because I am in effect wishing they had been hurt too but also because I remember then that I am less than they. I must be, because what happened to me didn't happen to them.

It is my interpretation of what happened that causes me such pain. There would be pain anyway from prolonged and horrendous abuse but it is the interpretation that gets in the way of the wound's healing.

It was an unbearable interpretation. Part of what drew me into the cult was the temptation to trade it for an easier one: perhaps I was being hurt more than my brother, not because I was worth less but because I was superior, I was being tested, trained. I could become one of the elite. My mother might have rejected me but perhaps my father had chosen me. I longed to feel chosen.

My mother was not the only one I felt had tried to protect Bill at my expense. I had too. I couldn't bear to see him being hurt. I would do what I could to stop them.

10/15/91

Saw Rich.
Finally decided to go down into elusive anger place (hadn't found it re Liz in spite of my spasms of irritation — WHAT DO YOU WANT FROM ME?)
Go back to my brother, my mother protecting him but not me.
Rich lights a candle. I close my eyes.
Bam.
My brother is standing up. A lighted cigarette is approaching the back of his neck. I see it burn into him — I don't know if it really happens or is my imagining — I understand that I must not react. I understand that if I give myself to them, if I belong to them, they won't hurt him anymore. They give me a cup of human blood to drink and I do, gagging on the thick iron taste. When I have finished I look up. My brother is across from me, looking at me with horror and terror in his eyes. My face is covered with blood. I am one of them. That is how he sees me. As one of the people to be afraid of. I was trying to protect him.
I want to cry and rage, to hit and scream and weep.

I tried to tell myself it didn't count, drinking blood and doing what they told me to, if it was to protect Bill. But the cult seemed not to care why I agreed to do what they wanted: it was as if the acts themselves, regardless of my motivation, were enough to identify me as one of them. I clung desperately to the importance of my feelings and intentions, but as far as my brother went, these were hardly unmixed.

In everyday life when I was ten and eleven, about the time of this memory, Bill and I began to fight a lot and I remember clearly the white rage I would feel come into my fists and the message then in my brain, terse as a telegram: Stop. Stop now. I'd get up from the

Chapter Twenty-three

sitting room floor or wherever we were, and walk stiffly away, aching with the desire to hit and keep hitting.

Not all of my rage came from the ritual abuse. In Kenya servants had been paid (very little) to run the house. Back in England my mother expected me, but not Bill, to help with the housework. I was stunned and outraged at the blatant injustice of it. My anger was fueled by all the small wounds I'd suffered as a girl, all the ways I'd been told I was worth less, both inside and outside the family. I'd protected myself with the fantasy of being a boy but as puberty approached my fate seemed to close in on me. Everywhere I looked I learned that women were lesser beings. I tried to hold to the clean anger which refused these reflections, but I couldn't keep out the worm of doubt.

The ordinary anger of a spirited girl tends to become a source of guilt in this culture, even without ritual abuse to muddy the waters. With the abuse, and my mother's and my efforts to protect Bill, came an even more shameful sort of rage, a rage I know still: rage at the weak, at anyone I feel I have to protect because, experience tells me, in order to protect you I will have to abandon myself.

In 1980, near the end of my solitary travels in Asia I met two English women, Hilda whom I knew from Oxford and her friend Jane who was eighteen, three years younger than us, and quite naive. We were walking down a mountain in Kashmir at dusk when three men came out of the woods and tried to rape us. I started fighting rather ineffectually and then I heard myself think, "They mustn't get Jane, they mustn't," and I began to fight in earnest. The men ran off. We had another mile to walk down through the woods and we suspected they had gone up to get the taxi-driver who had offered to drive us down from the top. I walked the rest of the way carrying a rock. I remember the feel of it in my hand, rough and dry. When we heard a car we hid in the woods, covering ourselves with leaves. The car stopped at the next bend and the men got out and searched for us, four of them now. After a while they gave up and drove on. We waited a long time in the leaves before we walked the rest of the way down. I knew I would fight now, if I had to, with my whole being, for myself, and the knowledge was as unfamiliar and definite as the weight of the rock in my right hand.

When we got back to the houseboat Hilda told me she too had been unable to fight back until she thought about Jane and making sure Jane didn't get hurt. It stunned me, that we had learned so deeply not to fight for ourselves that the most basic animal instinct of self-defense had been suspended. Jane had barely fought back at all. Was it that we believed it was only all right to fight if it was for somebody else? Did we believe we weren't worth protecting? Or that we couldn't protect ourselves and so it wasn't worth the effort? I have no idea whether either of those two women had been abused as children. Perhaps just being a girl in this culture is enough to teach a woman not to look after herself.

I tried to protect Bill, not because it was the right thing to do but because it was even more intolerable to see him being hurt than it was to be hurt myself. This was a true and spontaneous response and I'm glad I was capable of it, however complicated the other feelings that came with it. Since then, though, I've often tried to protect people when the situation didn't merit it, when in fact it was a form of arrogance. And somehow the impulse to protect became the stopper in a cask of rage and then it was me, my rage, I was trying to protect people from. And not just my rage, my truth too. When all that fermenting anger finally built up enough pressure to drive out the cork and the rage spilled out onto the pages of my journal, it was rage at a whole world whose innocence I felt I had to protect as if I were its older sister. There's a crazy hubris to this.

When a friend said, "Your truth is a gift you have to give to the world," I cried. My truths felt like grenades hurled into a crowd of Christmas shoppers.

10/14/91

L. cried and cried Saturday night, desolate and lonely, feeling the relationship gone between us.

I had been about to write in here my wonderings — would Clair and I really end up lovers again? I'd wondered through the day. Up at the look-out in the state forest with C., reveling in the color and our pleasure in the color, in perception — which is the real bond between us, is what I miss in other people — C. said, "You should have married me." I said, "It's not as if I've never thought that too. It wouldn't work."

"I don't see why."

I didn't say anything more. Neither of us did. She wore a sweatshirt hood pulled up. I saw her fingers touch her face, the slump of her shoulders, looked back to the shining yellow birch, the rivers of color, the hemlock rocks directing the flow, didn't speak, wondered was she right, afraid how dead things with Liz feel.

10/15/91

I dreamt about knives last night — what would be small enough to fit in my pocket but not too small for the job.

Folding knives. Penknives. I put my hand into the bin and weighed each one.

The job was to collect wild food.

10/16/91

After the SIA meeting tonight I felt warm, warmth coming from inside me, comfortable in my skin, alive: anger — other women and me talking about anger — Lois exhilarated by the Thomas hearings — what came out into the open — can't be angry about the stuff until it is in the open....

I was talking too about women betraying women — what made me angriest in the whole hearings I think: some Chicago bar/BBQ joint — cheering when the result of the senate vote is heard. A woman's voice: "And she got what she deserved."

That smug vindictiveness.

10/20/91

Happy today, that strong happiness, taste of iron, crisp autumn day, the scarlets almost over but flares of orange, tawny oak leaves, lemon yellow swamp maple, beech.

10/22/91

Saw Rich.

Homesickness for England — a kind of humanized country, gentle land, the boundaries between human and wild blurred — feeling like a stranger here.

Lots of pain in my voice — Rich asks about it — too much mess, too much pain, too much horror.

Rich made connection: longing for England = longing for a time before I knew —

The civilized landscape, landscape of repression — easy to sentimentalize — what about everything that gets pushed down and resurfaces? My father emblem of what British culture produces — no feelings, no reactions.

So, grief for my lost innocence — lost long ago — I could never quite believe in civilized England.

I was filled with yearning as well as rage: for home, for innocence, for a place to belong. Perhaps I could feel the desire for reintegration into the human world more deeply once I had allowed my rage at that world to surface.

When I built my house I sited it consciously on the border between the human and the wild worlds: to the east, forest I left untouched; to the south, woods I thinned and planted with daffodils; to the west, my garden and, beyond that, Liz's house. Though my house was living proof that I was not alone — without other people's help I could not have built it — it also enshrined my solitude, my place on the margin of human community.

I could give you a thousand reasons why the margin is a good place to be, a better place even, but the more I faced the ritual abuse the more I began to feel, under the veneer of choice, compulsion. It was as if I had sentenced myself to life in exile in expiation for the blood on my hands.

How to come out of exile? I had no idea how to be at home with myself, how to feel at home in the world, with all that I now knew. I wasn't even sure what it meant, home.

Like many immigrants I longed for the old country, but it was sentimental, my longing for England's green and pleasant land. Rich was right, I was longing for the innocence to believe in the civilized veneer of upper-middle-class British life, to believe in the well-groomed garden, the well-turned phrase, the well-dressed man my father appeared to be. That wasn't a world I could go back to. I would already have gone if I could.

Something held me back from making a home in the new world too. There was something that kept me on the outside, something that wouldn't let me send down roots, however hard I tried. My dreams pointed to the Greek story of Orestes who murdered his mother, Clytaemnestra, and the Furies who pursued him, never letting him rest, clamoring for vengeance. Intuitively I knew that the unconscious forces which kept me moving from place to place, lover to lover, had been roused from their sleep by the violence and betrayal in my relationship with my mother.

Chapter Twenty-four

10/27/91

The north wind came in the night and blew the last leaves down, all but the beech. The wind blunders through the branches and the sky is winter blue.

Pain. Like no skin. Walking round the house. Dog in the armchair. Wood stove howling at the wind.

An unexpected light through the trees — moon lying low.

Sorting out old bank statements etc., reaching under my desk the dark corner looks comfortable. I huddle there, look through the rim of thin paisley hanging down from the computer it covers — and cry....

I feel scraped raw.

Dog on his back, paddling the air, sighs heavily.

To repossess my own life, my own experiences, redeem them with my grief and rage from the pawn shop o' my heart.

11/6/91

Dreamt I have a grandmother, a plump triangular grandmother who says, Oh I won't let you get into financial trouble. Something about the loony bin too.

I didn't want to wake up, it felt so good to feel taken care of, protected.

(After I'd talked at SIA about shame being bound up with feeling I wasn't protected because I wasn't worth protecting....)

The grandmother and I go on a journey, have adventures, but I don't remember what they are, only that I feel very secure.

11/12/91

Saw Rich, talked without a lot of feeling.... L. and I making *agreement [in preparation for the formal transfer of the land she'd given me] — money stuff — talked of her inherited money. As I talked I ran into a wall of loneliness and hurt — felt how desperation and isolation were the basis for whatever money skills I learned: I have to get out of here. I can't. I don't have any money....*

The huge ache of no family, nowhere to turn.

I started stealing when I was ten. I stole money from my mother's purse, and from shops I stole books and food to eat in the woods when I was playing truant. Soon I began to steal compulsively. At Elmsbury I stole money from other students even while, as a prefect, I was helping the housemaster to set traps — using dyed pound notes — for the thief. I was desperately ashamed of what I was doing but I did it anyway.

I think, by stealing, I was trying to take for myself what I hadn't been given and felt I shouldn't have to earn. I was trying to give myself the feeling of being taken care of, the feeling I had in my dream of the plump triangular grandmother. Money became a substitute for the mothering I missed out on.

At least that was what I think was going on unconsciously. In my conscious life money represented, even more than being taken care of, not having to be taken care of, being able to look after myself. Money was what I needed to get free of my parents. I thought about it a lot as a teenager but I didn't know how to earn it. When I was at college, my father gave me the equivalent of the grant the state would have given me if his income had been lower. I learned to live frugally enough so I could stretch that money to cover the holidays as well as the term-times. I moved out of College into a shared house my second year so I would have somewhere to live in the holidays.

Handling money carefully allowed me to limit my contact with my parents and that fact formed my habits around money. I had a horror of getting into debt. Even when I was drinking I lived within my means, however meager.

With Liz it was important to me that we keep our finances separate. Where they overlapped we were scrupulously fair in our dealings with each other. But cutting across all our small calculations was her decision to give me 5 acres of land to build on. I was stunned and moved and frightened by her generosity — and so I think was she. We talked a lot about it, probing for pockets of hidden emotion which might later cause trouble.

Chapter Twenty-four

Liz agonized about whether she should give me money to buy building materials too, but I didn't want her to. She told me how difficult it had been with her last lover, the fact that Liz had so much more money, and we congratulated ourselves on our sanity. And we were sane and it was easy, and then, as I began to thaw, to feel the anger and longing and hurt that was my inheritance from my family, I found my acceptance of the disparity between us was only skin deep.

Or perhaps I was changing. Perhaps, in one of those unspoken deals lovers make, we had agreed that Liz would be my mother and I would welcome the fact that she had the power (money) to take care of me and not try to take it away from her. Certainly there was something in the condition of being given to that I loved. I watched myself delay and delay the moment when the land was actually transferred to me: then I would be in the condition of having been given to, which is quite different. Eventually, though, I needed to grow up.

In whatever ways Liz had been my mother, she now had an adolescent on her hands. It was easier for all concerned when I was a grief-stricken child. Now I was angry and horny and demanding equality. I resented the disparity which had previously comforted me.

Liz was a good mother to me. I don't suppose it was the role she'd dreamt of when we got together, but something in her volunteered for it. She had a strong maternal streak. I used to joke sometimes and call her Our Lady of the Beasts. Stray cats came from miles around. They sat on her doorstep until she took them in. We called her house "The New England Home for Little Wanderers." I imagined her as a farmer's wife in Devon at the turn of the century, white apron and meaty forearms, happy and hard-working, held in a web of living beings, dispensing love and justice, casual and attentive as a mother cat licking the head of whatever kitten came within reach.

This wasn't the whole story of course — like many other women, she was able to nurture others far better than herself and there was at her core an unwarmed place and some at least of the same rage I felt. In her family too she had gone unprotected and felt unwanted.

11/13/91

I think I may be on the verge of some memory about a prostitution ring. Porn too?

11/14/91

L. and I had a little spat — her organizing me to pour concrete for her shed without asking — I felt furious and then a couple of hours later it was over and we made up. Healthy anger.

11/19/91

Saw Rich. Memory: I felt a man above me, saw money, notes being counted out, were they pound notes? no, Deutsch marks — the riding stables again in Germany — my resistance to going there, my mother's pressure.

Oh, the Saturday morning rides — all these men and me, stopping for schnapps at a bar, then on the way back — being passed around from man to man

back on the horse, very sore

sure my mother knew.

Perhaps they paid her as well as me.

At some point SM type stuff — me being beaten with a riding crop?

Very complicated mess of emotions with SM stuff — humiliation, being turned on, feeling small, wanting to be taken care of, feeling very split — under it all this horror of knowing my mother knew.

Anger in taking the money and despair — it signified my consent.

I had to write this stuff down for Rich because I couldn't make the words happen.

The fear of craziness — I felt so crazy then — I'd come back from the "ride" and Mum would say, "How was your ride darling?" and I'd look at her and hate her and already not know why, where the feelings were coming from, and just want to drink.

It didn't come as a complete surprise, this memory. I'd felt it surfacing. A few weeks previously another ritual abuse survivor had told me about turning tricks as a teenager, saving money to get away from home and the cult. I'd thought, much too vehemently, "No, I don't believe you. You're lying. You didn't do that."

The most shocking part of this new memory for me was the realization that my mother had known and had perhaps even made money off the transaction herself.

Throughout my childhood I heard my mother say to my brother, "Grow up and be a rich man so you can look after your mother in her old age," and to me, "Grow up and marry a rich man so you can" etc. This was the reality of the world she grew up in. In one way or another men exchanged money for the use of a woman's body — for sex, for reproduction, for housework.

My mother believed in traditional gender roles, she believed women were different but equal, holding the power behind the throne, a power rooted in beauty and the desire a woman could arouse in men. Women should depend on men, she said, men are the breadwinners.

I refused her version of the world, I despised it and in some ways I threatened it.

I think my mother enjoyed knowing I was prostituting myself. I think she enjoyed humbling her oh so intellectual daughter, just as she enjoyed punishing her daughter the queer, the one who had dared to fall in love with another woman.

11/26/91

Saw Rich — v. painful — I began to think how the cult was involved in a circle of pornography and prostitution catering to perverse tastes only I couldn't — again — make the word prostitution come out — tried and tried, stammered a bit — like last week — not somehow my own emotional charge but programming — okay, breathe — what threats did they use? What am I afraid of?

1) Whatever you saw will be evidence against you.

2) We'll get your mother.

3) We'll get your brother — immediate image of a boy — not Bill — being tortured, burned over and over with hot wire(?) — threat to his eyes.

Oh God.

Okay — finally able to speak, slow and strange at first — I was given some kind of job in the prostitution set up — watching over a room of young boys — men would come and pick one and take him away, sometimes just next door — brutal rape, sometimes boys came back with cane marks on their backs and legs, sometimes I didn't see them again. We could hear [what went on in the next room.] I read a book. I didn't want to feel. I wanted to save money to get away but everything I did trapped me further and further.

Terrible feeling — why didn't I run away? — Rich thinks I'm a horrible person — the black hole — asking him for reassurance — (don't please God refuse to give it.)…

A roomful of young boys, a girl watching over them, another room next door where men have sex with the boys: where? Where was this? Typing out these entries I think no, this couldn't really have happened. I feel almost sure it didn't. I look ahead in the journal. There are more improbable situations. None of it happened. I should call my publisher, explain, apologize. How embarassing. What a waste of all this work, two years writing this book. And the memories, three agonizing years. The memories. Could I have faked those? Only imagined what happened? The knowledge in my body, the way the images came, how they fitted together. Rich believes me. Liz too. Clair's not sure. I don't want anyone to believe I sat and read while boys I was guarding were taken away and raped.

Where could it have happened? I was 16 or 17 (if it happened.) In Germany then. In the Schloss? Is it so completely improbable? I think about Jenny (my lover just before I got sober) who graduated from Vassar and went to work in a brothel in San Francisco. She and the other women walked in a circle around the living room so the john could choose which one he wanted. This happened in an ordinary house in an ordinary neighborhood. Nanette, another lover, worked in a brothel in Maryland when she was fifteen. She was a dominatrix. The FBI chased her out of the state when a senator became one of her clients. It all happens somewhere, the porn, the prostitution, and it happens secretly and men are willing to spend a lot of money to get what they desire.

In my twenties I repeatedly chose as lovers women who had worked as prostitutes. Knowing other people who have passed through the shadowlands of this culture helps me trust my memories. I have no reason to deny the reality of their experiences. And so I come back to the same place. Each individual element I remember of the ritual abuse has already happened and been seen to happen in the world: prostitution, pederasty, cannibalism, torture, murder, incest, brainwashing. It is the combination of all these elements in one practice which feels so hard to believe.

The sheer organization of it is hard to credit. What about the boys, I think, where did they come from? They could have been the children of cult members, or runaways perhaps, stray children. Why should the cult be unable to arrange situations that the regular prostitution industry seems to manage easily enough? Businesses organize all sorts of complex transactions, and there are executive salaries to be made in supplying the more perverse

Chapter Twenty-four

demands in the marketplace of sex.

As a matter of fact I suspect that the cult financed its activities through pornography and prostitution. I can't prove it, it just makes sense to me. (The British NSPCC also suggested a link between ritual abuse rings and the prostitution and pornography industries in its report on ritual abuse.) I notice that I have particular difficulty believing memories having to do with prostitution, which in a way ought to be the easiest part to believe since we all know it goes on. Perhaps the cult put special effort into brainwashing in this area, precisely because a kid talking about prostitution might be believed where one talking about people eating babies would be dismissed.

I think too that the prostitution I remember happening indoors, as opposed to in the woods around the riding stables, did take place in the Schloss, and there seems to be an especially strong prohibition in me against talking about the Schloss. It must have been both risky and useful to the cult, to have a place fitted out for their activities. Obviously such a place would have to be kept very secret.

But what about me? It's one thing to think about prostitution out there on the street, another to work out how an upper-middle class teenager at home on holiday from boarding school was involved. How does it relate to what I know about my day-to-day life at home? That's the bit I find hardest to put together. Was this a regular "job"? I think I called it a job because I got paid, and it happened more than once but not often. Usually I spent the evening in my room, lying on my bed, reading and drinking. How can I not remember evenings spent reading in a brothel catering to sadistic paedophiles?

In among the pages of my journal for early 1992 I find a transcription of three journal entries written fifteen years earlier. One is from March 1977, when I was 18 and living on my own in London. I'd gone to have dinner with Jessica Turner, the woman who had lived opposite us in Germany. (It was through Jessica's son Dan that Evelyn had sent me the message saying my parents were returning her letters.)

> *We talked a little of mother who was apparently thoroughly unpleasant about Jessica behind her back in Germany — I hardly remember — my memory disposal mechanism at work dealing with a very unpleasant time in my life.*

The other two entries are the only entries made while I visited my parents in North Africa after hitching around Europe with Katarina.

8/27/77

"Man, if though knowest what thou dost, thou art blessed; but if thou knowest not, thou art accursed and a transgressor of the law." (Luke VI, 4. Codex Bezae)

8/28/77

I wonder why I remember so clearly and with such discomfort my father pointing out that if I did not accept a Christian morality I must seek some other. My reply was that one must never do anything that will hurt anyone else (all this at the time of the Evelyn troubles). In saying this I had no objectivity, I spoke only from my own dark pain and did not see the pain I was causing — perhaps I carry the guilt of this yet. I know that an inner turbulence when I think of this makes me turn my mind away rather than face it. It, and my other 'crimes' such as shoplifting, used to haunt me in my dreams, fill me with a dreadful dark and sweaty anxiety. This they no longer do very frequently but not I think because I have faced and accepted them which is what I should do if I forced myself. Such thoughts and memories react with my conscious mind as do two south polarized magnets pushed together — mutual repulsion in a strange slithery way. To accept and learn from one's own guilt is so necessary if one is not to be weighed down and perhaps even destroyed and yet, and yet...

I have strayed, as usual, from my initial idea but never mind. It is strange that every new idea that emerges in my consciousness makes the past recede into some swirling and uncomfortable mist.... I know that at the age of 12 or 13 I had a similar sensation of emergence after the dreadful two years at the day school.

The truancy, shoplifting, pretending to be sick etc. are so far away and dark that I know only the inner pain I felt then, particularly as, towards the end, I knew I was in a dream from which I must wake, a chrysalis from which I must emerge.

I think that my fourteenth year, the Upper Fourth at Westwood, was a well-earned respite when I had friends and was away from my parents (did being away at boarding school aid my emergence or was it purely incidental?) But slowly I was submerged again — that feeling that I was a divided person so different at home and school, that I had perhaps no real me, the feeling that my ability to detach myself — to *become a pew stand or a dry leaf called Humphrey — was becoming frighteningly real, that "I" was no longer really in my body.*

I wrote that long before I remembered any kind of abuse, when I thought there had been no violence of any kind in my family. It helps and saddens me, to see myself struggling to name and make sense of my "memory disposal mechanism." It is not so hard for me to believe that the person who wrote these paragraphs was living a life divided between grotesque abuse and apparent ordinariness.

In the end perhaps the main reason for the wave of disbelief that came over me as I was typing out the journal excerpts about my "job" watching over the roomful of boys, is the oldest, simplest reason for denial: I don't want to face my guilt. The Schloss was the center of activities during the time when I was being transformed from victim to perpetrator. Was some of my shame at this memory an acknowledgment that, furious at my brother for being protected, a part of me was glad to see other young boys being hurt, all the while thinking I was doing what I could to protect Bill?

Chapter Twenty-five

11/27/91

Woman at the SIA meeting tonight — Kate — who came to the Newcomers' last week — so SEXY — lots of long thick auburn hair, severe glasses and a little lipstick, a white sweater, oh I don't know — quintessential wild big-passioned straight girl with intense intelligence — I was moved by her, liked her last week, more so this week — felt her looking at me after the break a little — felt me looking at her — felt too the surge of vital force through me, that high wild sense of being alive.

Uh oh. I don't have to act, can try to enjoy the sensation of lust — just as I did this time last year with Sandy.

L.'s and my anniversary time.

Hmm.

But I do love the feeling.

It helped then to have sex with Liz.

Oh but I want wild we don't know each other but we see into each other's souls sex.

How sexy long hair is — how sexy women who use femininity, claim it as their own.

12/3/91

Saw Rich — no tears — a piecing together — my attraction to Kate at the meeting —

to a cut off part of you? said Rich

Mm yes. Femininity (but not as victim); vulnerability; sensuality.

Later

Outside the trees stagger under coats of ice. Feeling of being alone *with experiences too weird, shameful, horrible to tell — must have been how I felt then.*

So good to come into L.'s house, with light and the smell of fresh baked bread and sleeping cats. Unfreezing — the tree shedding its ice aches. I hear tree branches coming down.

12/5/91

Connection at the SIA meeting — my trouble and rage re being taken care of by a Higher Power stem partly from the messy confusion of being hurt/feeling taken care of which is coming up around sexuality and prostitution.

Which makes me think of my fury at Susan [when I was a year sober and getting involved with Nanette and SM], her saying because I'd been abused I didn't know what pleasure was — my sense of pleasure was distorted.

And sure enough there's Kate who I'm drawn to talking this week about compulsively going out looking for rough sex — wanting to be hurt.

Wanting to be hurt: my friend Susan was arrogant but accurate when she told me my sense of pleasure was distorted. Somehow, out of the whole scramble of messages in all the different abuse, I'd ended up with an association between being hurt and feeling taken care of. Perhaps it started with my mother using me to masturbate and then punishing me. Perhaps it was when I was three and, after days of pretending I didn't exist, she was raping me with a hairbrush and I didn't want her to stop because the pain was better than nothingness. Perhaps it was a kind of self-protection, to translate people hurting me, which I couldn't avoid, into people taking care of me. Perhaps it was simply that the people who took care of me, hurt me. Physical pain was sometimes a relief: compared to the emotional and spiritual pain it felt safe. Probably it was all of these and more.

I discovered, through my brief involvement in the lesbian SM scene, that physical pain could be like a drug for me. I had an appetite for it. I could imagine craving more and more. That frightened me. People say it has to do with endorphins, that pain triggers the release of the body's own opiates. Runners get high on the same body chemistry. But there is a psychological dimension too: it is pain in a particular context that is desirable. Even the most dedicated masochist does not enjoy stubbing her toe.

Chapter Twenty-five

I find it difficult to write about wanting to be hurt. The concept of female masochism has been used too often to blame women for men's violence. But there is something in me that wants to get hurt and I know I'm not alone. I've listened to a lot of women — far more women than men — talk about the same tangle of feelings.

I suspect that the opposition between masochist and sadist is false, that in fact they are two sides of a coin, the impulse to hurt and the impulse to get hurt. This is not a palatable thought. I share the general moral prejudice in favor of masochism: "It's okay so long as the only person you hurt is yourself." But my hunch is that masochism is, in part, a way to control one's sadistic impulses. When Kate went out compulsively looking for rough sex, wasn't she perhaps looking for an outlet for her rage, someone to express it for her, and at the same time a way to contain it, to protect other people from it by taking it into herself?

Rage again. The desire to hurt someone. I have an impulse to hurt somebody else as I was hurt, a longing to end my loneliness by making other people feel the way I feel, a part of me that would enjoy having the power to inflict pain.

It is difficult to admit this. Any violent impulse or behavior I find in myself feels like proof that I am a perpetrator, one of Them.

12/10/91

Saw Rich.

Eventually closed my eyes, saw an elderly German man, grandfatherly, white hair, a girl (me?) in a dirndl, a pink and white gingham bouncy skirt, a bonnet even. He gives her money and then he spanks her. Under her child's clothing she wears a red satin corset and garter belt.

When I am trying to think how to say this to Rich, to get the words to come, another image crosses and recrosses, of me having sex with a young boy — of us being watched — my brother I think.

I tell about the girl (me) — how I was caught up emotionally — grandparents giving me money signified love — ... such a mess of feelings.

But worse the sex with Bill(?) Grief and falling down and down into the vortex of self-hatred. "Help," I made myself say, but Rich didn't hear, said "What?" I couldn't reply, just prayed and prayed for him to help stop me falling into the pit of self-hate which he didn't. My hands and arms started to shake. I felt an almost independent desire in my hand to hit my face, to hurt myself, smash myself up — hating the part of me that did this, Very frightening journey down. Belatedly I got Rich to help a little and we talked about needing him to jump in sooner and not necessarily at my request — to provide a view of land.

As a teenager I used to sit in my bedroom in Germany dripping hot wax on my skin. And once, drunk, I cut my wrist with a razor blade. It wasn't a serious suicide attempt — I held the razor in my left hand and I'm right-handed — though I still have the scars from it. I remember the relief of cutting into my own flesh.

Hurting myself was a way of expressing my rage while protecting other people from it, and it was a way of punishing the perpetrator in me, but there was something else going on too. I couldn't integrate the knowledge that I was both perpetrator and victim. It takes time to grow a self capacious enough to hold the knowledge that I am the hurter and the hurt. In the meantime there was a split, a contradiction. Either I was a perpetrator or I was a victim. For a moment, in the act of hurting myself I bridged that gap: I was both.

I haven't had to struggle as an adult with cutting myself the way my friend Leslie and other survivors I know have, but I think, from what they have told me, that they too are trying, by cutting themselves, to hold their pieces together.

Compulsive cutting and other forms of self-mutilation are fairly common behaviors among survivors of sexual abuse, but they are particularly common among ritual abuse survivors — precisely because, I suspect, ritual abuse cults make sure their victims also feel like perpetrators.

12/18/91

No Rich yesterday, series of mishaps, a snow storm.
I feel out of sorts today.
Denis has Karposi's sarcoma in his throat. I took lunch to Sarah Johnson who just had a mastectomy, was organizing an AA meeting for Karen who's still in bed after surgery for cancer on her labia, and Rich was called away because one of the congregation was killed in a car crash.
Yikes.
I feel our vulnerability as bodies so strongly these days... feel more tender towards bodies now.
Powder blue sky, powder snow.

Chapter Twenty-five

I love the shadows, every hummock mapped in its relation to the sun.

Full moon and Solstice 12/21/91
Raw and sad tonight — feel the two years of bruising memory, how even when I'm cheerful and busy (or cheerful and idle) some part of me is swimming with the monsters, monsters with their familiar, familial faces, their brutality. It is still so hard to see it all at once.

I'm reading Louise de Salvo's book about V. Woolf and sexual abuse. Stunning some of it, how it was all there, so visible and unseen, irritating when she stretches evidence too far.

1/2/92
Saw Rich.
Talked of oddness of things coming up and I feel them a bit and then they sink back underwater and I go about my daily business but aware something is going on under the surface.
Winter like, only the roots alive, vital signs slowing.
Rich saying Jung says there is a first stage of life, building up the individual ego but then often lose touch with the ocean, get just the island aware of itself, second stage is a surrender of individual will to something greater
— but not the cult who posed as a false ocean.
Turn my life over to my spirit.
Yes, said Rich, to the spirit within me which is also not-me.
A kind of denseness to the self, like rock. I've been swimming underwater round the island, touching rock under water.
Rock and water.
I feel a little calmer for writing things down, though still unsure what is moving me.

1/7/92
Dream: I saw an ocean and Sudha and Parvati's [Sudha's daughter's] heads sticking up like islands. I thought, they're sitting ducks.

All through December and January of 91/92 I felt as if I were swimming underwater. My center of gravity was somewhere deeper than my conscious self. I've had patches of time like that before and since.

Ordinarily I work hard to keep up my sense of separate selfhood, my feeling of agency. I am hypervigilant, on red alert for any threats to my precious individuality. This is hardly surprising, given the effort the cult made to take it from me, but it is exhausting and stressful. I experience the island of individuated self as a sitting duck, an easy target. The solution, mostly, is to spend a lot of time on the shoreline, where land and water meet — in dreams and poems and passing thoughts — but sometimes, and this was one of those times, I need to dive in, feel the rock from the water not the water from the rock.

In this particular time of feeling that I was underwater, I think I was undergoing some kind of initiation, an initiation into womanhood, in a way. My strong attraction to Kate (who, probably fortunately, left for San Francisco two weeks later) was one of the currents drawing me under water, and Kate bore a certain similarity to a number of my past girlfriends, women I'd been drawn to because they seemed so much more at ease with being women than I was. There had been an addictive quality to most of those relationships: I was looking for a missing part of myself and I needed whoever it was at the time if I was to feel whole. There was also, often, in those women, a quality of turbulent sexuality which reminded me of my mother.

This particular initiation, this descent into the labyrinth, had to do not only with an entry into womanhood but also an entry into knowledge, in particular knowledge about that place inside me and in other women that seemed to want to be hurt. Somehow it wasn't a surprise to discover that Kate, to whom I felt such a strong draw, was struggling with a compulsion to go out looking for rough sex. I needed to lose my innocence about this masochism, to face the fact that, inside the impulse to hurt myself lay coiled the wish to hurt other people.

Seeing this in myself was bound up with facing my mother's sadism and her victimhood. In part my refusal to be a woman had been a way of saying I was not like her. Acknowledging that I was, like her, a woman, felt like acknowledging that I too had both sadist and victim in me.

1/18/92

Strange sense as I was cooking supper — seeing Mum cooking (as she was in the Mill House?) — the most vivid sense of her presence I've had in years. So this is the woman who did all these terrible things. Some movement of acceptance in me. I kept on thinking about her, a calm intensity, while my supper sat on the plate in front of me (potato and carrot and salad and cold roast beef — fitting tribute to her cooking.) I wondered if she were dying or in danger. I found myself thinking about forgiving her — not as abstract as that, picturing her looking happy, joyful — could I be glad to see her so? Yes and then no and then another layer of yes — forgiveness an act of will said the preacher in Levitt's Corner church — accepting the sense of her as sick I found myself acknowledging what I had done to her, my hatred and rage — how the circle had turned (as she once turned it on Granny) — and I asked her forgiveness for my part. I called her Mum.

And then it was gone and I was eating my supper, thinking a little about the Second World War and how Mum's story is bound up with the scars of war, the killing of her father — what was it like to be a young child in that maelstrom — what sense of safety in the world?

Such an odd, strong but unemphatic tone to this experience. Oh, I also realized and said, "I have hated and loved you more than I will ever hate or love another woman" and knew that was true and said also "I love you" — as an adult somehow, not only the kids.

The longing for connection with my mother, when I let myself feel it, is, in its depths, a longing to dissolve my boundaries, to join with her again. To hold onto my separate selfhood, I fight my longing, fiercely.

It was no coincidence that, immediately after talking to Rich about the experience of my mother's presence in my house, I remembered the following experience:

Closed my eyes — I am laughing hysterically, wild-eyed, hair tangled, a man slaps me — after that everything is very close up, bits of faces, body parts, a frenzy, my rage held in this circle of men, a crazy lust, a loosing of the bounds of self — the unhooping of the self, the staves fall outward — a kind of safety to release the bodily experiences of years of abuse.

Once you have known this level of coming apart, of abandon, you no longer have the ordinary boundaries.

Somewhere in here got onto my mother watching and enjoying pain pushing me past the bounds — her pleasure in watching me experience the collapse of self (at the end one is left punctured, deflated — after being sex, being rage, being lust one is left being nothing.)

How can one forgive someone who did that with pleasure?

Don't bother about that, look for it in yourself, says the voice and

I realize on a smaller scale, making love to someone, when they reach the point of abandon, there is sometimes a sense of power — I made them do this.

Rich identified but said that wasn't why he was doing it in the first place.

(What difference does that make?)

The thirst for abandon — a place of renewal, death and rebirth — surrender of self, hence religious links — a very deep thirst in me, a longing to push the island back under the water.

Not surprising, says Rich, considering the knowledge you have to bear consciously, what is growing on that island.

Is this Thanatos, the death wish, the longing for annihilation?

I do go on feeling in some way corrupted — once you've had these intense experiences you can't unknow them — it's like somebody who's always traveled on foot traveling by car for the first time: the experience that it's possible changes everything.

I don't mind the knowledge in a way, am glad of it as a writer — but I'm not sure how one lives with it.

Healing from ritual abuse has taken me into the bowels of this culture, to the core question of what we do with the shadow, individually and collectively. Reason is a weak flashlight in these realms, relying on it merely prevents one's eyes from adjusting to the dark. Dreams, intuitions, memories are the thread in this labyrinth.

Over and over my dreams during this time probed my relationship with the shadow — most often in the form of an angry young man — and they underscored the necessity of ambiguity. Everything alive can go either way, they said in their different ways, everything has the potential for light and for dark. Consider anger, consider sex. If you try to make things go only one way, you kill the life force, and you yourself will turn to stone.

The dream image which has stayed with me is a pattern of four fish painted on the panels of a hexagonal summer house. The fish, tails out, noses not meeting at the center but interlocking, made a pattern that was both compact and alive. It had something of the movement of a swastika, but the fish were delicately painted, in the style of a Chinese watercolor, and somehow humorous.

Even now, picturing that image, I feel a prickling, an electric response in my solar plexus. It has a sort of specific gravity. It comes from the shoreline where conscious and unconscious meet but it's not

• CHAPTER TWENTY-FIVE •

just flotsam, tangled and salt-stained. It feels shaped, artful. It feels as if it exerts a magnetic pull, as if it is capable in some way of repatterning me.

I think it is, for me, an image of wholeness, that pattern. It represents a system which is both stable and alive, whether that system is an individual psyche, an ecosystem, or an entire society. A swastika-like shape, delicately painted. A shape like a swastika only, instead of "feet" which point to the left or the right (the way of the dark or the light in many traditions), the tails of the fish point both ways at once.

Chapter Twenty-six

1/31/92

We talked about calling the lawyer, doing the agreement. L. said she hadn't, feeling neither of us had enough money — she figured it would cost $500-600 — oh shit — felt the bottom dropping out — was crying, hugging Esau, then L. touching me and me talking about feeling it'll be taken away at the last minute, I won't really be able to have it [the house and land], and then Esau pounces at Peter and Liz's screaming something at him over and over (three times), advancing on him, and I'm screaming at her "You can't do that to my dog" and she stops and I'm sobbing and she's yelling about how her cats don't feel safe in her own house.

I cry and cry (I don't know what she does) — going down the pit again and praying — eventually can say I'm sorry I yelled at you and she's talking about the bloody animals.

I say it felt v. scary to go from kneeling on the floor sobbing into Esau's furry back to a moment of comfort from her to her advancing on him, raging. She muttered she could see how that would be scary.

I feel v. uncared for.

She feels exhausted.

I feel utterly alone again — we hug and I say it seems silly for us both to feel so alone — she says she just feels exhausted and desperate, pulls away then says she doesn't mean to push me away like that.

I can't tidy away the feelings so easily — I watch myself falling down and down the pit of utter aloneness, talk to L., the intensity of feeling in my voice then, saying I don't know what to do to get away from them, they're getting their claws into me, I don't know how to get away — the naked desperation of that shakes me — L. saying but you *did get away, that's not now. I know, I know, but then the only way in the end was to kill myself.*

Nobody will help is the strongest feeling.

I don't like feeling grabby and ungrateful.

Jesus.

That's the first time I've screamed at L. in almost four years, since our one and only dramatic fight on the street.

2/4/92

Something I can't bear about lying under that warm big soft comforter [Liz's mother gave her for Christmas], L's face so happy — looking taken care of.

& Jesus I grew up white and upper-middle class — guess at some of this fury in people who didn't.

Called L. and asked if she'd come down because I felt v. alone and she did and we sat in the armchair and talked ....

How she also feels alone — with building her shed for example.

I see then that I feel about time as she does about money — scarcity mentality, hoarding, not enough for what I need — don't know how to make more.

It helps to see this.

We agreed that maybe what's going on is a shift to more partnership — she says she's gotten so used to being so careful around boundaries she's not quite sure how to move, change.

Sense too of her depression, of how much her everyday living is a struggle — what I do have is energy. (I'd rather, given the choice, have energy than money.)

2/16/92

Congregational Church, Montague.

"Dear God, When we trust in You, we can stand firm, nothing can hurt us. We thank you for Your help. Amen." The prayer for children's time — a fury in me — don't bloody well lie to children and then muse in your sermon about how to teach young people about God, waffle on about woe and tragedy and then say when we trust in God nothing can harm us.

What's a kid who has been hurt supposed to make of all this? That they haven't believed enough.

Arrant nonsense.

In a religion whose central symbol is the crucifixion — exactly the

Chapter Twenty-six

tension between real human suffering and faith in a power which does not protect us from suffering.

The service started out with a particularly revolting Victorian hymn to the tune of *Adeste Fideles,* full of polysyllabic assurances from the omnipotent God that He tries us only to refine our gold, burn away the dross.

Oh fury in me.

2/19/92

Saw Rich.

Talked mainly about beginning to let out the inconvenient, messy, angry, needy child I've kept packed away — fear I'd alienate people — under it all I want Rich to be my parent.... Do I really? Part of me does, wants to know life as a child in a safe home and is angry that I can't.

He says that self grows up quickly when allowed out into sunshine and air.

I felt a little like he was going to get rid of me before I'd even been born.

I'm embarrassed by some of these journal entries. I wish that when Liz said she was feeling exhausted and desperate I had said, "Oh you poor darling, of course you are. I'm sorry this is so hard for you too," instead of going down into my own pit again to focus on my desperation. Liz could have ignored me, gone away and looked after herself, but that would have been a violation of her own compassion. In my neediness I put her in positions where her kindness led her to abandon herself. Her anger at this came out indirectly: my dog was threatening her cats. They didn't feel safe in their own home. Meanwhile Liz was getting more depressed.

I'm not sure how I could have behaved differently and at the same time I can see what enormous stress I was putting on Liz. I saw it then and felt bad and tried to talk about it. She said mostly that no, it wasn't me, it was the ritual abuse that was putting so much stress on both of us. In that way she shouldered some of the burden of it, but with far less support than I had. She had organized a group for partners of sexual abuse survivors, and that helped some, though mostly she came back grateful for how good our relationship was by comparison, which was nice but not perhaps useful. She had also been involved, for a number of years, in a self-help network for people who have a tendency to lose themselves in other people. But still, she didn't have a Rich to talk to, nor did she find it easy to know what was going on inside herself.

Looking back, I wish I'd pulled out of child mode into my adult self, recognizing that the brief eruption of her rage was a sign that she had gone beyond the limits of what she could give freely. Friends remind me that it was her responsibility to take care of herself, but that's a legalistic version of love and human interaction, a helpful simplification, a rule of thumb: it doesn't take into account the tides that pull us about under the surface.

Liz was the youngest in her family and had been bullied mercilessly by her two brothers. I felt this child clearly in Liz, and found it easier to love her than Liz did herself. I wanted to show her the world was a safe enough place for her to come out and play, but just when she was beginning to do that, I started to remember ritual abuse, reminding her how terribly unsafe the world is. It cannot have been easy for her child self to separate the messenger from the message. I was the big bad dog who made the house unsafe for the little animals. At the same time I was one of the little animals myself and Liz warmed me with her love, played with me and praised me, while her own child self huddled, neglected and miserable again.

An ideal in which we each parent only ourselves is both chilly and unrealistic, but it is dangerous not to take on the responsibility of being one's own parent. For Liz it was less painful to be a parent to me than to deal with her own feelings about her self as a child — that she was fat, drab, smelly, cowardly, angry. For me, having to be my own parent meant accepting that I'd had the only mother and father I was going to have. I could not bear the full weight of that loss, the feeling of having been ripped off, and all the self-hatred that went with it. A part of me was still opting for the fantasy in which I am the child and you, whoever you may be, are finally going to give me what I did not get and still need.

When I was fourteen I read Margaret Mead's *Coming of Age in Samoa*. She described a society in which the burdens and pleasures of childcare were spread widely: children kept an eye on each other, an aunt took in a child who was having difficulty with her parents, grandparents lent a hand. It was a revelation. I was aghast at the stupidity of the nuclear family and longed for something different.

Through SIA and AA and a network of friends, I tried, as an

Chapter Twenty-six

adult, to make for myself an extended family. I didn't want to need too much from Liz and Rich. But I didn't grow up in such a family. When I'm frightened and hurt I try to get what I had as a child, what I almost had, what I feel angrily I should have had: my mother's love and primary attention. The pit of need I go into feels as if it pulls me back to being three years old. That was when I had my mother most to myself: my brother wasn't born yet and my father was only home at the weekend. Having my mother to myself was hardly an unmixed blessing: she used me to masturbate herself and hurt me afterwards.

But still I hunger for what I knew of love as a child — I remember the red and white material of the pushchair my mother wheeled me about in when I was two and three, and the toy shop window where we stood and looked, and the gollywog I longed for and which she eventually bought me, having saved a few pennies each week out of the groceries money, and Big Ben, the Old English Sheepdog on wheels with a red handle to push him along, a dog the size of Esau in whose fur I buried my face when I was upset. But just as it is too much for one adult to try to feed that hunger now, it was probably too much then. For my mother it meant giving too much, giving more than she could afford. Women are supposed to do that. It is supposed to come naturally. The rage it engenders is buried, turning to depression. Or, as in her case, erupting into violence.

My mother's abuse of me when I was a young child was not just a result of her own childhood, it grew out of her situation, an ordinary enough situation for the 1950's: a woman in an unfamiliar place, deprived of adult company, without transport or money, alone with a three-year-old day in and day out.

So we were both victims of a humanly untenable version of the family. Still it leaves me with the hunger for what I almost had. What to do with it, this wanting too much? The fear of being too much is deep in me. I was too much for my mother. That wasn't my fault. But nor exactly was it hers. The fear makes it difficult to take in what I am given, so the pit sometimes feels bottomless, to me, to other people. What will be enough? Enough love, enough care, enough attention?

Chapter Twenty-seven

2/27/92

I notice I haven't recorded that L. transferred the land to me on the 22nd, signed the deed at Donna's office, hand poised, pen tip touching the paper, she kept asking Donna questions. Come on, sign, I thought.

Took L. out for an extravagant meal that night.

No big deal in the end.

3/2/92

The other day I realized with surprise how vividly I could remember the countryside surrounding the Mill House, plants and fields and feel of the land. I treasure this clarity and am startled by it. Something integrated.

And then, cresting the anxiety of the day — pre-menstrual tension, the quickening of the book in me — I wrote in an hour the whole shape of the plot I think — it flowed out, pieces falling into place and working backwards and forwards — a shape which will allow me to talk about RA and trust and reality and horror and daily beauties. A little while later I found my period had come.

It felt like working in concert with my body.

3/3/92

Saw Rich.

Can't talk — watching a man being crucified — the Schloss banquet hall — high stone walls — a lot of people — a Jewish man in his 30s (33?) with a beard is nailed to a cross. I watch but as if I am a solitary eye looking out of a sort of box, no feelings. After he's been hanging (I think) they castrate him and slice up his penis very finely into — wafers — passed around some of the people, including me — "This is my body" — bawdy atmosphere.

This memory shuddering, half-retching, yet somehow not fully feeling it.

They collect the blood from the wound, pass it in a silver cup/tankard (?)

3/4/92

Hard time today — not surprising I suppose — walked the dogs — lovely spring day — worked at Cathy's a bit — home for lunch I felt raw and empty and alone with the gruesome details — inclined to tough it out — go check the sap buckets — I called Erica and felt better.

Oh dear, this vulnerable needy self — at a time when L is — self-confessedly — a bit withdrawn, indrawn.

Where do they get the victims from? Eastern European immigrant? Shiny cheap old-fashioned suit.

3/10/92

Saw Rich.

Talked of the brief image last night, pale face upturned, blood and thick bloodiness dropping onto it. I turned then from the image, afraid of it, afraid I'd start to see blood everywhere and be crazy. Now I was quiet and waited, as I almost always do at some point, and then my mind began fighting — practical objections — a blond boy, 13 or 14, either refused the "wafers" of penis or gagged — they stripped the clothes from him — a white robe? — and he was forced to kneel under the cross, his face upturned — a spear point under his chin — while someone with a billhook ripped open the crucified man's innards so they spilled down on the boy's face.

Then — and this is where my practical objections grew loudest — how could a boy get an erection at such a time — I was to fuck him for his first time — I lay under him, a piece of human intestine slippery under my right shoulder. The smell of offal.

I felt then as if, in my remembering, I was putting on an act which I watched from elsewhere, play acting. I'd felt earlier odd dislocations in time/space in the process of remembering — falling into gaps between moments/events.

Christ.

"When did her mind split?"

Chapter Twenty-seven

Later Rich said perhaps to perceive yourself as play acting, as not really doing what you were doing, was the only way for you to retain your integrity — I cried then — somebody seeing what I have seen.

3/11/92
A wild and blustering March morning, mild and wet and English. I found the first snowdrop here two days ago. I feel drained by this new memory.

I want some way to express it in the world, the presence of this — look, this happened to me... this happens — sometimes I hate my own ability to carry on, day to day — the old longing to break, find an edge to go over, say no, look, this affected me, this terrible thing which is absorbed into the fabric of day-to-day life.

3/19/92
Outwrite Conference, Boston
Dorothy Allison gave a wonderful keynote address: "I want my writing to be so good it can break the heart of the world and heal it."

How she wrote out of rage, the emotional start of the stories [in Trash*] was I hate you. Now, harder (for her), writes out of grief, out of caring. I miss you.*

To keep what is lost, what is forgotten.

A woman now with access to her full range of emotions. Gone is that hard doughy quality in her face.

"Write for me.

"Write the truth, the hard, terrifying truth of your life."

I didn't want to write about ritual abuse. I didn't want to have to go on thinking about it. I didn't want to make it any more real to myself than it was already. But I observed that I was going to do it. I felt a book forming in me and I decided not to abort it.

At the Outwrite conference, a conference of gay and lesbian writers, I attended a session in which a friend of Clair's, Janis, was to read her poetry. Before we got to Janis though, a woman named Sandra read a story in which the narrator killed her father, mutilated him, then cooked and ate his penis. The words were venomous, triumphant, sticky as blood. Clair leaned forward, blocking her ears. I tried to cope by writing in my journal as she was reading but in the end I walked out. I went and stood in the bathroom, holding my hands under cold running water until the shaking stopped.

Not half an hour before Sandra's reading I had listened to descriptions of the terrible brutality inflicted on Native peoples by the Europeans as writers of color responded to the quincentennial of Columbus' "discovery" of America. I didn't enjoy listening to those descriptions either, but I was grateful to the writers for giving me that information, and I felt anger and grief and disgust and shame at what had happened. Why was Sandra's reading so different? A friend of hers tells me Sandra thinks of her writing as revealing the violence and depravity of this culture, not endorsing it. And yet neither I nor the friends I was with could escape the feeling that her story was a glorification of the violence she described, an exploitation of the gruesome. Listening felt like being implicated. Other people in the audience were laughing. Perhaps they hadn't listened to the details of genocide half an hour earlier.

How to write about violence without doing violence? It comes back to telling the truth and telling it all, to making room in a piece of writing, often but not always through the character of the narrator, for the widest possible range of feelings. In Sandra's story the narrator was the mutilator and there was no other viewpoint, nowhere to stand other than in her crude rage, her vengefulness. Part of what was powerful in the responses by writers of color to the quincentennial, was the way many of them wrote about complex truth, mixed feelings, about being Indian and Spaniard, about complicity as well as oppression.

I thought I was going to write a detective story about ritual abuse. I had read a lot of detective stories when I was eleven and twelve and then again when I started remembering ritual abuse. I liked the English village mysteries best: murder reveals the evil lurking under the surface niceness of village life and then there is a detective (who always survives no matter how many other people are killed) to uncover the secrets and bring about some sort of justice. My detective would be Muriel Norridge, the postmistress in the story Liz and I were inventing on our way up to Maine the day I found I couldn't say, "No, this didn't happen to me." She would want to find out the truth and she would be strong enough to bear it. She would respond with her heart as well as her head. She would be a comfort to me as I wrote and she would cushion the impact on the reader of the atrocities I was describing.

But I discovered, thinking about this, that the idea of giving readers this comfort angered me. I didn't have a Muriel Norridge to look after me when I walked through hell, so why should they? My anger made me look into my motives for writing about the ritual abuse. Perhaps I didn't just want "to break the heart of the world" in order to heal it. Perhaps I wanted to use writing to wound, to inflict on the reader the pain I felt.

The motive underlying this impulse to pass on the pain is the longing to feel less alone, and that I certainly feel. But I do not, in most of myself, want to plunge the reader into the experience of violence. Writing can bring me company in a better way than that. I want my writing to make a bridge between the public, visible world and that world of secret, unthinkable violence, and I want the reader to walk out and meet me there. I don't need more victims, I need more witnesses, people who will look and see, not only with their eyes and minds but with their hearts also.

I want the particulars of my experiences to be known, to be recognized not as unique but as frighteningly more common than any of us want to believe. This is why, in the end, I decided against writing a novel about ritual abuse, not to deprive the reader of the comfort of Muriel Norridge but because part of what I have to say is "This happens, this really happens. In England, in Germany, and here, in your country." I can't make you believe it, but I can at least say what I saw.

It is more frightening for me to tell it this way. I feel so alone when people don't believe me. I tell myself that, if there are people who say the Holocaust — the most well-documented atrocity in history — didn't happen, then of course there will be people who won't believe what I have to say. Sometimes I can't believe it myself. But there the rage returns. I have to believe it. I know it in my body. I don't want to but I have to, otherwise I'm living a lie. Why should other people have the option of turning a blind eye?

In writing not just non-fiction but autobiography I am not only bearing witness, I am witness. I am both the reporter and the reported. I am completely involved in the story — I know the events in my body — and I am exercising judgment as a writer, selecting what of the journals to include, deciding at which point to interrupt the flow of the journals with commentary, where to start a new chapter.

This could easily reproduce for me the split I experienced during the abuse, shrinking me to "a solitary eye looking out of a sort of box, no feelings." I could become the kind of detached detective narrator I used in "The Sea, The Sea," the story I wrote just before I got sober. In that story, the central question was "Why did her mind split?" I barely knew what I meant, and I certainly did not have the answer then, but I described the split clearly enough: on the one hand the detective narrator, rational and detached, modeling herself on Holmes and Hercule Poirot, and on the other, the inchoate, passionate child. The story also imagined the healing of that division, the detective self listening to the child, sleuthing for sense and being told stories from the past, and, in the listening, being brought to the place where land and sea meet, where reason and imagination, logic and emotion, live in the same body.

In a strange way, ten years later, I am living out that story in the writing of this book. I have not made for the reader a fictional detective but, in following the chronology of my journals rather than organizing the information thematically, I have chosen for this book a shape of discovery and made of myself a sort of detective narrator. The story I am telling now is not only the story I uncovered but also the story of how the uncovering transformed the detective. I am no longer a solitary eye looking out of a box, observing. I am in my own story.

I am in my story *and* I can tell it. As much as I needed to bring the observer into the story, I needed also not to become so identified with my story that I would lose the ability to see it and tell it. There were times when I longed to fall apart, to go crazy so that in my being I would bear witness to what happened to me. Functioning, going on with life, felt like collaboration in the silence. To make the wounding visible I felt I had to be the wound. Anything else was a lie.

Writing, I think, helped keep alive the witness self. Without it perhaps I would be a case history, narrated in the "objective" voice of a psychiatrist. To be the narrator in one's own story is to embody not the wound but the healing of the wound.

Chapter Twenty-eight

Just before I went to the Outwrite conference, I dreamt about being in a room where ritual abuse happened. There was a steel countertop and a mahogany ruler or yardstick on which somebody had scratched more calibrations. I knew this detail would eat into me.

Telling Rich about this dream a memory surfaced:

> *A child is being stretched in a modern rack on a stainless steel countertop, a ruler beside him/her (I think of the child as 'it' — never see the sex — keep my eyes pinned on the ruler by the child's shoulder which is pulled out of joint.) There is a camera suspended from the ceiling, filming, the ruler heavily marked so the camera can read it. I have to watch and not react. A tall man stands behind me. He has an erection. Sick monster. Sometimes I focus on his erection, the sensation of it....His hands are on my shoulders except when he moves his right hand to press the button which makes the machine pull the child further apart. The child is screaming then they cut out its (his?) tongue and blood wells from its (his) mouth. The room is like a basement, light from small high windows, the floor and walls white.*

I feel sick and cold and shaky just typing out this memory. It is unbearable in itself and unbearable to admit to myself who that tall man was.

4/7/92

A three-sided sharp spike is driven into the tortured boy's heart. My father watching, standing behind me — comes as the boy dies.

It all goes into me, all of it enters into me — what's in front and behind me.

My father. Who taught me to read, to ride a bike, to swim.

Mining the body for the ultimate sensation.

Jesus.

All the last two weeks I've been thinking — my father, doing these things — and Dad with the wheelbarrow in the garden.

4/12/92

Dream. I am out in rough garden near a bonfire site. A man comes there — I'm not sure if I see him as my father at this point. I see the man as somehow saturnine, a dark, heavy feeling to him — (satanic) — I have been masturbating? or am feeling sexual? — he watching. I ask him to fuck me and he says he doesn't have time — has to get back up to the house — but then he does.

When he's done and has walked away I find, lying on the ground in the half dark, a video camera. I think oh, it will get ruined, lying on the ground out here, and I don't care. I fiddle with it a bit. It's too dark to see the controls. I'm able to see title pictures of what's been filmed — mostly Hollywood thrillers, one sort of game show with a band of men stripping off. The title hides below their waists but the implications are clear. I am glad there is something less innocent on film — proof — but see no RA stuff yet. I'm a bit afraid of what I'll see but then it's stuck on some glitzy movie and I can't get it to move on so try to find the off button and it sort of winds down in mid-film. I wonder if I am ruining the tape.

My father appears again with a flashlight — my father definitely this time — looking for the camera which he takes. I can't find my glasses — do in the end, half buried. I skulk up to the house, looking through the windows, but I don't want to be caught/seen — light and my mother and Bill inside.

4/24/92

The night before last L. went to listen to a Holocaust survivor speak. He told how he escaped being shot with the other children by obeying a voice which told him to hide in the outhouse, burying himself in the shit up to his neck. When it was over he called to the inmates to get him out. There was no water to wash him with as the water was only turned on for half an hour a day.

My heart was pounding, my vision felt funny as I asked L. to stop

talking, I was about to get a flashback. It took a while to calm down.
Aaarg.
Today I'm burying Melanie's water line in 300' of trench, a third of it 2' deep in muddy water. Oh great.

4/28/92

Saw Rich.
Growing sense of Dad's sadism — the missing piece of the tension at home, physical memory of that tension — was Dad hurting Bill in the house?
This is not so dissociated as other memories, more connected to daily life — I felt like an adolescent, thinking about it.
I can't really bear to think about it.

"I just want to cry and watch the bulbs come up," I said to Rich. I needed to go slow, not to try to take control of this terrifying material by hurrying myself through it. There was an old struggle going on: how much did I want to see? That question was there the first day I got sober, sitting in the eye doctor's chair, trying on contact lenses, thinking, "I don't want to see this clearly." In the dream about the camera I couldn't even find my glasses.

I knew I had to face what I was remembering but forcing myself to look at it felt like being forced by my father to watch torture. He had wanted to make me into a recording I/eye like him, a detached observer. Now if I tried to absorb more than I could cope with emotionally, I dissociated and that made me feel like the watcher he'd wanted me to be.

There is a difference between looking for and looking at something. I was always, in life as well as in my dreams, looking for the warmth and light of the family life I missed, looking in from outside, hungrily. My father I associate with looking at things, the camera his tool, his weapon, his protection.

That camera lying in the grass in my dream was not merely symbolic: in the first full memory I had of my father's participation in the ritual abuse, he was the camera man making a snuff film of the murder and dismemberment of a girl. Now there was another camera in the memory of the boy being racked, this time mounted from the ceiling. And again my father was watching.

I think of him watching the death agony of a child, his only response an erection, an orgasm. I feel sick and slightly dizzy and I believe it (and then I don't.) I can believe it in a way I couldn't believe an image of him in a frenzy of blood lust. During the time this memory was surfacing I read an article in the New York Times about the National Front, a neo-Nazi group, holding a dance in the quiet English town of Bury St. Edmonds. It described the dancers, all male, slam dancing themselves into a frenzy while, at the edges of the room, men in suits, the organizers, watched. Not for them the ecstasy and release of the dance, of group violence, that submersion of the separate self in the depths of the collective unconscious. They were interested in harnessing the forces that came from the depths without themselves being sucked in. They didn't get their hands dirty. I thought that was how my father was: an administrator, a scientist of pain.

I was being trained to follow in his footsteps. The story Liz repeated to me about the boy who survived in the concentration camp by immersing himself in shit in the outhouse affected me strongly not just because it reminded me of actual abuse involving shit but also because it gave me a potent symbolic image of how I had myself survived. I was beginning to grasp how I had used sexual abandon, how I had taken cover in the sexual sewage, seeking out sex with my father when I was a teenager, walling off the part of me that didn't want that, didn't want orgies with unknown men, didn't want to be used, to be fucked like an animal.

It wasn't just that, by merging with what threatened me, I avoided being broken, nor that, in the frenzy of sex I could obliterate what I had seen. I tried to use sex to escape the watcher in me. I wrote about the racking memory:

> *I have to watch and not react. A tall man stands behind me. He has an erection. Sick monster. Sometimes I focus on his erection, the sensation of it. (3/18/92)*

Better to be my sexual self than the watcher self. But in the end they weren't separable for me. What I saw in front of me — the boy being murdered — and what I felt behind me — my father coming — went into me, entered me — that's how it felt, like being penetrated. It wasn't pleasurable, far from it. It was the boundarylessness that felt sexual. There was nothing between me and what I saw, what I felt.

When I think about a man who has an erection while he is

Chapter Twenty-eight

watching a child being torn apart by a machine which he controls with the touch of his finger, I think his erect penis is the concentrated expression of all his longing for human connection, all twisted, all reduced to this.

But perhaps that's not it. Perhaps his erection is above all a statement about the eroticism of power. It is not only that power is erotic but also that power uses the erotic to express itself. Sex becomes emblematic, a representation of control and the power to degrade.

Somehow I think both versions are true. Sex becomes the sole locus of the longing for connection with other people and it is emptied of emotional content, rendered abstract.

Either way, everyday life is drained of meaning. There is only sensation to fill the void, sensation sought in sex and violence. The man who feels nothing in the rest of his life gets an erection torturing a child.

But is this man my father? I would rather dwell on my difficult, shameful sexual fantasies than think about what he did, what he wanted. But once I'd had this memory I knew in my gut that what he most wanted to do was to torture young boys. He wanted to watch their pain. This was part of the unconscious life of my family, the water Bill and I swam in. He wanted to hurt Bill. I can't explain how I know this is true. It is confirmed by a myriad unnamed impressions. It simply fits. I think my mother knew it intuitively. Perhaps that was part of why she tried harder to protect Bill than me. I think in a way my father tried to protect him too. I don't think he did act on his sadistic impulses with him overtly, as he did with other boys.

So under the surface of my apparently happy upper-middle class family lay the effort to placate my mother, to keep her stable, and the unspoken knowledge of her abuse of me; and under that lay fear of my father's sadism, our collective need to keep it out of sight and under control. Ritual abuse gave him a way to act on his strongest desires outside the family. In a strange way all the abuse that did happen revolved around something that didn't happen, that everyone tried to make sure wouldn't happen.

Or am I romanticizing him, trying to save my version of him by giving him this much goodness at least, that he tried to protect his son from his desires? I can't be sure that was true. I don't even know for certain that he wasn't actually hurting Bill at home.

And what about his daughter, what about me?

He raped me when I was three and when I was eight or nine and when I was fourteen and fifteen, and then there was the sex when I was seventeen which was rape too only it felt different because I sought it out and it felt warm, a human connection with him, unlike the other times when he was either using me to get back at my mother or kow-towing to her scheme to straighten me out.

There are so many questions. Was it a coincidence that sex which felt like real connection with my father began to happen after the cult had done its gender bending number with me? Was I in some way becoming a psychologically safer object for his desire, being his son but in a woman's body?

Was my mother's venomous hatred of homosexuality due in part to suspicions she had about my father? If so, there is something even more haunting about the thought of her watching her husband fucking her daughter: was it to straighten us both out? She once, when I was about seventeen, started to say something about what the single-sex public (i.e. private) school system did to English men and their sexuality. I cut her off. I recognized the intensity in her voice. She had already tried to hint about the affair she was having with her acupuncturist. I didn't want to hear what she had to say about my father. So she said, "Not Dad of course. He's a wonderful husband." It was patently not what she had been about to say.

That my father got off on watching young boys being hurt does not mean he was homosexual. I'm not sure he had reached the stage of being either homo- or heterosexual. It's as if his primary sexual relationship was with his own child self. Ritualistically he presided over the annihilation of the child, making himself watch it. He was toughening himself as much as me, his "son." He was proving that he had triumphed, but, in the need to prove it, showed he hadn't really. Just as my masochism was in part an effort to control my fury, especially the wish to hurt my brother, perhaps my father's sadism had at its heart an attempt to control his vulnerability.

Perhaps my mother's hint was right, my father had been so brutalized at school that he got stuck, trying endlessly to rid himself of the hurt boy who stood between him and survival. He must have been an outsider, a scholarship boy from a lower middle class family, an easy target. Ashton, the public school I went to, was only about thirty miles away and a similar type of school. The stories I heard there about the way the school was before it went co-ed were pretty horrific, replete with bullying and fagging and caning.

Chapter Twenty-eight

Then too my father's childhood, like my mother's, was dominated by the Second World War — he was born in 1929. Two of the small number of facts I know about his childhood are that his father returned from the war uninjured physically but given to sudden and frightening rages and that my grandmother "went batty" when she reached menopause, so much so that my father's youngest brother had to be sent to boarding school when he was only six. I only know this much because my mother told me. Except for the ham radio he built when he was thirteen and one story about a joke my grandfather played on him — sending him to a pub to buy a jug of steam — my father never referred to his childhood. His life seemed to start when he left home to do his National Service.

I think about the photograph my mother always kept on her dresser of my father in his Naval uniform (it occurs to me as I write this that I never saw any of him when he was a child), eighteen, the long hook of his nose, his pale eyes, blond hair looking almost white in the black and white photo. He's not quite handsome, his face too smooth, wax-like, untouched, untouchable. Had he endured abuse at school, at home? Were his parents involved in ritual abuse too? Or did he just come into the world with an overwhelming desire to hurt, to feel the power that comes from hurting another being?

I doubt I'll ever have the answers to those questions, but I come back to the two World Wars and the scars they left and the soil they grew from, which was the soil he grew from too. England and Germany each had a ruling caste whose educational policy, especially in relation to boys, was to annihilate the child with measured doses of abuse, creating men who were invulnerable, rational and self-controlled. These were the administrators of empires whose subject populations they viewed as child-like, irresponsible, emotional, in need of discipline.

Not everybody who went through that educational system turned into an active sadist like my father, but he is not an improbable plant to find growing in such soil. The way he treated children has everything to do with the way he felt about and treated his own child-self.

How much I long to excuse him, to understand at least. Then I think of what I saw him do, what I felt him enjoy, and I only want to scream at him, "You sick monster, you sick monster," to shout away the despair in me.

How could I have sought out sex with such a man?

He never stopped being my father. The worse he was, the more I longed to connect again with the warm, human part of him, and the only way I knew how to do that was through sex. Perhaps too I believed that, if I could keep that part of him alive, he wouldn't be a monster again.

Re-reading these sentences I think I sound just like a battered woman talking about her husband.

Consciously I couldn't admit my father had ever been a monster. I couldn't bear it. I still can't. I write this chapter with a howl of grief. This morning I crawled into bed and sobbed and sobbed before coming to my desk. Why can't he be the man with the wheelbarrow in the garden, the tall man in his old green sweater with leather patches at the elbows? My father. I want my father, this man I haven't seen since 1981. I'm losing him now, again, writing down what I saw. I don't want to have seen.

5/10/92

I think what is most intolerable is that my father wanted to be who he was. Mum did not, half-crazed by pain and secrets and fear, but Dad — this is what the label sadist conveys — wanted, he desired another's pain, his cruelty was not incidental.

I remember once saying to Sudha that at least I was not cruel, I had not deliberately inflicted pain on anyone, nor taken pleasure in someone else's pain. I knew as I said it that this was very important to me, not to be that sort of person.

But then so it is to many people — it is at the root of English culture, to eschew cruelty, especially towards animals. My father, I remember, could not drown a litter of unwanted kittens. I suspect that cruel people are often sentimental.

"Cruel" comes from the same root as "crude," the Latin "crudus" which mean "raw, undigested, unripe, rough, cruel." My father was unripe. That feels true. He was urbane, knowledgeable, ironic, but he wasn't somehow full or mature. Something in him longed to be pure, was repulsed by my mother's physicality (which had a quality of over-ripeness, of a fruit splitting its rind, seed spilling out.)

Purity is a kind of immaturity, an unripeness, and purity is often found in the neighborhood of cruelty: I'm thinking of the Nazi ideal of racial purity; the Inquisitors' efforts to cleanse the Church of the stain of heresy. If one is to feel pure, somebody else has to carry one's shadow. And one has to disconnect oneself from whoever is carrying the shadow. So the lust for purity gives rise to the impulse to persecute whoever carries the shadow. The particular kind of cruelty my father went in for was scientific, sterile: he kept his hands clean. That was his illusion anyway.

But in fact purity and filth are never far apart. The psyche, like any other part of nature, seeks wholeness. To go to one extreme is to attract to oneself its opposite. And so my father, the fastidious, hyper-rational man, found himself in a cult where they drank blood and smeared shit on children.

It is sexual desire, in particular, that so often messes up the effort to disown one's shadow by projecting it onto somebody else. That somebody else becomes suddenly, mysteriously attractive. It is as if, when one separates from one's shadow, an electrical charge is set up and the air between crackles with sexual energy.

So there was my father, trying to disown his vulnerability, sexually drawn to the most vulnerable of humans, children. And there he was, torturing a boy, demonstrating his indifference to the child's pain, secretly turned on.

My father. I have a headache, writing this. My kin. The root of kindness, etymologically and otherwise: kin, the sense of kinship. Why then is there so much cruelty inside families? Is it that cruelty grows, not so much out of the absence of connection as from the desire to disconnect, and that is fiercest where connection is most tangible?

My thoughts feel like cobwebs. They catch at my face, my hair. I want to beat them away. I want a well-swept room of truth, a simple room, a table and a chair. Somewhere — pure.

But the path away from cruelty is not pure, it is a sort of willing impurity. "This thing of darkness I acknowledge mine," says Prospero of Caliban at the end of *The Tempest*. What matters most is my ability to accept my shadow as a part of myself. Otherwise, however hard I try to be kind, I will be cruel to the people upon whom I have projected those parts of myself I cannot accept. I know. I've done it. I was cruel to Clair the seven years she was in love with me. Not consciously, intentionally cruel, but cruel nonetheless. She was all the vulnerability, all the yearning for love and warmth and touch I could not face in myself and I was enraged and terrified by her. I tried to drive her from me, and at the same time I couldn't let go of her.

Vulnerability, yearning for human connection, don't sound like especially "shadowy" attributes but they were what I could least tolerate in myself. In this I was like my father. I do not want to acknowledge the similarity. But I have to. My father is part of my shadow. I have to accept my father's existence in me, his fear, his cruelty, his pleasure in cruelty, the possibility that I too might take pleasure in cruelty. To become my father's opposite is not enough, it will lead me back into his arms.

Chapter Twenty-nine

5/2/92

Yesterday, wandering in the garden — scarlet tulips — Praetens Fusilier — coming up behind and around, astilbes which emerge brownish bronze, and in front of these heuchera Palace Purple — set off by the green of iris, campanula, hosta — an unexpected, unplanned joy, a cello and a flute — the physical pleasure of color.

5/10/92

Linda McCarriston reading.
"People of goodwill always are willing to lose their ignorance."
She read a horrifying poem about the Inquisition burning Joan of Arc's war horse before her eyes — I wept and wept — and stopped hiding my tears — why should I be ashamed of my response to cruelty?

5/12/92

Saw Rich.
Creativity — gardening, writing, making of the self — partnership, the unexpected, how things come together and make sense suddenly — how gardening reassures, the antidote to RA. Where for Linda McCarriston the horse was "the spirituality of flesh in the field of time" [her phrase], so for me plants — the physicalness of gardening, how you are in the space bodily, moving, participating not observing.

5/18/92

Hard conversation with Laura last night — a friend of hers had dropped dead two hours before and she was calling people who had meant something to her. I was present for a bit — tried — then she asked how I was and I talked about anxiety re working with Liz and how I was being a jerk. Have you talked it through with her? Sort of. Pray about it, she said. Who the hell to, I thought. I felt slapped in the face and angry. I wish I was the sort of person who said right off, "Well, that shut me up." Instead I began to shut down.

She talked about a family visit — a funeral — finding she had a lesbian cousin, feeling less alone there, how Janet [her lover] had gone with her.

I was jealous I suppose, shut down and began to do the washing up. Felt bored and not present.

Later I went for a walk and realized how angry I was — I feel there's no room for mess and pain and suffering — my mess and pain — at the same time aware I wasn't really present for her either and that, being out of myself, I was droning on a bit.

Beyond that though I'm angry at her and ashamed of my anger — I'm angry that once we felt like siblings, brothers really, but she worked through her incest stuff, reconciled with her family, and here I am with no family, pulled further and further down into this nightmare of cruelty and sadism and murder.

I wanted to yell "You wouldn't talk to me about your fucking family if all mine had been killed in a car accident. Well fine, my father's a murderer and a sadist. My mother's crazy and I don't know where the fuck my brother is." I'm crying and crying as I write this, as I did last night talking about it to Liz.

Damn.

Oh my God, could it be self-pity?

Oh fuck off.

Anger and integration — suddenly this spring I've felt drawn to hot colors, reds and crimsons and maroons... have had an inspiration to plant a whole hot border....

Saw Rich.

Fear of anger — having the memory in my body of stabbing a woman to death in a blind rage — I cried and cried, a desperate sobbing — the kids needing Rich to say again "You're not a bad person" as I needed him to when the memories of abusing were first coming up.

Tonight Blasphemous Rumours, the RA book Sudha bought for me in England arrived.

Turned to the section on "Abused to Abuser" — there it is, exactly my sense of it — but nothing takes away the memory of having done it.

The book even uses the image of mind control entering very far

inside a person, lodging there like a psychic semen deposit — my image of having let them all the way in and being left with death inside me.
Read bits of this book slowly!

5/26/92

Saw Rich.
On the drive down I was thinking about writing a book about ritual abuse — and growing very sleepy as usual.
A kind of diary of recovery — following the chronology of memory not of the events themselves — the process of coming to terms with reality. (Now I feel self-conscious writing in here, having thought I might use journal excerpts as well as poems and bits of novel.)
Starting with the afternoon before the night of reading "The Sea, The Sea" — sense of my life hanging in balance then.
Talked about this with Rich who was enthusiastic and encouraging — how much is this the writer self, how much the part of you healing from all this who feels the need to go back and bring your story together?
The two fears — of having to encounter my whole story — of going public (I obsess about whether it should be under my own name.)
Image talking to Clair last night about the book idea.
"Guide to the underground," she said. "Bring a thermos, sandwiches."
"A big ball of string," I said, "and make a garden that smells so sweet the smell will reach you in the bowels of the earth."
Like the Greek island sailors could smell from the sea.
Good use of anger, fuel to do this. From reading Blasphemous Rumours, *the battles over whether RA is real or myth. Instead of feeling deadened and scared by the denial I feel angry, invigorated: well then, I'll put in my pennyworth too.*

I'm glad I didn't get hold of *Blasphemous Rumours* when I first started remembering ritual abuse. When my own emerging memories tallied with the stories Boyd recorded, I would probably have told myself I was just being suggestible. By the time I did get a copy, after two and a half years of remembering, that argument wouldn't work. The book both drew and repelled me. I wanted to know and I didn't. The headings themselves read like the names of subway stops on a familiar journey. Under "Common Threads" there were "Locations; Rituals; Animal Sacrifice; Human Sacrifice; Cannibalism;

Pornography;" under "Methods of Control," "Drugs; Blackmail; From Abused to Abuser; Mind Control; Threats."

> *"'You've only got to watch an act of abuse to feel like you're an abuser in that situation, because you didn't stop it.'"* (p. 104, quoting Nigel O'Mara, a counselor who works with adult survivors.)

> *"'If it's a child, they may have a knife in their hand and it's actually an adult who's doing whatever is necessary, but they say, 'You participated in the death of someone.'"*
> (p. 79, quoting Vera Diamond, psychotherapist.)

> *"'My children have talked about all those things and worse. They've talked about having to kill other children.'"* (p. 79, quoting Kathleen Sorenson, victim's adoptive mother.)

My head aches and my heart feels too big for my chest, typing out these quotes, rereading a couple of chapters of *Blasphemous Rumours*. I still haven't read every section in the book.

Once, when I was about nine and Bill was five or six, he asked my mother if she had ever gotten drunk. I remember the surge of anxiety in the silence that followed, the sense that the world was teetering, might fall, like Humpty Dumpty, and be smashed to smithereens, the relief tinged with disappointment when my mother laughed and said, "Of course not, darling." And then Bill said, "Yes you have, I've seen you," and my mother said, "Don't be silly, I've been tipsy now and then but never drunk," and I glared at him, willing him to shut up and he did. But later, when my father came home, he asked, "What's tipsy, Dad?" I don't remember exactly what my father said. I think he glanced at my mother and said it was something grown-ups did, and it was time for Bill to go to bed.

Truth was potent, obviously: grown-ups handled it with such caution. It could break the world apart. I'd learned to fear it long before threats and brainwashing and implication in murder and cannibalism had been used to ensure my participation in the lie. But it was fascinating as well as dangerous.

When Bill was asking my mother about getting drunk, a part of me was willing him to shut up, but another part of me was excited, and proud of his daring. And on his part it wasn't a completely naive question. He knew he was taking a risk. But he wanted to know.

Among all the weapons available to the cult for maintaining their secrecy, the most powerful is the enduring will of people not to know, not to see what they look at, not to listen to what they hear. Most of us don't want truth to shatter our worlds. But, equally strongly, we do want to know. We want to hear the truth and tell it. The astonishing fact is that this wanting has been strong enough to break the circle of silence so elaborately constructed and enforced by the cults. I go on asking myself, what keeps the will to know alive? What is it about truth that is so compelling?

I am not an especially honest person. There probably are people who have never knowingly told a lie, but I am not one of them. I've lied to get out of tight corners, lied to save face, lied sometimes for no apparent reason at all. But it is a relief to tell the truth. It was a relief finally to decide to write about ritual abuse directly, to say this happened to me, I am writing from experience. I knew I would be poking my pen into a hornets' nest, within myself and in the world, but under my fear I felt calm. It was the next right thing for me to do.

The process of remembering has taught me the same lesson over and over: fighting against the truth is more bruising than the truth itself, however awful. It is a sort of surrender, to let the truth be more important than what I want the truth to be. Telling the truth has meant shedding layer upon layer of wishful thinking. Almost everything I most wanted to be true about myself, about my family, about my country, has turned out not to be true, or at least to be only partially true. The story I am telling, the story that tells me, has grown harsher, more frightening, harder and harder to believe, but even so I am glad I know it, I am glad I am telling it. Perhaps growing up among so many lies sharpened the hunger for truth in me. Lies fester. Truth hurts but the hurt is the hurt of healing. When I'm facing and telling the truth, I'm aligned within myself so life can move through me, and the moving and being moved through matter more than pain, or joy, or any particular feeling.

Sometimes I find myself day-dreaming about writing a surprise ending to this book: guess what, I've realized it was all a fantasy, an elaborate confection of my unconscious, psychologically accurate but not literally true. This isn't just wishful thinking on my part: I am testing my willingness to tell the truest truth I know, however embarrassing or disturbing. I think, I hope, that if I had come to the conclusion that my memories had no basis in external reality, I would have written that story.

Our versions of truth are approximate and changing but the willingness to seek truth out and speak it is a rock I can build on.

6/9/92

Saw Rich.
Talked about my speedy heartbeat these days — is it
a) caffeine
b) anxiety
c) programming — the bomb in the heart set to go off if I tell.

Fear of programming — what can I trust inside myself — how I ignore this brainwashing stuff but I have been saying Oh I'll have to deal with programming to write this book.

Finally breathed and was quiet and right away had an image of a baby, its chest exploding open from the inside — a sort of popping sound. Perhaps somebody was holding a remote control.

I kept looking and looking — it can't be true, there must be an explanation. They don't really have magic power.

The terror behind that — I'll go crazy with fear if I really believe they have that power....

A biggy, this.

Thought I saw a shadow of Satan's head in the memory — a great horned shadow high on the wall. Lots of us were being shown they had this power.

I've avoided dealing with the supernatural element.

I talked too about them burning Granny but I could not say burning, with all the will I could summon I could not say it — the Satan's head appearing on her white robe — a trick, invisible ink — but I can't be sure.

How can I be sure? When someone describes something that happened within the boundaries of what is commonly agreed on as ordinary life, their story is easily credible. It may or may not be true but it seems likely to be true. On the other hand, when something seems incredible it is tempting to think it is impossible. The incredible and the impossible both exist on the far side of the line separating the ordinary, plausible world from that other shadowy, frightening, fascinating realm. The far side is the special province of the

National Inquirer, the *News of the World,* it is the land of three headed babies, adolescents with stigmata, Loch Ness monsters, UFOs, Satanists. These stories hover on the line between the imaginary and the real, expressions of the collective unconscious dressed up as news.

Looking out from inside the boundaries of the credible it doesn't matter too much whether they are literally true or not. It would ruin the fun to be sure either way. But when I remember seeing what appeared to be a baby exploding, I need to know, did this actually happen, and if it did, how did it happen? Approximate truth no longer feels like enough.

The cult laid claim to the whole realm of the incredible, from the improbable to the impossible. They staged supernatural effects to coincide with tangible acts, and they used the paraphernalia of science to give weight to esoteric claims. They used these tactics in particular when they were instilling in us the necessity of silence: they wanted us to believe they had the power to reach us across space and time.

A part of me is still afraid. Do they know where I am? Do they know I am writing this book? Will something bad happen to me because I am?

I tell myself, you were terrified, the first time you told Rich one of these memories, that he would be hurt or killed but it didn't happen. The only way they will know you are writing this book is because someone tells them you are, and that is not very likely. Yes, something bad could happen to you as a result of writing this book. Somebody could hurt you or people you care about. But it will be a real person, driving a real car, who harms you, not a ghost or some device they planted in you eighteen years ago. And if they planted in your mind the suggestion that you would kill yourself or go crazy or go back to them if ever you went public with this information, well, you're here, you're talking, you've already proved you don't have to do what they told you to do.

In order to tell my truth in public, to be a part of breaking the circle of silence, I had to — have to — overcome this fear that they will magically know and punish me. To do that I remind myself that anything that is impossible in daily life is impossible in the realm of ritual abuse too. It is all happening in the same world.

But it's not so easy, this. Ritual abuse does feel like it happens in a different world: so much that seems incredible in the ordinary world happens regularly there. Throughout my recovery I have felt painfully aware of the gap between the worlds, an abyss I'm straddling, a chasm I stand over on my slender rope bridge. How can I say the abyss doesn't exist? It has been central to my experience, the root of so much loneliness, anger, sorrow.

It does exist, this abyss that seems to separate the worlds. It is a perceptual gulf, a line we draw to separate ourselves from our shadows, as real as the border between two countries — and as unreal. Life in each country is defined by the border, but the soil is no different ten feet on either side of the line.

Not a bottomless chasm after all but a line drawn in the dirt, not two worlds but one in which people wait for the bus and people eat babies. If I can't grasp this myself, can't get other people to grasp it, my story will seem no more real than a story in the *News of the World*, another report from the far side.

But how to grasp it, how to hold this knowledge? I know about double vision, about trying to see the world of bus stops and the world of cannibalism, trying to see the two worlds simultaneously, to hold the knowledge that both exist, both are true. But this is like double double vision: there are two worlds and a chasm between them; there is one world and all the different things that happen happen in that one world.

Iron Curtains fall, national boundaries are drawn and redrawn but the earth goes on being one planet. The unity beneath the apparent divisions in the world is a profound truth. But so is the experiential reality of the divisions: an East German and a West German living a block from each other on either side of the Berlin wall will have led very different lives.

Integration, reunification cause dislocation. The boundaries which divide also organize. When they are gone there is the threat of chaos. In order to tell my truth I have to reunite my two Germanys, a task I'm not sure is any easier on the individual than on the national level.

6/15/92

Knives frighten me at the moment. They catch my eye. It is as if, holding one, it might acquire a life of its own and stab me. Their presence is like the passing of voices in the night, intrusive, barely distinguishable. I don't think this is me feeling suicidal, it is much more like the earlier messages: Drive off the road, drive off the road now.

• CHAPTER TWENTY-NINE •

6/16/92

Saw Rich — talked about the knives — felt v. anxious — breathe — "You'll hate me. Everyone will hate me." Breathe some more. I am raping Mum with the handle of a knife. Savagely, repeatedly, enjoying her face gray with pain, sweating. She is being held down, her face turned to the right. I feel elated, ten feet tall. Finally I push the blade of the knife up her vagina. It is the culmination of some sort of ritual.

Remembering I feel sick, horrified, ashamed. I cry and cry. Think how on Wednesday I talked about cruelty and how I had not found in myself a pleasure in causing another creature pain. Yet, I added, a little nervous as always because such statements seem to invite contradiction.

Rich said we have that part inside us but ordinarily it is held in check, balanced by other elements. The cult cleared away and blocked off all other elements, created an artificial situation.

Yes. I feel sad I have that part in me. I hoped I didn't.

I felt oddly calm after the earlier crying — no longer as if I would be sucked into the vortex, no longer so desperate for Rich's reassurance that I'm not a horrible person. I hovered for a moment, crying, wondering if he would jump in and reassure but I realized that the self-hate really wasn't there.

Solstice 6/20/92

Heavy with this memory — I've been running around getting ready for my garden party tomorrow, worrying a thunderstorm will strip the peonies of their petals — but now at the sink I think, I raped my mother with the handle of a knife. With the blade. My stomach clenches. All day I've noticed the tightness of my face muscles.

I don't know how to take this in, like the memory of killing. I didn't talk about it to Clair on the phone last night. Haven't told Liz. Have talked about it at two meetings.

I don't even think I'm making this up. I just feel sick. Her face gray and sweating, twisting from side to side. I felt so tall, exultant — high — on a drug? on power? It was a feeling of invincibility I tried to get back through booze and drugs and angry music.

I'm a little numb I think.

I want to read Blasphemous Rumours *— unwise? I don't know. Perhaps to feel less alone, to remember the context.*

I do think about Hobbes' Leviathan *a lot — as I lose my own sense of essential goodness, have to accept in myself the frightening mixture.*

I think too about context — in a context in which brutality and cruelty is encouraged and compassion punished, each of us is more likely to act sadistically, to act in ways which later, in another context, seem inconceivable.

The gap between the worlds again.

So I am neither a saint nor a hero. Each of whom transcends context, circumstance?

Worse, I was consumed by such hatred (for the woman in me as well as for my mother) I raped her — with a knife — the castrator's implement? Oh Freud, oh Freud.

But yes, there is something in this. I remember the first RA memory — me with the handle of the knife shoved into me, the blade pointing down, a steel penis. A prick.

So I do read a little of Blasphemous Rumours *and find this quote from Anton La Vey, founder of the Church of Satan: "It is a blatantly selfish, brutal religion. It is based on the belief that man is inherently a selfish violent creature, that life is a Darwinian struggle for survival of the fittest, that the earth will be ruled by those who fight to win."*

Nasty, brutish and short.

One RA effect [according to Boyd]: anything you love will end up being hurt and it will be your fault. YES!

6/22/92

Today, after putting up roof trusses all day at Diane's, I planted the second Golden Ninebark and then started on Constance Spry [a climbing pink rose] — thought, out of nowhere in particular, I could plant this for my mother — suitable — her favorite cookery book [was written by Constance Spry] — the other good and nurturing thing she gave me. An emblem of forgiveness, this planting, and asking forgiveness, which I did, kneeling in the brambles and leaves in front of the hole. It was a genuine amends I think because I was able in my heart to focus on what I had done to her.

6/23/92

Saw Rich.

Went back into the memory of raping Mum. Waves of cold through my body. Sense of a separate part of me 6 feet over saying, "So what if you're cold. You've forfeited your right to feel by doing this." That part of me drifting further and further from the frenzied angry rapist. Crying

Chapter Twenty-nine

and crying — feel so ashamed. Horrible pain, pray and pray — I think I can't bear it and where's the end, there's no end to this feeling. Pray pray pray.

Rich saying you're integrating the action and the feeling — not that you were fully responsible for your actions back then but now it's good to feel.

Cried, cried, cried. Lambent voice of self-hatred: "Stop sniveling."

"Whose voice is that?"

Surprised I say, "My father's."

See him put his arm around me — as if to say good job, son, after I am done. I am numb and stunned and feel little and start to cry. He tells me to stop, I'm past all that, look at what I have done. I see the knife handle sticking out of my mother. I have pushed in the blade — I didn't know I did that. She is very still. Is she dead? He tells me the knife is my penis. In me they are making a new kind of being.

A monster I think, howl. I'm not a monster. Cry and cry. Tell me I'm not a monster. You're not a monster [says Rich]. Rich says it's time to stop. I can't stop crying. I'm crying partly because I see this, this is what I had to do, to be, to win my father's approval. Angry then, half crazy with it. Him in Chile. Think about Brazil where they pushed 300,000 street kids out of sight for the Earth Summit and nobody knows where they've gone. Him with my mother. Is he still doing this shit? It makes me so angry.

Rich points out that as I feel closer to my mother I can be angrier at my father.

6/30/92

Saw Rich.

Made to look at my mother — I didn't know if she was dead, if I'd killed her — I felt numb, just staring at the handle of the knife protruding from her vagina, the twin silver curls of the hilt against her vulva and ass. Someone used her blood to make an upside down cross on my forehead.

Something then about a room, a big old book I sign my name in — I keep getting sleepy or numb — then a sharp wave of the impulse to hurt myself.

This part is set around with programmed warnings?...

Sense there may be fireworks coming — Rich away next week.

Feeling monstrous.

Fear they were trying to make a serial killer out of me. L. saying knife as penis is classic sadism.

They don't have the power to get me, do they?

7/1/92

Talked at the SIA meeting about fractured narrative, not being able to believe in one omniscient narrator — not being able to see with both eyes together — now speaking from myself in Double Vision *and how frightening that is.*

Lots and lots of nodding round the table — reassuring.

7/4/92

Grief again yesterday, like last year at Jean and Helen's, crying among the raspberry bushes.

I found myself thinking about the high percentage of Holocaust survivors who eventually commit suicide (Primo Levi, was it last year?)

I thought how surprised Jean and Helen would be if I killed myself.

Raking dry grass to cover a black plastic mulch I just wanted to lie down in it, under the ferns and brambles, like when I was little.

Liz came about 5 to see if I wanted to go to an auction. I couldn't decide, cried. Told her this week's memory and then couldn't breathe, felt my throat closing — frightened — felt/thought, this is programming, I've been told I won't be able to breathe if I tell. I thought, I can breathe, I prayed and breathed in gasps with gaps in between. At last, breathing more normally, I felt a kind of current running from the back of my skull down the upper part of my spine. A thick vibration, not pain. I've never felt anything quite like that.

Did they try to do brainwashing that would affect involuntary reflexes such as breathing? Did they use electric current? or subsonic sound I experienced as vibration?

This memory of raping my mother with a knife had surfaced before, in March 1991 (see Ch. 18). That time I remembered using the handle and being on some sort of drug and then, "Stuck after this, no feelings." I didn't remember using the blade nor the exchange with my father, nor signing my name in the book, but the emotional silhouette was there already: guilt and self-hatred, the longing to be chosen, an awareness of the "complicity and bond between my father and I" (3/28/91).

The memory surfaced each time with the same companion

Chapter Twenty-nine

concerns too: programming and feeling suicidal. Both these, I realized now, were connected to my official induction into the cult as a perpetrator. Programming was particularly dense around that book I signed my name in, and suicidal feelings were strongest in me when I felt there was no other way to escape being made into one of them.

It is confirming for me to see this combination of consistency and change in a memory: it feels authentic. I know that not every detail of all the abuse I've remembered can be literally true. There must be places where I've filled in gaps, rationalized, projected my own fantasies, but I doubt I could invent stories so densely woven as these.

Starting to reread my journals at this time, in preparation for working on this book, supplied me with other examples of odd details which had surfaced years apart but belonged in the same picture. The most striking thing, though, was to reread the dream I had when I first went into therapy after I got sober.

3/29/84

I go to an AA meeting early, talk to this middle-aged woman. She wants me to open the door. I have keys to the bathrooms. She gets me to unlock them. I say, "I haven't done the fourth step yet but I can show you upstairs."

Inside this building are two bums decapitating a pure black, healthy cat, slicing off its head, ready for food, the bright red of blood and flesh, the neck like salami. There's blood all over the floor. I scream at them and someone else, "There's blood in my house." It's everywhere, in fat drops and rivulets. "There's blood in my house."

Later I think I'm glad not to do my fourth step until I've done one, two and three.

This from somebody who believed she had never experienced any violence. And six months later, when I tried to do a fourth step — taking a "searching and fearless moral inventory of myself" — and then a fifth — reading it to someone else — I didn't feel the relief I had hoped for. Instead I felt as if I'd forgotten to mention that I murdered somebody. That was how I put it to myself.

Eight years later I was still opening doors to more rooms with more blood. Though it was hardly fearless I was just beginning to be able to look at what I had seen and done without spinning down in a vortex of self-hatred.

7/5/92

Need to take some time, let the waters still, the monster shape emerge, not do or talk or look or even think. I'm ragged, easily hurt, sure I'm being judged by Liz. (When in truth I am judging myself, can't feel loved — only she does also seem distant — overwhelmed by her own life.)

I feel forgiveness for my mother, a softness in me — is this real or just a response to having abused her myself? I think it's real.

Is this in a twisted fashion like the way in which daughters, when they become mothers, find themselves forgiving their own mothers?

Graduating to perpetrator, to member, to a circle above hers, I see how abuse fuels abuse — have some intuitive sense, an inside knowing....

Chapter Thirty

7/12/92

Talked with Laura last night on the phone…talked a bit about RA, felt her pull away, felt the tight throated tears in my voice. Asked how it was for her to listen to me talk about RA.

She went into a long rap about how she wondered how I was doing with the 6th, 7th, 8th, 9th steps as I still seemed to be carrying the weight of my family around, wondered about acceptance and letting go and forgiveness.

I got madder and madder listening to her — and didn't shut down. Finally I interrupted, said "This is exactly what I feared you were thinking. You really don't get it, what I'm talking about. I'm talking about torture and sadism on a huge scale and it's still going on."

She said, Yes, maybe she didn't get it, didn't have hooks of her own to identify with, it seemed like a movie when I talked about it.

I said, "Well that might partly be how I talk about it" — I started to cry then — "because if I talk about it any other way I start to cry and it's hard to talk, also to trust that the other person cares, wants to know, will ask questions. Most people don't want to know, don't want to take it in. I talk about it to Hazel and she asks how the weather is."

"Oh, how is Hazel, where is she?"

I brought the subject back. "Thank God for Liz who has not tried to keep her world safe from this knowledge."…

"Yes," said Laura, "I guess I don't want to take it in. It's not that I haven't thought — huge chunks of my family were wiped out in the Holocaust. But I guess I don't want to see what you're talking about. It horrifies me and I shut the door."

"Which leaves me feeling shut out," I said, "because I can't divide myself anymore the way I did back then and have for so long. So if you shut out that aspect of the world you've shut me out. I don't come in a package with detachable suffering anymore."...

7/14/92

Saw Rich.

Talked through the jaw clenched tension of the last two weeks, the bouts of self-hatred, the episode of not being able to breathe.

Eventually breathed deeply — aargh. I am shut in a small dark space with a child who is shut in a box with rats. The child is screaming. At first I think, as I'm remembering, what a fiendish torture, for the child (who had tried to tell) and for me. Then I realize the box was not locked, that I had been told it was not locked and I had the option of opening the box and letting the rats out and that they would then probably start eating me too. I couldn't do it. I couldn't open the box. I lay there and listened and hated myself and couldn't do it.

When they took us out of there, they opened the box in front of me. Fat, bloody muzzled rats looked at me, the child's face and eyes had been eaten. I think the child was dead. I don't know.

They congratulated me on passing their ordeal, on being strong enough just to save myself.

I felt numb with horror and self-disgust, and confused.

Remembering is rebellion, said Rich.

7/18/92

Dreamt the last two nights I had blood on my hands, caked and thick. Tonight I went somewhere to scrape it off, hand it in as evidence.

Over and over it is the administrative aspect of evil that drives me crazy: who orders the rats, decides how many, the box, coffins, electrical prods? In the Holocaust who ordered the gas vans, wrote to the manufacturer with recommendations for greater efficiency?

Yes, said Judy, a friend of hers had told her how, when her father raped her, he put duct tape on her mouth. Judy keeps thinking about him going to the hardware store to buy the tape, waiting on line, talking to the clerk. I think about him going up to her bedroom, remembering to bring the roll of tape and take it away again afterwards.

7/18/92

Hazel here. She wants me to be her shaman in the woods, her magician, her writer friend, but she doesn't want to deal with the raw

Chapter Thirty

grind of change — "transformation" — I can only use those long words in quotes.

7/19/95

Last night having supper with Hazel and Cora I almost started crying — having twice tried to talk about the ritual abuse book and had Hazel ask no questions and change the subject.... I went along with it in best little well-behaved daughter mode — for god's sake don't make a scene.

But it costs me too much, that game.

7/21/92

Saw Rich.

Talked about feeling v. tense, stomach sore, voice flat. About talking to Hazel and how well that went — her warm response and apology.

About her saying she's always seen in me a streak of goodness, a real kindness. I found this very hard to say, crying and ashamed and then intense emotional pain — fear he'll say, no, you're bad; sense again of forfeiting the right to feel pain because I didn't lift the lid. Think of how that kid felt, knowing there was someone there who did not lift the lid.

How that short circuits my anger: the very thing I am most angry about — not being rescued, people refusing to see what was happening — was what I did to that child — couldn't bring myself to do otherwise.

Talked earlier about kindness, empathy, and their failure to kill that in me being linked to the survival mechanism of flooding my boundaries, merging — remembered them opening the lower section of the lid and me seeing the rats had gnawed out the child's stomach and then bam, I'd merged with the child, was feeling it as if it were happening to me (no wonder my stomach hurt) — I began to cry hysterically and they shoved my face into the bloody cavity. Someone told me the reason I didn't open the lid was because I couldn't, I belonged to Satan now.

Rich said a defining moment — I merged with the victim not the abusers.

Asking my friends (and now my readers) to open themselves emotionally to my story is in a way asking them to do metaphorically what I was not able to do literally: to lift the lid and let the rats out. Out of the box, into one's own space. To risk being eaten by the rats. Not to stay on the other side of the barrier, listening to the screams of the victims.

Acknowledging that someone is screaming in the first place is a crucial step, but it is only a beginning. I was taking a second step when I began to let myself imagine how it must have felt, to be the child shut in a box, being eaten alive, knowing somebody was there and wasn't opening the box. Mostly in the memories up till now I had focused on myself, my feelings, my reactions to the violence I witnessed. Beyond visceral and horrible moments of identification when memories were coming up, I had not really let myself imagine how it felt to be the boy being torn apart on the rack, the man being crucified. I was frightened of all that pain, felt overwhelmed by the pain I felt already.

Imagination opens the door, lets the rats in. Empathy, the ability to feel with, to feel for, someone else's pain as if it were my own, empathy ignores frontiers, insists we are made of the same stuff, whatever country we live in.

Laura said that what I told her about ritual abuse felt like a movie, by which I think she meant it felt unreal, distant. But not all movies feel that way. Some touch you deeply, make you cry and rage and laugh. I told my stories flatly to Laura, was not yet able to tell them with feeling, and that must have added to the feeling of unreality. But also she was not willing to reach across the line between her life and mine with her imagination, to risk feeling my life as real, as real as her own. She said she did not have experiences of her own to hook onto mine, to let her identify with my story, but I don't buy that. We all share a common language of emotions, feel pain and fear and pleasure. If one is willing one can imagine all manner of experiences one has never had. Not perfectly, not completely, but enough to start with.

For me the greatest aid to imagination is detail, specific information, like that roll of duct tape Judy's friend told her about. Perhaps that is why my memories are often short on details of faces and surroundings: perhaps this has to do not only with programmed prohibitions against recalling information which could identify specific people or places but is also an effort on the part of my psyche to protect me from the emotional impact of what happened: details would make it all even more vivid. Certainly the fight I was having with my friends about their refusal to imagine, their assorted tricks for distancing themselves, was a fight I was having with myself too.

The memory of the rats took a long time to surface. This even though I had a hunch there might be something about rats because, eight years earlier, the rat torture scene in the film of 1984 had left me sobbing in my seat long after the movie ended, Nanette sitting anxiously beside me. I couldn't tell her what was happening. I couldn't make any words come. All I could think was, "I can't move."

The radioactive core of my feeling of being bad was buried between this memory, my grandmother's death, the memory of raping my mother with a knife, and the memory of having killed a woman. Believing that I was essentially bad felt like saying the cult had won. I had somehow to take in that I could be this bad and be good too. It was as if I needed a new muscle. I needed to imagine the agony of that child and I needed to imagine my own terror. It was not enough to imagine only one or the other.

Imagination can heal the split inside myself, and between the worlds. It already operates from the knowledge of unity beneath all the divisions. It is the opposite of the impulse to separate myself, to say "I am not like you." But at the same time, wonderfully, the imagination loves distinction, the specificity of who you, in particular, are. It is bored by forced unity, by generality. "We are all one." Yawn. Imagination is a spark leaping between poles, able to join them because they are separate. Paradox is the staple, the potato in imagination's diet.

7/26/92

I've outrun the lions! Turned 34 today.

I felt such a sense of lightness and relief all day — a sense of liberation, of having escaped.

When I was weeding the raspberry patch I heard a man bellowing, in rage I thought but wasn't sure. I walked out to the street and listened, inclined to dismiss it, but went inside and asked Jean and Helen if they'd heard anything. "Oh dear, is that the man living next door to the Nortons'?" A batterer, so Janis Norton had told Jean. Helen and I walked up the street. By now there was very loud music coming from the house which was spooky. Over the music we heard two, maybe three, screams — sped back and Helen called the cops but by the time they got there all was quiet and neither wife nor child showed signs of abuse.

I wished then that I'd gone and knocked on the door after calling the cops.

I felt myself slip into neutral when it was all happening — only later did I see the parallel to lying in the dark next to a screaming child, not opening the lid/door.

Still I did something.

Jean asked me if I took credit for being a hero.

I said, "Well, it's hard to when you're remembering doing nasty stuff to other people."

"Well," she said, "but look, you survived and you've built your own house, you write novels and poetry and help other people out. Look at the garden you've made, you add beauty to the world."

It was lovely to hear that, really felt like a birthday present.

7/28/92

Saw Rich.

Letting go of self-hatred.

Breathe. What's in the black box?

Indifference: the choice not to care. Nobody can get me ever again.

So for ever after I feel inhuman — very strong feelings here, shame, fear of saying this aloud to Rich who really cares, sense of touching a truth in myself.

Rich said "No, it doesn't invalidate your feelings of caring, it's more that when you care it wakes up this other feeling, that it's dangerous to care."

I sobbed and sobbed then. Some relief....

How much I wanted to be a good person. Good people, especially good women, care, they empathize, they accept and tolerate and forgive. Some of my fury when Laura said she felt I should be letting go of the past and reconciling with my family grew out of my own unease at being this angry muckraker. But it's still going on, the ritual abuse. I have no reason to believe that the complex organizational structure of the cult folded when I walked away. How can I let go, go on with my life, having had my spiritual oil change, having felt forgiveness for my mother, the beginnings of empathy with my father? I cannot forgive on behalf of the child eaten by rats, the boy my father tore apart. I can see I share a common humanity with abusers and victims, I can try to accept that I am a mixture of each, that we all are, but if I open my heart to the suffering I witnessed, if I let myself imagine it, then I know I must take sides. I must resist, denounce, condemn.

The more I integrate myself and my worlds the less inclined I am to play the diplomatic daughter. I have somehow to take sides without believing in the sides, accepting that there is no absolute boundary between us and them but acknowledging the necessity of opposition.

I am not, by temperament, an activist — I can hardly organize my own grocery list — but at Oxford I threw myself into the socialist world of action groups and demonstrations. I needed to side with people who were saying, "Something's wrong, something bad is going on," and I needed to assert my identification with the victims, the oppressed. At a party once I said to a fellow student, "As long as there's someone starving I can't be happy."

I couldn't care enough — I couldn't care enough to compensate for the numbness in me, my secret indifference. I felt my indifference as monstrous and I set about fighting the monstrous indifference of the world.

Nowadays, after a long fallow period, I am part of a group of citizen activists monitoring and publicizing the health problems caused by the nuclear reactor fifteen miles from where I live. We are also educating people about nuclear waste. It is oddly familiar, the struggle to grasp, really grasp with heart and mind, the corruption and folly of the nuclear industry; to understand the toxic legacy which will be passed on now from generation to generation.

Like ritual abuse, nuclear waste is such a terrifying and intractable problem that it seems unreal. The time spans alone feel unimaginable: it's hard to believe that human beings, in the last fifty years, have manufactured substances which will still be dangerously radioactive three million years from now. In order to deal with the problem of what we have created, we, I, have to believe that it exists. Really believe it, which means, I know from facing the ritual abuse, letting the details enter into me, letting my imagination take hold of the information which will otherwise just be facts on a page. If I can do that myself, I can tell other people about it in ways that make it real.

It's good work for me to do, this. My activism is no longer driven by the need to expiate crimes I can't remember committing.

Instead I'm using what I've learned from facing the ritual abuse. Being able to do it is one of the fruits of the reunification that began in me in the summer of 1992. Gradually I moved from feeling as if I lived in two worlds separated by an abyss, to feeling like a divided city, to feeling like one person who had inhabited different contexts in a single world. My experiences could then become useful, a source of knowledge, a basis for action.

Chapter Thirty-one

8/5/92

Double Vision: *what does it take to make something sacred out of waste, out of violence?*

8/12/92

I have a kind of furious boredom, a great disgruntlement upon me — I think of spending the rest of my life with Liz and I want to scream.

8/18/92

This morning at work I found myself day-dreaming about living in Ireland with Clair, helping her raise the child she wants to have. It surprised and pleased me, that picture.

Tonight on the phone she said, "This is why there should be three of you, one to live with Liz, one to write on your own, and one to live with me in the west of Ireland. We could be quite happy, driving around in an old station wagon, and it wouldn't be so bad if there were a curly head bobbing in the back."

I couldn't say how good it sounded, how I'd been thinking about it — this rising up in me of the thought, I'm really in love with Clair, that's who I want to spend my life with.

I feel sick at the thought of causing Liz such pain and loss of trust.

I feel confused because I don't know if this is another storm in a teacup — after all last year I was lusting after Sandy (or was that the year before?)

How much is all this because I've been keeping myself hidden, and I need to stop that, need not to protect L. and I from discrepancies, clashes, things that are missing? But somehow I don't emerge in a vac-

uum, am sung out by the presence of a like mind?

I've felt strangely, strongly, that I could make a commitment with Clair, could say, "This is the one," in a way I can't quite with Liz.

God what am I thinking about. It frightens me to write it down.

8/28/92
Bristol, Vt.

Sleeping in the back of my pick-up in the woods. So happy, relieved to be on the road, away from my life.

8/29/92

Battell Shelter on the Long Trail. Cold and windy but as I hauled myself up the trail I did feel myself becoming more "transparent to the transcendent." (Joseph Campbell)

Even a mythic edge to the people I passed climbing the mountain. Two small girls. "How far to the bottom?" one asked. A man with two canes, dark glasses. At first I thought he was blind. People saying, "You're going to sleep up there?", and then a couple saying "Good for you," me saying "Well you wonder sometimes as you haul yourself up the rocks." The woman said "No, it's wonderful. I affirm you." The odd stiff words reverberated.

Liz is so solid, stolid, won't respond, won't be permeated, locked in herself, her kind and playful spirit entombed in flesh, as her face is sometimes. The light in her grows dimmer.

But when I see it shine in her face I love it and her.

Do I think by patience and kindness I can bring L. out, make a room warm and safe enough for her to flower, me with my heart full of affection, yes, but also my hot impatience?

"Do not be afraid of what you are becoming." (Jamele Highwater)

9/8/92

Saw Rich.

My urge to run is fueled by feelings I had when I was eighteen and was finally making a break for it.

Sense of being in transition from dealing with the past I had no control over — childhood — to one where I had choices — adulthood.

I told him about going to London after Elmsbury, about Frieda and Henry and Isabella.

How did I get away? Again it comes back to the suicide attempt.

Chapter Thirty-One

9/15/92

Saw Rich.

Memory: in an underground(?) room — rough stone floor, a stone altar/slab on which I was tied, spread-eagled, naked, the room full of men in black robes like academic gowns, full face masks, a sort of growling male chant in the background. Some of these men were teachers. The men were raping me one by one — just penetrating briefly, a ritual of violation — then they spat on me. I was looking down on myself, ugly female fat victim writhing — I felt the contempt for myself that they felt for me, was completely identified with them.

A ritual of repudiation.

Remembering, I could not say the word "teacher" — it was like walking towards an open doorway and running into a pane of glass. Had to write it down eventually.

Don't tell. But I can write.

They were punishing me by expelling me from the cult. I never realized they could see it as punishment. I only ever thought about it as a fortunate escape.

9/18/92

Liz and I did have a good talk — me feeling I can't talk about the RA with her unless it's really urgent, her feeling shut out and that I talk to other people but not her, especially about the larger framework (which I don't talk about to anyone much.)

Me feeling it's been too much for her. She said in some ways it has — is — she needs someone to talk to — something wrong when a woman at a meeting said her mother gave her an organ for her birthday and Liz wondered which one!

I talked about how I'd felt rejected, even though I knew I shouldn't, when she told me earlier in the year that she was feeling burned out. How after that she never asked about the RA (much.)

The corrosive effects of silence.

9/21/92

A bleak day weeding the long daylily border, the earth unyielding, the old weight in my chest.

Last night on the way to the Harvest Festival contradance L. said "I love you," and I thought, "Who do you love? You don't even see great chunks of me."

I tried to talk about the feeling and L. felt on trial and cried and

I quit trying to protect her and cried too and realized how lonely and lousy I've felt. When she was crying and I felt like a brute, I felt for a terrifying moment all the horrible things I ever did in the cult come rushing at me, accompanied by a sickening self-loathing.

9/22/92

Saw Rich.
"How do you feel different now than when you got together with Liz?"
"Older and tireder. I know too much and I'm tired."
At some point I remembered my father was among the men performing the renunciation — I recognized his eyes and the top of his nose which the mask left visible. I yearned to connect with him, sexually if need be, and felt repulsed by this need, looking down on myself lying there.
He treated me exactly as the other men did, acknowledging no relationship.

I did not know it at the time but this memory of the group of men, one of whom was my father, expelling me from the circle of the chosen, was the last major memory of ritual abuse to surface. It is fitting in a literary way, of course, that my psyche held this memory until the end, but that's not why it took me so long to remember. It took so long because it was surprisingly, shamefully, painful to be rejected by the cult.

I had assumed that getting out of the cult, however I'd managed it, was my choice, the successful culmination of my long struggle not to become one of Them. Though I'd remembered enough to know I was no hero, still I felt there was something heroic in the fact that I had, in the end, escaped. When I remembered, in September '91, men jeering at me after the suicide attempt, I'd remembered my despair and my resolve: 'I kept thinking "I've got to get away."' What I hadn't remembered then, what I couldn't bear to remember for another whole year, was that the cult had made it clear that *I* was not good enough for *them*.

When I became a "male" initiate in the cult I was no longer subjected to routine rape. But when I fell from favor, my suicide attempt having revealed, I suppose, an unforgivable weakness, I became once more a female body to be used and discarded. And I saw myself that way.

• CHAPTER THIRTY-ONE •

It was difficult, in the remembering, to acknowledge the sense of loss I'd felt at being rejected by the cult: loss of a version of myself (male, strong) that I had wanted to believe in, loss of what I felt was my only chance to belong anywhere, loss of my promised success in the world. How could I feel loss when I should have been rejoicing?

Worst of all was my father's participation in the ritual. He raped me like the other men, contemptuously. He made it clear that losing my status in the cult meant I had lost his respect. More than that, it was as if I no longer existed as an individual, as a person, in his eyes. I yearned, ashamed, for any connection with him, but now I wasn't good enough to make love to, in the way he had sometimes during the two years or so when I was an initiate, tenderly, urgently. The way he raped me in this ritual told me all that was over. I was nothing.

9/29/92

Somehow got on to programming — my feeling that there was a space between thinking a word and being able to say it — a creepy feeling. I ditched my body early on — too vulnerable to violation, couldn't protect it — but in the end I couldn't protect my mind either.

Breathe — image of scalpel held in front of my right eye, a bright light flashing on and off — but I feel no anxiety, feel utterly relaxed and unguarded (v. strong physical memory of this feeling of relaxation — heroin?) I think there's a voice but I can't hear it. The light gets closer and closer — it is looking into me, illuminating. I feel empty, no anxiety to hide anything.

Was this some kind of final boost?

"Like activating programs already installed?" said Rich.

Yes, that's right.

Oh and programming is up too because I'm trying to write about RA and can't.

When I first typed out the memory of the ritual of repudiation in this chapter I left out the reference to teachers. I felt uneasy but I justified it to myself: the book is too long, I'll probably have to come back and cut this, might as well do it now, and anyway there's no context in the book for this information. It'll take too much explaining, and besides, it just seems so improbable that this shit was going on at Elmsbury too.

There is no context because, I realize now, I have consistently edited out all the other little hunches that ritual abuse might have been going on at school. I wanted to do this with other fragments of information too but I made myself include them, aware that the impulse to omit them might come from suggestions planted in my psyche rather than from authorial wisdom.

Why did I fail to include the references to Elmsbury, in particular then? The cult might have devoted special attention to making it difficult for me to talk about what happened at school precisely because it is an identifiable place. I could show you the town on a map, and it is a small town.

But programming is not the only possible explanation. Perhaps nothing did happen at school. It's possible that the teachers in my memory weren't schoolteachers but my cult teachers. Perhaps I should trust the depth of disbelief I feel at the thought of ritual abuse happening at Elmsbury.

How could cult rituals have taken place on school grounds and gone unnoticed? The meetings of the Masonic Lodge were supposed to be secret but they were common knowledge: lights burned in one of the classroom buildings and there were extra cars around and teachers and other grown-ups were seen going in there. There is not a lot of privacy on a campus of six hundred school children. The grounds weren't huge, most of the buildings were not tremendously old. I find it hard to believe they housed secret underground rooms with stone floors and altars.

Three days after the memory of the repudiation ritual, driving behind Liz on an unfamiliar road at night, I was filled with the same sort of impotent fury I'd experienced in the summer of 1991, a fury I'd linked to being driven to the Schloss. Perhaps the room where the ritual happened was not on school grounds but somewhere in the surrounding countryside, somewhere I was driven to at night.

I have compelling reasons other than programming to censor the possibility that ritual abuse was going on at school. I counted on school as a haven from home. However regimented, it was at least safe, predictable, or so I thought. To face the possibility that ritual abuse was happening there too is like discovering that the worlds on both sides of the abyss are equally terrible. The division I erected to protect myself crumbles.

The references to Elmsbury I omitted from earlier chapters fall into three rough categories: uneasy hunches without particular content, just a feeling about Elmsbury; a shadowy memory of a group sex rite which I thought included boys from the school; and some musings about the school and my paternal grandfather. It was my grandfather and my uncle who got me into Elmsbury after I'd been expelled from Westwood.

I've wondered off and on whether my grandfather was involved in ritual abuse himself. It seems likely that my father was shaped by cult abuse. Ritual abuse is generally thought to be passed down through families. There also seem to be geographical concentrations of cult activity. Perhaps the small market town where my father grew up and where my grandparents lived for sixty years was in such an area. Elmsbury was only about thirty miles away. There could even have been a place somewhere midway where rituals took place, an isolated farmhouse with a cellar perhaps.

I don't know. It's hard to get a bigger picture. So much of it is speculation. I'm not sure that any ritual abuse took place in or near Elmsbury. But as I write about the possibility of a place I was driven to from school, it feels right. In an odd way, the consistency with which I tried to eliminate references to Elmsbury inclines me to believe something did go on which involved teachers from the school.

When this memory first surfaced in September 1991, I was vague about location:

> *Memory I think — being laughed at by men after the suicide attempt — somewhere — if you die it will be because we kill you.*

The memory poses a logistical problem. I am sure that my expulsion from the cult took place shortly after I tried to overdose, and that was in September or October, 1976. My parents had been posted to North Africa the year before. I've had no memories of cult activity there. And I don't think I went back to Germany during this time so the ritual must have taken place somewhere in England. It could have been in Surrey again, I suppose, but I think the Mill House was rented out at the time. So perhaps it really did take place somewhere near Elmsbury.

This is the nub of the issue with programming: even if it doesn't work perfectly, it is effective enough to be confusing.

I'm lucky in that the cult did not (so far as I remember) get their hands on me until I was ten. My parents did plenty of damage without group back-up, but they didn't go in for sophisticated brainwashing. Other survivors who were subjected to this at a much earlier age seem to have a different experience of programming than I do. I know that on this topic in particular my experiences are not representative.

I find in myself different layers of programming. There are the specific interdictions which make it hard for me to say the word "teacher" in the context of a memory, the sort of interdictions which may have led me to censor references to Elmsbury from the book. These are the sort I felt I needed a manual for, a way to enter the language of programming in order to reverse it. Such commands are localized and relatively easy to circumvent. But there is another layer which is turning out to be more persistent and difficult.

This sort results from the combination of explicit suggestions made by the cult and lessons I learned from my experiences in the cult, experiences which were often crafted and manipulated in order to teach a way of being and feeling.

Perhaps the central idea the cult tried to embed in me was, "You belong to us." As an adult I carry, in the core of me, the belief that I don't belong in the ordinary world, there is no place for me, no home. Buried in this feeling is the belief that I belong to and in the cult, that I will never belong anywhere else. When I try to belong in the world, in a group of friends, in AA, when I try to make a home with a lover, I find there is a part of me that doesn't believe it is possible. The feeling that I can't belong is so painful that I don't even want to try. I'd rather live by myself in a little cabin on the edge of the human world.

That's what I told myself for years anyway, but it's not true, not entirely. I hunger for human company, for intimacy and family. It's just that, in my heart, I don't believe those things are possible for me.

I don't know what to do to shake this belief. Logic can't touch it. There's no manual to tell me the code for delete. And if there were I'm not sure I would use it: to wipe out this feeling of not belonging would be to erase the self who lived through all those experiences.

I think I can only follow my hunger for connection and be patient with my contradictions. After all it's not uncommon, the feeling of not belonging: it's the cliché of our time. It's the recurrent feeling in just about every AA story I've ever listened to. And I have to live with myself as I am now, whatever made me this way. But it is a little easier to have mercy on myself when I acknowledge some of the forces at work.

Chapter Thirty-two

10/5/92

Pensive today — because I finally corralled myself into writing about the ritual abuse directly, well copying from my journal the first memories anyway. An inevitable detachment, looking back on oneself, the trace of oneself left on the page?

The sky so blue, a dense blue, and against it crimson and burnt orange, all the smolder of fall, and the brilliant oppositions, red and green, orange and blue. I was delivering a load of firewood to Judy, wondering what I believe in. That within me is a fragment of spirit, part of a larger Spirit, the whole whole. That there are tendencies, laws of probability but that equally there is a world of possibility one can enter. That you can live towards or away from your spirit. That fear clouds you, mostly. That these probabilities have little to do with justice. It is, for example, more, not less, likely that an abused child will be abused further and that s/he will go on to abuse others.

But equally there is a tidal pull towards potentiality, wholeness, the intent of the seed — as a hazelnut becomes a hazel tree, so a God seed becomes God.

10/6/92

Saw Rich.

Talked about starting to write Double Vision — has it been programming or just my fear which has made the effort feel like trying to push the same poles of two magnets together?

How does one authenticate programming when, by definition, it does not come from within and therefore is not validated by the accumulation of feelings, images, obsessions etc. In fact if it carries those *things it's probably not programming.*

10/7/92

Interiority — the sensation of being full of feelings, all sorts, like water ruffled by wind playing in different directions. This is how I felt at 18, and earlier too, sitting on my windowsill in Germany, smoking and drinking late into the night. I wasn't numb. Even in that house, in the room where my father raped me and my mother watched, I wasn't numb. I hid this place of feeling from other people, still feel protective of it, but it was there, when I was reading and alone, and so it must really be very tough as well as tender. I like this self who sat in Germany and longed for England, who felt alone and invisible except with Katarina, Evelyn, later E.A. What I keep coming back to is the sense of newness, of discovering a room inside, not the immediacy of childhood feeling but a more refracted sense — the wind stirred water, not the wind itself. An interior room to be glanced at in passing, not stared into.

A key aspect of adolescence, this discovery of self.

A bowl brimming with water.

I like feeling and being open.

Can I live from this place more in the world? With less fear of people?

It was like being a bud in April, sap flowing into me, swelling me and cracking open the hard brown carapace in which I had rested, furled, waiting. Something in me knew there would be no more Arctic blasts of memory.

10/8/92

Dreamt I had gentle, kind, enjoyable, satisfying sex with a man — oral sex and penetration — neither of us ever came but that didn't matter. At one point he said something about not having been able to get hold of some form of contraception. I said, "Well, then we'll have to practice the withdrawal method." "Oh yes," he said, taking it for granted. Playful and fun.

Over the years of recovery I often dreamt about having sex with a man. Invariably we had been interrupted: either we didn't have a safe, private space or we didn't have any contraception. I was always afraid in my dreams of unprotected sex. (I just typed "self" instead of

CHAPTER THIRTY-TWO

"sex" which says it all.) This new dream was a breakthrough and I knew it was connected to my realization that the tender, full of feelings self in me was much tougher than I had thought: I didn't need impermeable barriers to keep myself safe, it would be enough to withdraw when I needed to!

10/12/92

Sex, like God, is all encompassing, inclusive, takes into itself everything, I said, talking to Ellen the other day. Rich's version is sex entering the world, going out from the self — suspect some core gender differences here! Both. I need to write with my going into the world Eros.

Lately I've been feeling flickerings of sexual interest in Liz and also have noted that my oft-repeated statement that I could give two shits about sex is beginning to sound a little hollow.

Scary though — a tremor of energy running up and down my torso talking about it.

Told Rich how Clair and I went to look at leaves in Vermont, how when we were there I told C. I still wonder, should we be lovers. She said it helped to hear she's not the only one who can't shed that thought. I still wonder if I should have said it — saying things to C. I haven't said to L.

10/13/92

Denis can't talk any more but when Joan held the phone to his ear and I said "I love you and I'm so sad you are dying and I'm going to make you a beautiful garden," he grunted and Joan said he raised his eyebrows.

10/14/92

L. and I drove down to New York and back today to see Denis, say goodbye. His hand felt warm and large with energy when I first touched it, some connection perhaps. He looked oddly unchanged, paler and thinner and a little balder, gasping into his oxygen mask. I talked to him a little, telling him about my sense in the garden after I talked to him on the phone that he could return to the leaves and the stones and the trees, let go — the sudden strong sense yesterday of the personality unhooping itself, releasing its own form and joining everything again. "Abiding in the fire is bliss. In the fire there is no fear of being consumed."

Denis. Damn he's good at enjoying things — he should get to do it for longer. I'd like to know him as an apple-cheeked old man and I won't.

Is it shut-downess or acceptance that gives rise in me to a sense of quiet, of it's OK for him to be dying. What can it mean to say he should live longer?

I'm going to miss him.

10/22/92

Haven't written down seeing Rich yesterday. Nothing major came up, more the weaving together of different elements, preparation for a more central revelation.

Denis, death, my acceptance of his death, something off-key in my feelings about this.... Connection to the deep cold cave I saw in myself in Thailand, the untouched and untouchable place, source of both safety and sadness. A place that cannot be changed, something always held back — a source of loneliness, isolation. I want to be — completely alive.

What might it mean to let go of that protection, the fragment of self I buried so far inside nobody could get it (I hoped)? Kelly says her [protected self] is outside herself, a blue child separate from herself and sometimes a blue surround or skin to her whole body. She says it makes one a watcher not a doer.

10/28/92

Something is shifting in me — I don't know quite what — and I'm afraid. Plates shifting, continental drift and scrape.

10/31/92

Halloween — tense for days — thought perhaps it was just because I was getting my period — tonight L. came in from the outhouse clutching a piece of bloody toilet paper to put in the fire. I felt a wave of hysteria roll through me.

11/7/92

Letter from Sudha: "I have been feeling my way into 'rape' — particularly for a woman — the touching of the creative quick of one's being — the sense of contamination.

But one is not only a victim? Something was spared, protected by grace."

Protected by grace not by my efforts to protect myself with cold caves and all. They did not get me, I was protected. I can trust this. I've writ-

Chapter Thirty-two

ten this before. I can lean against my own self.

11/9/92

I think there's an obligation imposed by grace or strength and I've been afraid of it. Afraid, not that I won't go out into the world but that I will.

Is this true? It feels like a pompous, insistent voice.

I'm afraid of being crucified,
    of not being good enough,
    of being alone on the cross,
    of losing Liz.

Because if I tell I will lose whatever I love and mind about?

Aching chest and throat and tears in my eyes. I don't understand. None of this is what I think.

I'm frightened of becoming somebody different.

I felt afraid of losing myself and at the same time I was increasingly aware that my efforts to hold onto myself in the past were not what had saved me. I had been saved — I had a self — I could feel it now and I knew I'd had it all along, a place in me which had never been taken or tainted. But how could I entrust myself to some kind of grace I neither controlled nor understood?

Seeing Rich on the third of November I felt the old fog of despair at my core, the feeling that everything is only provisional, the whole fabric of the world flimsy.

"I'm not flimsy," said Rich, "I'm solid in this relationship to you, whatever you feel about it. I may be flimsy in other areas of my life but not in this one, and I bet Liz isn't either and other friends (which made me cry more). I don't know if this makes sense but perhaps you have to trust enough to not trust, to feel the not-trusting."

The next week, when we were talking again about trust, he said, "There is the center that holds which lies beneath the center of reactions we make for ourselves and which we need to allow not to hold."

I talked about the journal entry from January 1989 I'd typed out that day, the memory of the gang rape during which, on the verge of feeling myself shrink into nothingness, a circle of light with a cross in it had come to me, and taken me into itself.

I could see how where I was now, in 1992, spiraled over where I was then. I was again feeling my isolation and the price of invulnerability, and again afraid that there was a destructive force operating from inside me, something that was trying to change me. Three years ago I had feared this force might be a separate personality bent on my destruction, now I wonder if it were programming.

Rich suggested tentatively that the sense of a threatening, fragmenting force within me might be fear of the necessary death of the small self to the Self.

Maybe, I thought at the time. Now I think Rich was right: the threatening force I was feeling inside myself was not some programmed implant from the cult at all but the wise urging of my spirit. It felt threatening because it was pushing me to let go of a part of myself, to let my self die.

Ritual abuse put a spin on this ball. The cult wanted me to lose my self to them, and it was important that I resist. But it is no less important that I learn to surrender.

I am a child of my culture: death is to be conquered, passivity is bad, surrender is weakness. But my life teaches me a different lesson: admitting complete defeat in my long battle with booze brought me a new freedom. The whole of my recovery, from alcoholism, from incest, from ritual abuse, is rippled like sand on the beach by wave upon wave of rebellion and defeat, resistance and acceptance. I resist my own feelings, I agitate and cogitate to get away from them and then, finally, when I can't bear the discomfort of trying to live against my own grain, I give in and I feel whatever it is I didn't want to feel. And then I am relieved, calm again.

It is a muscle, this ability to sit with a feeling, to sit and feel and not leap into any of the actions which propose themselves, actions designed to change the feeling. Practice strengthens this muscle, and experience shows how powerful it is, simply to feel. But there is always more fear too. It took years for me to be able to sit in the feeling of despair, in the feeling that the whole fabric of the world can disintegrate in a moment.

I was afraid of being consumed by the feeling. It held within it all the experience I had of arbitrary power, the power of the cult to kill and torment. Just to sit still with this feeling for a few minutes was a liberation: I had spent so much time running from it, trying to stay out of reach of its scorching breath.

This "It," this monster, is death, is annihilation of the world as I know it, annihilation of myself. I fear it and I run from it, but I know in myself too a longing for it. "Abiding in the fire is bliss. There is no fear of being consumed."

Chapter Thirty-two

There are moments when I have known that death is only the unhooping of the personality. I knew it in the garden after talking to Denis that day on the phone. Mystical experiences, experiences of at-one-ment, are a kind of death, a death that brings one back to life. Death is necessary, all the kinds of death, little and large, and fear of it shuts me off from life, leaves me in a cold cave alone.

Change always involves death as well as birth. When I look back now at the fall of 1992 I see a great wave of change lifting me up and carrying me forward into a new life. It is mysterious to me that the cresting of that wave should have coincided so precisely with Denis' dying. I don't mean that one thing caused the other but that this is one more happening which I can't believe was "planned" but which does not feel completely arbitrary either.

Change always happens slowly, over time — the wave gathers far out to sea — but then there is the moment when it crests and breaks and hurls one forward in a tumble of sand and shells.

Denis died of AIDS on the seventeenth of October. Between the fifth of October and the tenth I began, finally, to write this book; I found myself brimming with feeling and aware suddenly that this tenderest, most receptive part of me had endured everything and was far tougher than I thought; I dreamt a joyful sexual union with a man; and, leaning on a bridge in Vermont, looking into the Winooski river, I yielded to the impulse to tell Clair I thought I might still be in love with her, had somehow never stopped being in love with her. It felt terrifying to say that, as if I were undoing all the years of cautious distancing, opening the door to all the demons we had summoned over the years, in each other, in ourselves.

I didn't mean, when I said it, that I had decided to leave Liz. I could barely face the thought of that, of the death of our partnership. I was afraid of what I was becoming, very afraid, afraid the changes in me would require me to live a different life, afraid I would lose my security, my life with Liz, my house, lose them through some inner necessity I neither understood nor wanted.

The thought of betraying Liz's trust was agonizing to me. I wanted to help her trust the world more, not less. She had taken a tremendous risk in giving me a piece of her land, had compromised the safety of her home on the strength of her trust in me, in us, in the possibility of us as partners. Yes, we had worked out a legal agreement in case we did break up, but it had all been done in the faith that we wouldn't.

Had I known, somewhere inside, that it might come to this even before she did the final legal transfer of the land in February? Had I deliberately remained unconscious of the depth of my discontent until after she had signed over the land? How deep was my betrayal of her trust?

Looking back now I see that, unconsciously, I was preparing to leave long before I did. A dream I had in April of 1991 presaged, with horrible accuracy, the way I felt eighteen months later.

> *I want to be with Zeus. I decide that means I have to move out and I tell this to Liz who is thunderstruck. It's out of the blue. Where am I going? I'm going to move in with Zeus.... I feel miserable. I can't believe I'm leaving my own beautiful house, the garden I've worked so hard for.... I am horrified at how much I am hurting Liz. She doesn't see why and I don't either. It's all out of the blue.*

The evening before I had that dream, Liz had said, "You're not leaving me are you?" I had just seen Clair and was, as always, feeling the draw to her.

So it wasn't out of the blue and yet it felt as if it was. I did not deliberately mislead Liz. I was so blind in part because I couldn't bear the thought of hurting her.

Such niceties wouldn't matter much to her. She would feel I had simply used her, taken her land, her love and support, her long patience and deep kindness, and then, when I didn't need her anymore, discarded her, no different really than a man divorcing his wife after she put him through law school, only at least the wife would get some sort of settlement.

How could I consciously choose to hurt someone, especially Liz to whom I owed such a debt of gratitude? But could I stay only out of the wish to avoid hurting her? Perhaps I was just acting out. Every marriage has its crises. What could I trust, how could I trust myself to make such a decision?

The internal urgency I felt, the necessity for change, whether I stayed with Liz or not, forced me to face my fear of hurting people. It was becoming obvious to me that some of my discontent with Liz was also discontent with myself: I kept myself shut away for fear of hurting her and then I was dissatisfied because the relationship didn't feel real and I didn't feel seen.

Chapter Thirty-two

My reluctance to cause pain was not due only to kindness: I was afraid of my own self-hatred, afraid of feeling that I was one of Them, afraid still that the cult had indeed made me into a monster, a fake man with a knife for a penis.

11/17/92

A slab laid across my heart all day long, a miserable day, bleak and gray, begun and ended in tears, made worse by feeling unable to ask L. for comfort. I took the dogs out walking in the half dark and cried more — for the disorder of my soul which I've been turning into discontent with job and this town and Liz — my grief, my desolation — ah and my implacable and merciless judge.

Bad bad bad, said my mother, said my father, raping me.

Bad bad bad, I said to myself, in order not to become them.

11/25/92

Saw Rich.

Talked about making L. judge and critic, the bad bad bad voice — how I need to be rescued from it, just as I wanted Rich to tell me I wasn't bad when I was remembering bad things I did — began to cry here, lots of pain, fear of being sucked down into the black hole — stayed with it into the core where there was a movement, a repeated downthrust, stabbing, me stabbing the woman to death, the split off watching voice saying bad bad bad, the stabbing rhythm, bad bad bad, stabbing me as I stabbed the woman I believed was my mother. Bad bad bad. I sobbed and sobbed, at first leaning back, arms along the back of the sofa, feet on table, and aware of vulnerablity, openness, but then the shame took over and I hunched, weeping.

Everything condenses in that memory, says Rich.

Later

I feel oddly happy, at peace somehow, after this (despite anxiety at having spent $28 on Thanksgiving dinner ingredients: salmon and asparagus and brie and goats' cheese and olives.)

A release obtained by descending the stairs into hell.

Who can forgive me but myself?

It does not sound like such a big deal, this time when I was able, in Rich's office, to let my own guilt wash over me without begging him in my mind to save me from it, but it was a moment of liberation for me. I could live with the knowledge of what I had done, with the knowledge in my body as well as my mind of stabbing a woman to death. I faced my own judge and my judge acquitted me: I would not have killed the woman if the cult had not set me up to do it. But it was not a legalistic assessment of my culpability that freed me. It was letting my guilt carry me down into the black hole I was so afraid of, and staying there while the voices crying "bad, bad, bad" swirled around me, that somehow released me.

11/28/92

What I learned at Denis' memorial service yesterday was that people love you and remember you for being yourself, not for concealing and easing but for expressing. Different men, his brother included, said he was difficult, thorny, he was honest, he insisted on his right to his feelings, exactly as they were. All this was part of his warmth, part of what helped people feel at home with him and acceptable, however they were feeling....

His AA sponsor stood up and said how Denis could not bear the hypocrisy of the Catholic Church, which made me and others cringe, his poor devout parents there, and then his father getting up and rambling on in defense of nuns and priests, and later I heard that Denis had made his sponsor promise he would do this. And I thought, well that's right then, that there should be this moment of difficulty and pain and embarrassment, everything not all smoothed out.

Art and a passion for life and honesty and concern, the important things, the bond we felt in pleasure, in appreciation.

So I came from there thinking there's no point in hiding, in trying to be good or nice, it's not important. Defects of character don't matter that much either — what matters is to give yourself to the world, to express yourself.

This is the place of growth for me — to risk sending myself into the world more and more without disguise, to risk exasperating and annoying and hurting.

L. pointed out I hold back on saying things I think about her when she'd rather I said them.

This after I'd felt so uncomfortable with her on Thursday that I couldn't bear to be in the same room, so I made myself start talking about us — said, "I feel I can't say this but I will — I wish you would find your imagination and find ways to express yourself."

She started to cry, said she wished she could believe that, she feeling that I thought she just wasn't good enough and sooner or later I'd

Chapter Thirty-two

trade her in. She's afraid there's nothing in her, nothing there.

I said I didn't buy that — I have a sense of her core self, the bright self without its wadding of fear, but that she won't let it out, or can't, and so I'm bored.

She said that self is somehow connected to her spirituality and that got stomped on when the ritual abuse came up.

I felt such sadness then, felt it was true, and anger at the cost of RA.

I said, it's possible to move through it — I am — but she said she doesn't have the tools I do. I said perhaps she should talk to Rich, get suggestions.

Maybe.

12/1/92

Saw Rich.

My fear that unconsciously I chose Liz to provide me with the security and care to get through the RA stuff — that I used her and now I'll discard her.

My pain and fear at the thought of hurting her....

I could see how last week's clarity, sitting with the bad voice, the murder, released something, enabled me to want with less guilt, to challenge and risk hurting more than usual.

Later

The moon belly Self pushing at one's buttons, gaping through, this butter fat waxing.

Felt again tonight a brimming aliveness, as if the myriad fibers linking inside and outside, me and the world, were being — had been — mended and once again life flowed freely through me-in-the-world.

Solitude wrapped around me, a cloak for this filling up of the vessel, the exact sense of interior, interiority. In the May Day Cafe watching people talk, animated, in myself that mingle of joy and sadness, the sadness welcomed equally as token of aliveness, of Self existing — how I felt as a teenager, hoarding my proofs of existence.

Now often it fills and flows over.

This is what I've found again, the rock lifted from my heart, this is the occasion of my loyalty and this is what feels unloved, unseen, unminded by Liz, this which is most precious to me. I felt her love for me and care when I came to her wounded, but in my wholeness I frighten her and she dismisses me.

This clarity pouring through me, water over the rock.

I've come to my senses.

Waking from three years of sorrow to a life made, perhaps, without true consultation with myself.

Perhaps there is a way through for Liz and me.

Let go of the result though, honesty for honesty's sake.

Because I cannot sacrifice this self and Self and Source and Spirit, the flowing of one through another.

Let go, let go.

12/3/92

The wounded self and the whole Self — how often and with surprise I've said over the last few months: they did not get me. I don't feel like a sick or damaged person — surprising. And important, not to buy into that view of the victim as sick — the psychiatric establishment's focus on the damaged victim, her (usually) problems and diagnoses, not those of the perpetrators and the perpetrating society.

It's snowing outside — the wild tangle of branches in deft black strokes, defined against a universal whiteness, here and there leaves dangle from young beech trees, a russet flock still enough so the snow gathers on each head, every shoulder.

Chapter Thirty-three

8/15/95

Dream. I was tricked and captured by a man, learned that when he'd done whatever he was doing they would take me upstairs and cut out my tongue — as they had with other people. How to get away? I was on a boat. I dove overboard and swam for shore. He shot at me. I swam underwater, trying to surface in unexpected places. I reached the shore and ran for the truck. The man grabbed me but I swung him off me, was at last able to get into the cab of my truck and then, time slowing, fumbling for my keys, everything moving so slowly, come on, come on, at any moment about to be captured.

That was when I woke.

That's how this time feels — urgent to finish — to get the book away — and time slowing, congealing around me.

This is the first dream I've remembered in months though often enough I've woken in the middle of the night so drenched with sweat I've had to get up and change my t-shirt.

It's been strange and difficult and wonderful, writing this book. Most of all though it's been exhausting. It took me from October '92 till April '95 to finish the first draft (this included a few breaks to make a living.) It was a fairly polished draft since I worked and reworked each chapter before moving on to the next one. I was teaching myself how to write the book as I went along and at the same time I was facing what had happened to me, taking it into me, sitting down with it four or five mornings a week. I soon noticed that the dominant emotions in whatever chapter I was working on leaked into the present so I would find myself unexpectedly angry or guilty or beset with loneliness. I had to learn to take this into account in the way a navigator must calculate the currents when setting a ship's course.

I needed a part of me to remain detached enough to keep an eye not only on the emotional leakage but also on my assorted tactics for avoiding the most difficult material. Sleepiness was the main one. Sometimes I could barely keep my eyes open. I peered at my computer screen through drooping eyelids and the words swam, as comprehensible as lightening bugs in a dark field. I don't usually drink caffeine, being quite anxious enough without artificial aids, but I started mixing a little caf with the decaf. I bribed myself shamelessly with home-made chocolate sauce and promises of time in the garden.

I found I had a great desire to write essays about the state of the world, ecofeminism, the nature of memory, Aeschyllus' *Oresteia*, Shakespeare's *King Lear*. I liked doing this much more than I liked writing about the abuse I experienced. Luckily, when I finished each chapter I brought it to my fortnightly meeting with Joan Larkin and Margaret Robison. At first gently and then with increasing firmness they told me they were interested in my story. I sulked and muttered about women not giving themselves permission to go beyond the personal and talk about the World, but eventually, grudgingly, I began to see what they meant. The essays were fine in themselves, some of them, but it produced a kind of vertigo in the reader to go from such immediate experiences to generalities. I began to notice that I was especially fond of ancient Greece and the view of the earth from space. Anything to get away.

Joan and Margaret didn't just criticize. They praised and were horrified and, best of all, they identified. Neither had experienced ritual abuse, but they had lived their half-centuries truthfully and deeply, and they had endured their own horrors. They recognized the feelings I described, they had felt most of them. It was a great comfort, this reminder that our hearts spoke the same language. When I picture having written this book without Joan's and Margaret's help I see myself wandering in a great flat expanse of snow, crossing and recrossing my own tracks.

When at last I reached the end of the first draft, it was 200,000 words long, and the contract I had signed with Trilogy Books called for 100,000. In the last three months I've gone back through the book, cutting and clarifying. Most of the essays have dropped away, like tadpoles' tails, leaving only a vestigial nub, some small reference. The content of each chapter still colors the days I spend working on

Chapter Thirty-three

it but now I'm moving so quickly from chapter to chapter it's like being inside a kaleidoscope.

The journey of recovery from ritual abuse has always felt more like a spiral than a straight line, and the writing of this book has been a part of this spiraling flight through time: the ritual abuse itself took place over a period of eight years, and that was the first loop of the journey, and then the remembering of it took three years and the writing the first draft two years and the second draft three months. Soon I'll reread the whole thing, quickly, in a day or two.

Once, years ago, when I was living in Manhattan and riding the D train into Brooklyn every day, an artist had painted on the subway wall a series of images of a rocket. When the train went slowly one saw each frame separately but when the train was rattling along you could see a rocket lifting off, rising higher and higher into the sky. When I move quickly through my story the image that comes to life is my own self, tortured and frightened and guilty yes, but suddenly, surprisingly three dimensional and intact.

One of the hardest things I've ever done was to leave Liz, which I did at the end of December 1992. We've barely spoken to each other since then. I still feel sick to my stomach when I think about the trust I betrayed and the pain I caused. I could dress it up in different costumes but, at root, it was an act of selfishness, a deliberate decision to do something which would hurt somebody else because it was what I wanted to do. I didn't stop loving Liz or minding desperately how she felt, but to have stayed would have felt like a betrayal of myself, and I wasn't willing to do that.

Clair and I did become lovers again. I sold my house in the end and together we bought an old farmhouse which we've been restoring. It's right on the road, though not a big road, whereas the house I built was quarter of a mile into the woods, and sometimes I think about the symbolism of that. I have been going into the world more, making new friends. I feel connected to the local community in ways I never have before. And often, when I walk through the rough pasture above our house, I feel astonishment and joy and gratitude rush through me: "I'm all right," I think, "I came through all right," and that's plenty among the juniper and Queen Anne's lace, goldenrod and barberries, the apple trees pruned by cows and deer and long hard winters.

Sometimes, when I look back on the three years of remembering ritual abuse I can't imagine how I got through them. Writing this book may have been hard but it was nothing compared to that. The passion for gardening which helped me then has grown into a business. Most of my income this year has come from designing and planting gardens for other people. I miss the purer passion of making my own garden for the first time, but when I think of myself back then, hacking beds out of the rocky root-bound soil in the fading light, I see myself surrounded by flames. I'm working in the midst of a monster's fiery breath. It scorches my neck, but mysteriously it doesn't char the wooden handles of my tools, nor the tender leaves of the plants I've gathered around me.

I think I should end this book with rousing suggestions for ways to End Ritual Abuse Now only I don't know what to say. I don't know how to put a stop to ritual abuse, any more than I know how to deal with nuclear waste. But I know where to begin: by being willing to relinquish my ignorance, by letting myself imagine. Somehow I have to let what is enter me before leaping to what should be. I can hardly bear to do that when it is all still going on: more children are being tortured, more nuclear waste is being generated every day.

But if I cannot sit with what is, all my actions will be driven by the need to avoid it, to escape feeling it. To become part of the solution I have "to jump into the river of grief and swim to the other side," in Helen Caldicott's words.

It is a wide river and I'm still swimming. I don't know what is on the other side. But there are things to do on the way. I promised myself a while back to pay attention to the children who cross my path. I want to be the sort of grown-up who recognizes the semaphores abused children send up, and who is willing to embarrass herself by interfering. I shan't respect the perfect privacy of the nuclear family and I will say what I see and what I know.

It's taken me a long time but I've reached a place now where, most of the time, I can both feel and know what happened to me, and know it happened, not in another world, not on the far side of an abyss but here, under the same sun, on the same planet. It doesn't make the world seem very safe, but then it isn't. Much of why I wrote this book was to return good for evil. I needed to compost the shit so that out of it flowers might grow. I needed, and need, to believe that that is possible. I think it is. The flowers want to grow, they yearn to become themselves.

Bibliography

This is not an exhaustive bibliography, by any means, but rather a list of books which I have found helpful, some explicitly about ritual abuse, others which have bearing on healing, belonging, guilt, evil, to name a few of the issues raised by experiencing or thinking about ritual abuse. Much more extensive bibliographies can be found in, for example, Oksana's *Safe Passage to Healing* and Sakheim and Devine's, *Out of Darkness: Exploring Satanism and Ritual Abuse*.

Bar-On, Dan. *Legacy of Silence: Encounters with Children of the Third Reich*. Cambridge, Massachusetts: Harvard University Press, 1989.

Bass, Ellen, and Davis, Laura. *The Courage to Heal: A Guide for Women Survivors of Child Sexual Abuse*. New York: Harper and Row, 1988.

Berry, Thomas. *The Dream of the Earth*. San Francisco: Sierra Club Books, 1988.

Boyd, Andrew. *Blasphemous Rumours: Is Satanic Ritual Abuse Fact or Fantasy? An Investigation*. London: Fount Paperbacks, 1991.

Browne, Ivor. "Psychological Trauma, or Unexperienced Experience." *ReVISION* 12, no.4 (Spring 1990): 21-34.

Campbell, Joseph. *Occidental Mythology: The Masks of God*. New York: Viking Press, 1964.

Campbell, Joseph, with Moyers, Bill. *The Power of Myth*. New York: Doubleday, 1988.

Gidlow, Elsa. *Elsa*. Booklegger Publishing, 1986.

Herman, Judith L., M.D. *Trauma and Recovery*. New York: Basic Books, 1992.

Hyde, Lewis. *The Gift: Imagination and the Erotic Life of Property*. New York: Vintage Books, 1979.

Klepfisz, Irena. *Keeper of Accounts*. Watertown, Massachussetts: Persephone Press, 1982.

Lifton, Robert J. *The Nazi Doctors*. New York: Basic Books, 1986.

Lusseyran, Jacques. *And There Was Light*. New York: Little, Brown and Company, 1963.

Marron, Kevin. *Ritual Abuse*. Toronto: Seal Books, 1989.

Miller, Alice. *Thou Shalt Not Be Aware*. New York: A Meridian Book, 1984.

Norberg-Hodge, Helena. *Ancient Futures: Learning from Ladakh*. San Francisco: Sierra Club Books, 1991.

Oksana, Chrystine. *Safe Passage to Healing: A Guide for Survivors of Ritual Abuse*. New York: Harper Collins, 1994.

Ritual Abuse Task Force, Los Angeles County Commission for Women. *Ritual Abuse: Definitions, Glossary, and the Use of Mind Control*, 1989.

Sakheim, David K., and Devine, Susan E. *Out of Darkness: Exploring Satanism and Ritual Abuse*. New York: Laxington Books, 1992.

Sinason, Valerie, ed. *Treating Survivors of Satanist Abuse*. London: Routledge, 1994.

Smith, Michelle, and Padzer, Lawrence, M.D. *Michelle Remembers.* New York: Pocket Books, 1980.

Soelle, Dorothee. *Suffering.* Trans. Everett R. Kalin. Philadelphia: Fortress Press, 1975.

Staub, Ervin. *The Roots of Evil: The Origins of Genocide and Other Group Violence.* Cambridge, U.K.: Cambridge University Press, 1989.

von Franz, Marie Louise. *Shadow and Evil in Fairytales.* Dallas, Texas: Spring Publications, 1974.

Wiesenthal, Simon. *The Murderers Among Us.* London: Heinemann Press, 1967.

Wink, Walter. *Unmasking the Powers: The Invisible Forces that Determine Human Existence.* Philadelphia: Fortress Press, 1986.

Wink, Walter. *Engaging the Powers: Discernment and Resistance in a World of Domination.* Minneapolis: Fortress Press, 1992.

Zolbrod, Paul G. *Dine' Bahane': The Navajo Creation Story.* Albuquerque, NM: University of New Mexico Press, 1984.